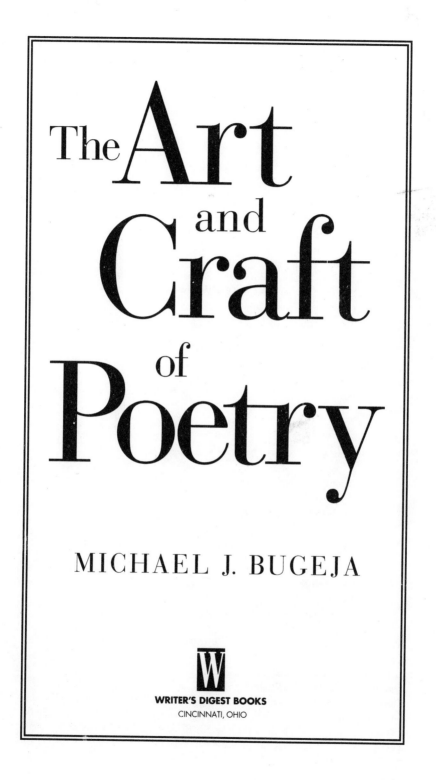

The Art and Craft of Poetry

MICHAEL J. BUGEJA

WRITER'S DIGEST BOOKS
CINCINNATI, OHIO

01 00 99 98 97   7 6 5 4 3

Library of Congress Cataloging-in-Publication Data

Other fine Writer's Digest Books are available from your local bookstore or direct from the publisher.

Bugeja, Michael J.
    The art and craft of poetry / by Michael J. Bugeja.
        p.   cm.
    Includes index.
    ISBN 0-89879-633-4
    1. Poetry—Authorship. 2. Poetics. I. Title.
PN1059.A9B84   1994
808.1—dc20   93-38192
                                                                    CIP

Edited by Christine Martin
Interior design by Sandy Conopeotis
Cover design by Sandy Conopeotis

The following three pages constitute an extension of this copyright page.

PERMISSIONS

Horoscope" appears in his book *Daily Horoscope*, published by Graywolf Press in 1986, and "The Silence of the Poets" and "Speaking of Love" appear in his book *The Gods of Winter*, published by Graywolf in 1991. "Flowering Plum" by Louise Glück is reprinted with permission from the author. The poem appears in *The House on Marshland*, first published by The Ecco Press in 1975. "How It Works" and "For Mary Who Was Killed Here Before I Moved In" by Corrinne Hales are reprinted with permission from the author. The poems appear in *January Fire*, published by Devil's Millhopper Press in 1984. "Redwings" by William Heyen is reprinted with the permission of William Heyen and Time Being Books. The poem appears in *Pterodactyl Rose: Poems of Ecology*, published by Timeless Press, Inc., in 1991. "Meditation of Mary, Mother of God" and "For Those Who Have Died at Birth" are reprinted with the permission of Martha Whitmore Hickman. "Meditation of Mary, Mother of God" appeared in *The Christian Century*. "Ann Howland" by Gerard Hilferty is reprinted with the permission of the author. "At the Heartland Cafe" by Art Homer is reprinted with permission of the author. Excerpts from the poem "An Abandoned Farm in the West" and "A Crazy Girl Brings the Rural Carrier a Dime" and "The Man Who Beat the Game at Johnny's Truck Stop" are reprinted with the permission of T.R. Hummer. "An Abandoned Farm in the West" appears in *Lower-Class Heresy*, published by the University of Illinois Press in 1987. The other poems appear in *The Angelic Orders*, published by Louisiana State University Press in 1982. "The Papal Saw in a Roman Blind" is reprinted with permission of Colette Inez. The poem appears in her book *Family Life*, published by Story Line Press in 1988. "Oil of the Pecos Valley" by Judson Jerome is reprinted with permission from Martha Jerome. "Damn You, America!" is reprinted with the permission of Harry Johnson. "Making My Peace" and "Remembering New London" are reprinted with the permission of Roger Jones and appear in his book *Strata*, published by Texas Review Press in 1994. "Reflections on the Sherwin-Williams Can" is reprinted with the permission of Debra Kaufman. The poem appeared in *Poems for a Livable Planet*. "The Universe Exploding" and "Faint-light" are reprinted with the permission of Robert Kinsley. The poems appear in his book *Endangered Species*, published by Orchises Press in 1989. "Walking on Ice" and "Tell Her" are reprinted with permission from Judith Kitchen. The poems appear in *Perennials*, published by Anhinga Press in 1986. "Tell Her" was first published in *Three Rivers Poetry Journal*. "West Texas, Ohio" and "Here and Back" are reprinted with the permission of Sharon Klander. "Here and Back" was published in *Kansas Quarterly*. "Tartine, for All Her Bulk" is reprinted with the permission of Laurence Lieberman. The poem originally appeared in *The Chariton Review*. "Norfolk" is reprinted with the permission of Rupert M. Loydell. "Knife," "The 1945 Poker Game Transcendence" and "Forty Years Later, the Father's Remaining Debt" are reprinted with the permission of R. Nikolas Macioci and appear in his book *Cafes of Childhood*, published in 1991 by Pearl Editions. "Knife" was originally published in *Artful Dodge* in 1990, "The 1945 Poker Game Transcendence" was published in *Sepia* in 1991, and "Forty Years Later, the Father's Remaining Debt" was published in *Spokes* in 1990. "A Sense of the Other Side" is reprinted with permission from Peter Makuck and BOA Editions, Ltd. The poem appears in *The Sunken Lightship*, BOA Editions Ltd., 1990. "Mirage" and "The Dance Teacher" are reprinted with the permission of Mary Martin. "To My Son, Growing Up" is reprinted with permission from Sharon E. Martin. The poem first appeared in *Byline* in 1990. "Not Only the Eskimos" and "The End of Science Fiction" are reprinted with the permission of Lisel Mueller and Louisiana State University Press. The poems appear in *The Need to Hold Still* by Lisel Mueller, published by LSU Press in 1980. "Miss Intensity Thinks About Her Name" and "Miss Intensity Meets the Holy Ghost" are reprinted with the permission of Katherine Murphy. "Miss Intensity Thinks About Her Name" appeared in *The Gamut*, and "Miss Intensity Meets the Holy Ghost" appeared in *Artful Dodge*. "Most of Us" is reprinted with permission from Jack Myers and Graywolf Press. The poem appears in his book *As Long As You're Happy*, published by Graywolf Press in 1986. "Welcome to Dallas!" and "$" are reprinted with the permission of Joyce Carol Oates. "Welcome to Dallas!" appears in the book *The Time Traveler*, published by NAL-Dutton in 1989. "$" originally appeared in *The Atlantic*. "The Issues" is reprinted with permission of Sharon Olds. The poem first appeared in her book *The Dead and the Living*, published by Knopf in 1984. "The Man Who Grew Silent" is reprinted with permission from Jim Peterson. The poem appears in his book *The Man Who Grew Silent*, published by The Bench Press in 1989. "What Happens" is reprinted with permission from Hilda Raz. The poem appears in *The Bone Dish*, published by State Street Press in 1989. "High Sea, Cow Point" is reprinted with permission from Stan Rubin. It appears in *The State Street Reader*, published by State Street Press in 1991. Excerpts from the journal pages entitled "Gracie Lou" and "Brown Shoes" are reprinted with permission from Grace L. Rutledge. "Assuming All Goes Well God Will Say" is reprinted with permission from Eve Shelnutt and appears in *First a Long Hesitation*, published by Carnegie Mellon Press in 1992. "Night Pleasures" is reprinted with permission from Dave Smith. The poem was first published in 1991 in *The New Yorker*. "Vespers" is reprinted with permission from R.T. Smith. The poem first appeared in *The Irish Times* and appears in his book *The Cardinal Heart*, published by Livingston University Press in 1991. "Three Ways to Tell a Story" and "A Love Note to Strunk" are reprinted with permission from Laurel Speer. "Three Ways to Tell a Story" appears in *Vincent Et Al.*, published by Geryon Press in 1985. It was first published in *The Indiana Review*. "A Love Note to Strunk" appeared in *Waterways* (a magazine) and *Sin* (a poem pamphlet). "Sand and Blue-Green Algae" is reprinted with permission from Michael Spence. The poem first appeared in *The Georgia Review* in 1991. "Tides" is reprinted with permission from William Stafford. The poem first appeared in *The Georgia Review*. "Mrs. Wei Wants to Believe the First Amendment" and "Mrs. Wei on Patriotism" are reprinted with permission from Hilary Tham. "Mrs. Wei Wants to Believe the First Amendment" appears in *Bad Names for Women*, published in 1989 by Word Works. "Mrs. Wei on Patriotism" appears in *Tigerbone Wine*, published in 1992 by Three Continents Press. "Modern Love," "On Alum Creek" and "One Dream" are reprinted with the permission of Ann Townsend. "Modern Love" first appeared in *The New England Review*, "On Alum Creek" first appeared in *Poetry Northwest*, and "One Dream" first appeared in *Green Mountains Review*. Journal excerpts and the poem "Oracle Bones" are reprinted with permission from Martha Vertreace. "Oracle Bones" was previously published in *Urbanus*. "Elvis at the Dollar Slotbank Sestina" is reprinted with permission from Diane Wakoski. "Early Brass" and "State Poetry Day" are reprinted with permission from Ronald Wallace. The poems appear in *The Makings of Happiness*, published by the University of Pittsburgh Press in 1991. "The Harp," "Short," "Temple Near Quang Tri, Not on the Map" and "The Last Lie" are reprinted with permission from Bruce Weigl. "The Harp" appears in his book *A Romance*, published in 1979 by the University of Pittsburgh Press. The other poems appear in his book *Song of Napalm*, published in 1988 by Atlantic Monthly Press. "A Hymn to God the Father" is reprinted with permission from George Whipple and appears in his book *Passing Through Eden*, published by Thistledown Press in 1991. "This Is Just to Say" by William Carlos Williams is reprinted with permission from New Directions Publishing Corp. The poem first appeared in *The Collected Poems of William Carlos Williams, 1909-1939, vol. I* copyright 1938 by New Directions Publishing Corporation. "When Angels Came to Zimmer" is reprinted with permission from Paul Zimmer and the University of Illinois Press. The poem appears in his book *The Great Bird of Love*, published by the University of Illinois Press in 1989. "Economy, August 31st" is reprinted with permission from Sander Zulauf and appears in his book *Succasunna New Jersey*, published by Breaking Point in 1987.

In memory of our first two children,

guardian angels of my daughter Erin Marie

and my son Shane Michael,

for whom this book is dedicated

ACKNOWLEDGMENTS

This book is a gift. I don't know how I got so lucky to write it. Included in these pages are dozens of poems by some of the world's most talented contemporary writers, most of whom donated their works, time and wisdom without compensation in an attempt to make *The Art and Craft of Poetry* an enlightening, enduring text.

Contributors to this project include Diane Ackerman, Terry Anderson, Tom Andrews, Nuala Archer, David Baker, Jim Barnes, Kevin Bezner, Charlene Blue Horse, Lady Borton, Kevin Bowen, Neal Bowers, Raymond Carver, Fred Chappell, David Citino, Stephen Corey, Ruth Daigon, Wayne Dodd, Frederick Feirstein, Carolyn Forché, Karen Joy Fowler, Lucia Cordell Getsi, Allen Ginsberg, Dana Gioia, Louise Glück, Corrinne Hales, William Heyen, Martha Whitmore Hickman, Gerald Hilferty, Art Homer, T.R. Hummer, Colette Inez, Judson Jerome, Harry Johnson, Roger Jones, Debra Kaufman, Robert Kinsley, Judith Kitchen, Sharon Klander, Laurence Lieberman, Rupert M. Loydell, R. Nikolas Macioci, Peter Makuck, Mary Martin, Sharon E. Martin, Lisel Mueller, Katherine Murphy, Jack Myers, Joyce Carol Oates, Sharon Olds, Jim Peterson, Hilda Raz, Stan Rubin, Grace L. Rutledge, Eve Shelnutt, Dave Smith, R.T. Smith, Laurel Speer, Michael Spence, William Stafford, Hilary Tham, Ann Townsend, Martha M. Vertreace, Diane Wakoski, Ronald Wallace, Bruce Weigl, George Whipple, Paul Zimmer, Sander Zulauf and others.

Almost two-thirds of the above not only allowed me to reprint their poems but also provided comments about craft in letters and telephone interviews. These quotations add another level of instruction to *The Art and Craft of Poetry*.

Also included are poems of great English and American writers: Lady Mary Wroth, Jonson, Donne, Shakespeare, Spenser, Raleigh, Herrick, Lovelace, Dryden, Matthew Prior, Milton, Swift, Blake, Wordsworth, John Clare, Walter Savage Landor, Keats, Byron, Shelley, Burns, Anne Bradstreet, Charlotte, Emily and Anne Brontë, George Meredith, Robert Browning, Elizabeth Barrett Browning, Herman Melville, Emerson, Thoreau, Whitman, Poe, Yeats, Longfellow, Dickinson, Christina Rossetti, Edna St. Vincent Millay, Eliot, H.D., Sara Teasdale, Frost, Edward Thomas, Williams, Housman, Lawrence, Sandburg, Edgar Lee Masters and many, many more.

You'll also be reading many of my poems. I have quoted from them and reprinted them because this book concerns the process of composing publishable verse — and I know that process intimately by trial and error. I want to share my successes and mistakes so that you may learn from them and save time in your quest to become a recognized poet. You also should know that poems by the other authors mentioned here have influenced or inspired me in some way. So think of the contributions of contemporary and past masters as the "art" in *The Art and Craft of Poetry*, and think of my work as the "craft" — or art in the making.

Finally, I want to thank Bill Brohaugh at Writer's Digest Books with whom I became associated early in my career when he edited *Writer's Digest*, the magazine in which my poetry column appears. I also want to thank Christine Martin, editor of this book and of *Poet's Market*, our yearly project, and Jack Heffron, another WD book editor, for their valuable insights. Most important is the inspiration of my wife, Diane, who encouraged me to share my life's passion with you.

ABOUT THE AUTHOR

Michael J. Bugeja is an internationally published writer and poet with more than five hundred credits in literary magazines, including *Tri-Quarterly*, *The Formalist*, *The Georgia Review* and *The New England Review*. He has won a National Endowment for the Arts Fellowship and the 1992 Strousse Prize from *Prairie Schooner*. He has five book-length collections of poetry. His most recent three are *Platonic Love* (Orchises Press, 1991), *After Oz* (Orchises Press, 1993) and *Flight From Valhalla* (Livingston University Press, 1993). In addition, he has written a book of social criticism titled *Culture's Sleeping Beauty: Essays on Poetry, Prejudice, and Belief* (Whitston, 1992). Forthcoming books include *The Visionary* (American reprint, Orchises Press, 1994) and *Academic Socialism: Problems of Merit and Morale in Higher Education* (Orchises Press, 1994). He is co-editor of *Poet's Market*, writes a monthly poetry column for *Writer's Digest* and frequently keynotes writing conferences and workshops across the country. He is also a full professor at the E.W. Scripps School of Journalism, Ohio University, Athens, Ohio, where he teaches ethics and writing.

PART THREE

Formats and Forms 215

INTRODUCTION

If you are just starting out as a poet, you should make a trip to the stationery store, the bookshop and the nearest library. Enjoy the aroma of a fresh ream of paper, the feel of a pen in your hand and the power of a library card in your pocket.

A working poet also needs notebooks, pads, pencils, pens, a ream of 20 percent bond paper, business envelopes (Nos. 9 and 10), manila envelopes (9″ × 12″), file folders, stamps, postal scale, a typewriter or computer, ribbons, correction tape or fluid, diary or journal, dictionary, thesaurus, rhyming dictionary, encyclopedia, reference books and *Poet's Market*.

If you can't afford all of these things, eliminate the postal scale (ask the postmaster to weigh your manuscripts); eliminate ribbons and arrange access to a typewriter or computer (ask a friend if you can use one, check to see if your library has a work station, or pay per hour at a local photocopying store); use scrap paper for your notebook, diary or journal; and take advantage of your library card so you can refer to the dictionaries, directories and reference books mentioned above.

You also will need a quiet place to think, read and write. If you don't have a room of your own, use the library again or ask the local clergy if you can spend time in a church facility. Perhaps you can use the town recreation center during off-hours, in return for some volunteer work. Or you can take advantage of the milieu of a café or restaurant whose owner doesn't mind your setting up shop at a table, as long as you order food or drink.

Make a commitment to devote at least fifteen minutes a day to write. Increase this, if you can, to an hour a day. If you have children and no support at home, hire a babysitter whenever you can and then hide yourself away. If you can't afford a sitter, trade off with other parents; let them watch your children during your writing time and then watch theirs during hours you are going to be home anyway. If you still think you have no time to write, try getting up one hour earlier when the house is quiet. Or eat a meal away from family, friends and associates, and use that hour to work.

Rely on your imagination to locate a corner somewhere for yourself. When Raymond Carver was just starting out, he used to write in his car. I did the same in a beat-up Plymouth when I was a teenager, using one hand to hold a flashlight and the other a pen, scribbling verse in a pad on my knee while guarding a factory all night. If you're serious about composing poetry, you'll find the time and the place.

A PARTICULAR ORDER

Look at the contents page again, and you'll note that this book is arranged in a particular order. We begin with generating ideas for poems and end with the total poem, summarizing key elements in the making of publishable verse. In between those two chapters is the making of a poet, and that usually takes time . . . and patience.

This book has three sections. In "Journals and Genres," you'll learn how to generate and record ideas for poems. You'll also become familiar with the established genres of poetry, helping you conceive more ideas. In "Tools of the Trade," you'll learn how to use each element of craft to construct a poem. In "Formats and Forms," you'll become familiar with the various modes of expression.

Each chapter takes a no-frills approach. In other words, I am concerned with conveying information to you in a clear, concise style and not with the politics of poetry, choosing works from one school of thought or promoting specific types of verse. Poets cited here represent a broad spectrum of the literary scene, past and present. Verse from such writers as the Brontë sisters or Christina Rossetti continue to inspire those who have access to their works. The time has come to rediscover them. Moreover, contemporary poets from different schools have much to contribute to the process of composing good verse; thus, I was democratic in selecting their works because my intent is to inspire you to follow your own muse, not my footsteps (or footnotes).

Furthermore, at the end of each chapter, I have included "notebook" assignments based on three levels of achievement. (Notice that I did not say "difficulty.") In this era of wasted paper, I have attempted to write an "environmentally safe book" that you can continue to use throughout your development as a poet. Think of Level One, Level Two and Level Three in the notebook as go-arounds in a rodeo or as sets in a tennis match. Go through the book once and do all the Level One assignments, and you should have a new understanding of the art and craft of poetry — along with your first chapbook (about ten to fifteen poems). Go through it again at Level Two, and you can see how you have developed as a poet in the interim. You'll have another chapbook of verse. Go through it once more, and you will have experienced three phases of development and composed one more chapbook of verse. Combine the best poems from your first three chapbooks — and *voila!* — you will have your first full-blown poetry collection.

POEMS HERE AND ELSEWHERE

I have researched thousands of poems for this book and selected the best. By best I mean ones that illustrate specific points rather than qualify as the greatest in the canon. The latter is a matter of taste, and my list of the greatest poems is bound to differ from someone else's.

In each chapter, however, you will find plenty of examples from the works of past and present writers. This is meant to give you perspective. You can see how a genre of poetry began, developed and evolved through the ages.

Moreover, poems in the various chapters are so powerful that they represent an anthology of sorts — individual works that, when read in sequence, convey information about the art and craft of poetry. So I have reprinted these works in "mini anthology" sections at the end of chapters to stress points made in the text.

In the first and last sections of the book, poems included in mini anthologies are contemporary, so you can familiarize yourself with the range of ideas and forms popular today. But in the second section, about the mechanics of poetry, I have reprinted poems by *both* past and contemporary poets. For instance, in the chapters on voice and rhyme (which affects voice), I use only contemporary examples because these best convey current tones of speech. In the chapters on titles, lines and meter, however, I use older works to show the prototypes of these aspects of craft. In chapters on the stanza, I include poems of past and present writers to illustrate a type of progression — how the tools have been sharpened over time.

Thus, if you are reading this book in a workshop or class, you'll have poems enough to analyze. However, by no means should you rely solely on selections in *The Art and Craft of Poetry* (or any book or anthology, for that matter) to sate your appetite for verse. You should read as much poetry as possible in your free time and consider assembling your own library of books, anthologies and magazines. The typical person invests money in a record, cassette or compact disk collection. Why not poetry?

Finally, keep in mind that your taste in poetry will likely change over the years, just as it probably has in music. When I was a boy, I enjoyed big band swing and then switched to rock and roll, bluegrass, jazz and classical. Now I'm into rap. True, trends have helped to shape part of my taste in music. But the other part developed over time because I needed more sophisticated fare or a certain sound to complement my emotional well-being.

It's the same with poetry. In fact, the first poets to excite me are now considered hack writers whose works, by the way, are not included in this book. I could name them, but that would be unfair, given what I have told you. The point is, don't be embarrassed if someone criticizes the poets who initially inspire you. Tell the critic you are working your way up the great chain of reading.

Nothing is more important than reading in your development as a writer. The more you read, the better able you will be to understand and employ the concepts in *The Art and Craft of Poetry*.

PART ONE

Journals and Genres

In this section you will learn how to conceive ideas for poems based on life experience, research and familiarity with traditional genres of poetry. In the first chapter you also will learn how poets use journals to keep track of their ideas. As you conceive and record your ideas, resist the urge to write first drafts. This is a time for observation, contemplation and discovery—talents that make for superior poets and that take time to perfect. When you have finished exercises in this section you should have as many as one hundred ideas for poems.

Chapter One

Ideas

The most important element of any poem is not its structure, rhyme, meter, line or language. It's the *idea*. That word does not mean *content* or *topic*. You can write about a tree just for the sake of writing about a tree and end up with doggerel, a nonsense poem that does not enlighten or entertain anyone. Poems that lack ideas merely state the obvious — they bore us. Ones that contain ideas, however, unify our thoughts or feelings. They shape how we perceive the world and excite us with images of beauty or moments of truth. Since ancient times, poets have been known more for their ideas than for the words they used to convey them.

So we'll begin with ways to recognize and generate ideas. Then we'll discuss ways to record them for future use. Once you have developed these skills, you'll be able to appreciate the various genres of verse — love, nature and war poetry (to name a few) — in the chapters that follow. You'll have new insights about the world around you and will be able to add your voice to the human chorus called poetry.

DRAWING FROM EXPERIENCE

When I speak at writers' conferences, I ask participants to do an exercise that generates ideas based on life experience. On a piece of paper, poets make a list of the high points, low points and turning points in their lives.

For instance, my abbreviated list looks like this:

1. Left home at sixteen.
2. Studied to become a musician.
3. Lived and worked in Salzburg, Austria.
4. Married at nineteen.
5. Divorced at twenty-five, no children.
6. Father died of cancer.
7. Met Diane Sears and married again.
8. Our first daughter is stillborn.
9. We have another daughter, Erin Marie.

10. We have a son, Shane Michael.

More than half my poems are based in some way on that list. You can almost tell by the titles of my books: *What We Do for Music* (about studying to be a musician), *The Visionary* (about losing a child), *Platonic Love* (about romance and relationships), *Flight from Valhalla* (about Salzburg), and *After Oz* (about family, faith and all of the above put into mid-life perspective).

When I was starting out as a poet, I composed my list and then thought about specific incidents related to each event. I tried to assess what I had learned from each encounter. I wanted my poems to be honest. As a reader of poetry, I knew that the best work of great writers was not based on mere description or observation but on epiphany or peak experience.

Let's define the two:

1. An *epiphany* is a moment of truth in which your mind seems at one with the universe. (In fact, I think what we mistakenly call the *muse* really is an epiphany that electrifies our mind.) During such times you realize something sublime or solve a critical problem in your life. Everyone has such moments: You wake at 3 A.M., bolt up in bed and proclaim: "Now I know why he (or she) left me. He never wanted a partner. He (or she) wanted *a parent*."

2. A *peak experience* is a moment of truth in which your body seems at one with the universe. Typically, an athlete feels this way after winning a race or while scoring the winning point. Many people experience peak moments after a triumph of some sort: finally doing a backflip or a difficult dance step or surviving conflict with another person, animal or even the weather. Almost all of us have experienced the most cliché of peak moments after a romantic encounter—our first kiss, perhaps, or a more intimate contact. You wake at 3 A.M., bolt up in bed and proclaim: "I never knew I could feel this way!"

Epiphanies or peak experiences usually accompany highs, lows and turning points in our lives. As you contemplate yours, ask yourself what you learned from each encounter and draw on your experience to express truth in the tradition of great poetry.

Let's look at my list again. This time I'll cite specific incidents along with epiphanies or peak experiences:

1. Left home at sixteen.
   Incident: Being attacked in Florence, Italy.
   Epiphany: "I have to survive now on my own."
2. Studied to become a musician.
   Incident: Auditioning at the Mozarteum.
   Peak Experience: "My fingers express feelings."

3. Lived and worked in Salzburg, Austria.
   Incident: Living on the same street as Mozart.
   Epiphany: "I'm starving to death."
4. Married at nineteen.
   Incident: Having a wedding at Mirabell Palace.
   Epiphany: "We don't love each other."
5. Divorced at twenty-five, no children.
   Incident: Claiming a no-fault divorce.
   Epiphany: "We're both at fault."
6. Father died of cancer.
   Incident: Being stoic when he died.
   Epiphany: "I have lived up to his expectations."
7. Met Diane Sears and married again.
   Incident: Telling her about my first failed marriage.
   Epiphany: "She loves me in spite of it!"
8. Our first daughter is stillborn.
   Incident: Trying to imagine her alive.
   Peak Experience: "This pregnancy is mine."
9. We have another daughter, Erin Marie.
   Incident: Holding her outside watching the stars.
   Epiphany: "She has taken away all my pain."
10. We have a son, Shane Michael.
    Incident: Holding him for the first time at delivery.
    Peak Experience: "My God, you look like me."

To give you an idea of how this method can result in verse, I'll
reprint a poem based on event number six in the above list:

SNAKE, ROCK: A POEM I CANNOT WRITE

I turn it over in my head
As a boy turns over rocks a hundred times
To find the snake. I chip it as a man
Chips a rock at odd angles for the gem.
I get neither reptile or ruby, merely a glimpse
Of snake, a fossil — a place the poem just left
Or lay so long it lithographs the stone,

A eulogy: how simple to leave it there,
A poem — sure — but not the one about my father
Dying. The dying part is easy: he phones me
At work to rasp what Mother claims is love,
A word we never use. The setting's wrong;
I am neither poet or professor, but reporter
Doing markets on deadline, barrows and gilts,

Up a quarter, or down. I put the phone
On hold, punch another line
To hear the rasp a mother has to translate,
And then hang up, a wrong number
In the hour of numbers. It delays me
Only a minute, and I return to the markets
With a peace I will not know again:

Somewhere here lies the poem, replete
With symbol, metaphor, and irony —
Everything but place, and time maybe:
This is the best I can do. Don't hope
For an ending. Don't ask me
Who was the snake in this matter,
Who was the rock.

It can be argued that all poems, in some sense, come out of our own experience because they come out of our bodies and minds. Yet sometimes I may *observe* an event that doesn't quite have an epiphany or peak moment, but I still want to base a poem on it. Perhaps the personal aspect of such an event would seem self-serving or trite or overly sentimental. In sum, I have yet to fathom the idea behind the poem and need to do some research.

When that happens, I visit the library and often come away with new insight so that I can complete the work in question.

RESEARCHING IDEAS

Incident: My one-year-old son Shane was under a tangle of morning glories on our outdoor deck, when a ladybug alighted on his arm. He marveled at its bright red wingcase that looked like a round piece of candy. I beamed at the sight, proud my son was learning about the beauty of nature.

Then, without warning, Shane popped the bug into his mouth, giggling as it slid down his throat.

I knew immediately that I would base a poem on this incident. (All poets must learn to observe life closely, ready to base an idea on any unusual incident or moment.) In this case I had witnessed Shane, in his innocence, admiring nature . . . or so I thought. Instead he *consumed* nature and went merrily about his business. That was irony, and irony makes for good poems.

Beyond that, however, I didn't know what the "truth" of the incident meant. Perhaps Shane was just hungry. The more I thought about the idea behind the poem, the more it eluded me. And I resisted the urge to write personally about my son swallowing an insect because only I might find that precious.

So I visited the library and read up on ladybugs (officially known as *ladybird beetles*). I began with the encyclopedia and learned some interesting facts. To wit: The bug is named after the Virgin Mary and considered divine because one variety, *Coccinella 7-punctata*, has seven dots on its back. Folklore suggests it can cure colic, among other things. Finally, the beetle helped inspire a popular children's rhyme.

I copied some references and did more research about beetles in general, consulting books on entomology and ecology.

The result was this poem, an elegy of sorts for the unlucky ladybug that landed on Shane's arm:

COCCINELLA 7-PUNCTATA

Biologists say the creator
Had a fondness for beetles,
Queenly colors of a wingcase
More angelic than seraphim

Aflutter at the seat of all-
Being. Whoever made you
Kept re-making you until
You were divine as the seven

Dots on your back,
Red and yellow like apples
Out of Eden. Kill beetles,
And the hop fields burn:

Lady bug, lady bug,
Fly away home,
Your house is on fire,
Your children do roam. . . .

Another judgment is upon us,
Our Lady. Blessed Coccinella,
Intercede as your namesake
Seldom does on our behalf.

I would not have composed the above lyric (a poem focused intensely on a subject to awaken emotions within the reader) if I hadn't spent time at the library doing basic research. Reading up on a topic can enhance an idea so that you can base a poem on it. You also can come across *new* ideas for poems by reading:

• **The encyclopedia.** Page through the books, scanning entries about people or subjects that stimulate your imagination or passion. Make a list of entries that might evolve into poems.

• **Quotation references.** Page through a compilation like *Bart-lett's Familiar Quotations* and make a list of quotes that excite or anger you. You can use them as epigraphs (brief citations placed immediately above or below the title of your poem). Then you can write poems expressing your views or imagining other scenarios.

• **Biographies.** Collect anecdotes about famous or important persons. Make a list of incidents upon which you can base poems, reconstructing the scene to express certain truths.

• **Published collections of letters.** Study them to get a first-hand glimpse of how famous and important people related to others. Make another list containing passages that you can use as epigraphs or upon which you can base poems.

• **Published diaries, journals and autobiographies.** Study them to get a glimpse of how famous and important people related to themselves or how ordinary people, living in extraordinary times, saw history as it happened. Base ideas on passages or quote them as epigraphs and reconstruct the events . . . from your point of view, of course.

Sander Zulauf, who edits *Journal of New Jersey Poets*, occasionally uses research to generate ideas. His poem below was inspired by the published notebooks of the great nineteenth-century novelist Nathaniel Hawthorne:

ECONOMY, AUGUST 31ST

In 1842, Henry David Thoreau sold
The boat he made with his own hands
To Nathaniel Hawthorne for seven dollars.
He had paddled the *Musketaquid* with his brother, John,
For two weeks on New England rivers.
In telling this fact to my literature students
I try putting it in terms of current dollars
Assuming this would mean more.
This would mean less.
Thoreau needed the money.
He had taken a trip in the boat with his brother.
The trip became immortalized
In his only other published book,
A Week on the Concord and Merrimack Rivers.
Hawthorne, being the genius that he was,
Bought something immortal for seven dollars.
Thoreau might have needed more than the money.
He might have needed to forget
His brother died.

Zulauf says that while paging through the notebooks he read Hawthorne's entry for September 1, 1842. The entry described Hawthorne's dinner and after-dinner boat ride on the Concord River with
a "Mr. Thorow" (and Hawthorne's subsequent purchase of the *Musketaquid* for seven dollars). "Mr. Thorow," of course, was none other than
the great poet and naturalist Henry David Thoreau.

"This especially rich passage documenting the meeting of two
American literary giants gave me the idea for my poem," Zulauf
says. After reading the entry, he combined the date of the Thoreau-
Hawthorne meeting with the title of the opening chapter in Thoreau's
Walden: "Economy."

"Now I had my title and my theme," he says.

Zulauf researched the topic further and learned that Thoreau's
brother, John, had died early in 1842. So it occurred to him, as it has
to other scholars, that the real motive for selling the *Musketaquid*
(named after the Indian word for the Concord River) might have been
Thoreau's desire to erase the painful specter of his brother's death.

But Zulauf, up until this point, resisted writing the poem.

Then the muse struck. "One afternoon my wife and I were sailing
our little dinghy on a nearby reservoir," Zulauf says. "Huge storm
clouds gathered in the West, and we brought the boat in just in time.
The storm let loose and it was coming down too hard to drive home,
so we sat there waiting. All the ideas came together and I began writing
on a brown paper bag. I knew I had the poem."

Like Sander Zulauf, widely published poet Laurel Speer of Tucson,
Arizona, uses research to generate work. One of her poems pays hom-
age to E.B. White and William Strunk, Jr., who wrote the classic
editing text *The Elements of Style*. In this case, her research entails
using an epigraph—a short passage from that book placed above her
poem's title. After the epigraph, Speer expounds playfully upon her
(and White's) respect for Strunk's editing skills:

From every line there peers out at me
the puckish face of my professor,
his short hair parted neatly in the middle
and combed down over his forehead,
his eyes blinking incessantly behind
steel-rimmed spectacles as though he had
just emerged into strong light, his
lips nibbling each other like nervous
horses, his smile shuttling to and fro
under a carefully edged mustache.
                                        —E.B. White

A LOVE NOTE TO STRUNK

Oh Will, why did we never meet?
I would've worshipped your pithiness, gone down
on my knees before the towering rightness of your
ideas, taken the mediocre grades you slapped
on my themes without even a "see me" to hold out
hope we might talk privately. I was born too late
to breathe your air, paddle your canoe, bear
your child, be known as the stylemaster's own
and never recant.

"Omit needless words."

As you can see, research can be simple. When you come across a passage in one of your favorite (or least favorite) books, cite a sentence that can serve as an epigraph and contemplate how you would respond or rebut accordingly. As the E.B. White citation illustrates, an epigraph serves to overshadow and generate the work in question. The poet's obligation, of course, is to transcend the researched material with enlightened verse.

Facts alone do not a poem make. As Sander Zulauf observes, "There is a truth in poetry that's always beyond the truth of the facts gleaned from the research. I believe a poet uses the facts in combination with everything the poet knows about making a poem and making a life, and if the poem is exactly right, it's always greater than the sum of its parts."

Now that you know how to recognize and generate ideas, let's consider ways to keep a journal.

KEEPING TRACK OF IDEAS

There's no one best way to record ideas. Typically poets keep diaries, journals, notebooks or idea files. Strictly defined, a diary is a daily chronicle of incidents and thoughts. A journal is less rigid, allowing you to make entries only when you think you have something important to relate, remember or observe. A notebook is less formal than a journal, usually a spiral pad in which you sporadically jot down ideas for poems or important elements of craft. An idea file is a folder containing loose paper outlining ideas for future poems. Of course, a dairy, journal, notebook or file can be easily created on a computer.

In casual talk, however, poets use one word to refer to all of the above: *journal*. Henceforth in this text we'll use that word to denote "a place where ideas are stored." Think of your journal—a fancy store-bought diary or slipshod idea file—as a warehouse and design it to meet your needs and lifestyle.

For instance, I lack the discipline required to keep a diary à la Sylvia Plath, dissecting each day in longhand and basing poems on entries. (I admire poets who do.) Instead I jot down ideas on the nearest piece of paper.

Case in point: Once I won a poetry contest and received a plaque with my last name spelled wrong. I ripped a deposit slip from my checkbook and wrote: "Base a poem on the *j* in *Bugeja* and recount all the trouble it has caused you in life." I put the slip in my shirt pocket so I wouldn't forget it. Later at home I typed out this paragraph:

J: This letter kept me from the close-knit community of Italians in my neighborhood. Everyone knew *Bugeja* wasn't Italian because there is no *j* in the Italian alphabet. It's been my scarlet letter. Worse, my name sounds like *bluejay* with a silent *l* and an *a* at the end: boo-jay-ah. How to explain?

Underneath the paragraph, I mapped out what I thought would be basic elements of the poem:

- Use *j* as the title.
- Include scenes from Lyndhurst, New Jersey.
- Explain that there is no *j* in the Italian alphabet.
- Focus on bluejay (or birds) as central image.
- End with understanding my name, Maltese (or Phoenician), a type of "song to myself."

Then I put the idea in a folder and let it cool for a few days, pondering the poem and holding back the urge to write. I do this because I want to visualize a work in my mind before putting it down on paper. Often I'll tell my friends or family members what I have been thinking about—a great way to sharpen an idea. If you're reluctant to speak directly about a topic, talk about feelings or images associated with it. For example, when contemplating the idea behind the poem "J," I didn't say, "I'm going to write a lyric about a letter of the alphabet and I want to run some thoughts by you." Rather, I asked my sister, "Did it ever occur to you that having a *j* in our name was a liability in Lyndhurst?" This way she could respond with some tidbit I may have overlooked. Meanwhile I had the benefit of focusing on my idea and envisioning my poem. Finally I composed several drafts, polishing lines, stanzas and the title (more on that in the "Tools of the Trade" section).

Here's the final draft of this particular poem:

"J"

On the page, in the right font,
It resembles a jay,

Swoop of the serif like a tail
Guiding the ascender,

Quotations around the beak
Vibrating the backdrop
Of erasable bond, an endless
Expanse of sky. My name has

A history, thirty years' war
Fielding questions, teaching
Friend and foe how to call
Or curse me, lovers unable

To pronounce declarations,
Rivals, vows of vengeance.
Even my blood brother,
The serious Sicilian, disowns me,

No "J" in the alphabet, Giacomo,
A confused pigeon, as if paisan
Opened the wrong coop,
The homing sense lost,

So when I sing of myself,
Nobody joins the chorus,
Nobody hears the screech
Bluejays make as they sully

Line or limb, preen a feather
As I want to preen
The scarlet letter from my name,
Phoenician, phonetics of fate.

To summarize my system:

1. Write a paragraph about an idea for a poem.
2. Sketch out key elements of that poem.
3. Think about the poem.
4. Hold back the urge to write.
5. Discuss the poem with friends and family members.
6. Compose the poem.

My method seems very reportorial, perhaps because I worked as a reporter for United Press International for several years. As you can see, I jot down a story idea as a reporter jots down facts on the nearest scrap of paper. I sketch out a strategy to capture the idea, think about where to find information, and then "interview" sources for details. I hold back the urge to write as if on deadline . . . and then get the job done.

This approach may or may not work for you. Perhaps you want to keep a journal like Dana Gioia's. Gioia had a busy career as a vice-president for Kraft General Foods, but that didn't stop him from writing poems and essays for publications like *The New Yorker*, *The Hudson Review* and *The Atlantic*. Now, as a full-time writer, he still uses several types of journals.

When I asked Gioia to share his methods, he wrote me, "I keep one notebook for prose ideas, one as a sporadic diary, one as a commonplace book of quotations (taken from books he reads), and others for poems and fragments." He adds, "If I were to share one notebook, it would be a little 5″ × 8″ binder I have. It's small enough for me to take along for a walk. It fits into my coat pocket. I jot down lines as they come to me. Or images as I notice them. Sometimes I'll even work out a stanza."

Gioia sent me pages from that spiral notebook and, reading them, one can see why he is such a powerful poet: He has a keen sense of perception. His journal enhances that gift. These phrases, taken from two sample pages of his binder, are printed carefully, with plenty of white space separating ideas:

. . . And one phone ringing down the hall

the circle of mist around the moon
like something dissolving in water

the dark veined hand
that you must learn to look on as your own

and memory becomes a well ~~into~~ down which
we whisper all our secrets and then hear
our own voice answer ~~back to~~ us with lies.

the light exactly right, the water calm
and leaning over the edge, we can see
not only our own face
which does not look away
but patiently returns our scrutiny
unashamed.

our own sad face which does not look away

and from that moment that we realize
that we are going to die

I studied these entries to see how Gioia captures his muse. Typically he focuses on the senses — "... And one phone *ringing* down the hall" — or combines a visual image with a simile: "the circle of mist around the moon/*like* something dissolving in water." He'll also explore metaphors — "and *memory* becomes a *well*" — in an attempt to articulate truth: "and from that moment that we realize/that *we are going to die*."

Reading Gioia's entries is like reading a long, disjointed poem that resembles a dream in which images and ideas meld into more images and ideas. Nonetheless, he claims, those entries in his binder seldom evolve into finished work.

"Someone might reasonably say that the book is largely a waste of time," Gioia observes. "I have noticed, however, that when I use this sort of book regularly I write more poetry."

Gioia believes that notations in a journal, however fragmentary, keep a writer's imagination open to more stimuli and help to focus mental energy in a creative manner. "One begins listening to one's own unconscious mind," he says, "and taking dictation. This sort of attention eventually creates the right attitude toward writing."

In addition, Gioia says, a journal is a practical tool for writers who have nonliterary jobs (as I did when I was a reporter and as he did when he worked as a marketing executive). "It gives poets something to jot down — momentary flashes of inspiration — so that they won't get lost."

Gioia knows that ideas for poems can strike at any moment. To record the unexpected visits of your muse, you may want to use Gioia's method to:

1. Keep the imagination open.
2. Set the mood for writing.
3. Catalogue ideas for poems.

As you can see, Gioia's system takes the pressure off the poet: It doesn't obligate you to compose, and yet you end up writing almost every day. Productivity is bound to increase.

"Sometimes years later," Gioia says, "I notice something looking through the book and suddenly a poem will start. I have given the imaginative seed enough time for it to germinate into a real poem."

Earlier I noted that you should design a journal to suit your needs or lifestyle. One of the most interesting adaptations I have seen is the journal of Martha M. Vertreace, an Illinois-based poet whose book *Under a Cat's-Eye Moon* (Clockwatch, 1991) has been widely praised because of the range and depth of ideas behind her poems. Her "journal" is part calendar, art catalogue, historical document and diary.

Her custom-made journal is, actually, a spiral calendar the size of Dana Gioia's notebook, featuring paintings by Vincent Van Gogh in the upper left corner and excerpts of letters by the famous Dutch artist along the top margin. The rest of the page is relatively blank, with seven horizontal lines to mark each day of the week.

At the top left, in her handwriting, is the salutation, "Dear Vincent," followed by a letter to her phantom painter about an idea for a poem (or a revision or some other artistic matter).

"I chose to address the journal to Vincent Van Gogh as a literary device to help me achieve some objectivity in evaluating my poems," Vertreace says.

She sent me pages of her journal that tell "the story of a poem, 'Oracle Bones,' " which she wrote and revised in the summer of 1989. An early entry in Vertreace's calendar occurs on July 4:

Dear Vincent,

Two strange, disconnected stanzas about ? perhaps home memories — I want more — perhaps [the poem] lacks a source of tension. [It] definitely lacks a source of tension. Interesting images. I like the line lengths. I think I will type it and tape it to the next page.

Here is an excerpt from one of those "two strange, disconnected stanzas":

Weekends I played with a cigarbox full of Betsy McCall
paper dolls while I watched
Flash Gordon's squadron of Mixmasters conquer
piano-wire space:
or I followed my brother around the edge of Burrville
    playground our Little Toy Hunt —
pennies, Cracker Jacks prizes, bits of yarn
    for a string ball —
whatever survived
the hot water bath my mother gave it.

Two days later, Vertreace writes:

Dear Vincent,

The version coming up is certainly longer — still only a catalogue of pleasant images — still no real metaphors. I am still not certain where I am going with this. . . .

On the next page, a new stanza appears containing more memories of the poet's childhood — "women ice skating/in costumes my mother/ would make" — and then another letter:

Dear Vincent,

This version still lacks a clear focus — a clear sense of direction.

The images do not seem to cohere — except in the all-too general sense of their being memories — most of them — of childhood.

Three days later, the poet writes the painter another missive. Vertreace has found a title for her work-in-progress, "Oracle Bones," and comments on the inspiration that she received after reading a book on the artist Georgia O'Keeffe. Then more drafts of the poem appear with commentary in her calendar. In all, it takes her about a month to finish the poem. Here is a portion of her last letter, dated July 18:

Dear Vincent,

I think I have reached the point of abandonment. The changes I made in the previous version are not that crucial — at least not in the sense of changing thematic drift. . . .

Writing about each substantial version forced me to slow down the process, in one sense, although I actually produced more versions, I think, than I would have, had I not done this. . . .

I found the process to be extremely interesting. By commenting on the versions, I was forced to confront the weaknesses as I saw them, and build on the strengths. I am convinced that inspiration is not merely a haphazard occurrence.

Let's summarize Vertreace's method, too. She uses her calendar as a journal to emphasize:

1. The power of imagination, suggested by the dialogue with Vincent Van Gogh — a good way to put distance between her memories and the concepts behind them.
2. The link between the visual and written arts, suggested by reprints of the paintings.
3. The evolution of a poem, from idea to final draft.
4. The importance of memory and the past, as suggested by individual days in the calendar.

All poets, in a sense, are timekeepers. They have to be or their unique ideas, like snowflakes, will melt and be gone. It's important that you record ideas for poems, but again, *where* you decide to record them is entirely up to you. Be bold! If you want to write a lyric about a maple tree whose trunk is ringed with carved hearts and inscriptions, but the tree is deep in woods along a trail, rent a camcorder and take a hike, videotaping the trail and the tree as you ponder your poem aloud.

Pick a method to suit your taste. The goal is the same: If you record your muse, you'll increase your output as a poet. You'll also become more aware of epiphanies and experiences.

Now let's preview the poems in the mini anthology:

- Dana Gioia's "The Silence of the Poets" contains a heightened moment of truth like those we've been discussing.
- Martha Vertreace's poem "Oracle Bones," mentioned earlier in the chapter, is included so you can see how that work turned out.
- You probably know Terry Anderson as the Associated Press reporter who was held hostage in Lebanon from 1985 to 1991. I knew of him as a competitor when I worked for United Press International and then, with millions of others around the world, followed his plight during his captivity. Upon his release I learned that he wrote poems and began corresponding with him. I've included one of those poems to underscore the points made earlier about highs, lows and turning points.

Additionally, it is interesting to note that Anderson never had the opportunity to keep a journal during those agonizing years. "We weren't allowed paper or pencil," he told me. To keep track of his poems, Anderson had to recite them in his head each day, a tedious process, because he always feared that he would forget his poems and ideas. On the day that two other hostages were released, Anderson was allowed one hour to write a letter. He did, along with eleven poems that he had created and memorized.

This dramatic anecdote only proves the importance of a journal, something we take for granted that helps preserve our experiences and thoughts so that we can share them with others.

Mini Anthology of Idea Poems

THE SILENCE OF THE POETS

is something to be grateful for.
Once there were so many books, so many poets.
All the masterpieces one could never read,
indistinguishable even then
among the endless shelves of the unreadable.

Some claim the best stopped writing first.
For the others, no one noted when or why.
A few observers voiced their mild regret
about another picturesque, unprofitable craft
that progress had irrevocably doomed.

And what was lost? No one now can judge.
But we still have music, art, and film,
diversions enough for a busy people.
And even poetry for those who want it.

The old books, those the young have not defaced,
are still kept somewhere,
stacked in their dusty rows.

And a few old men may visit from time to time
to run their hands across the spines
and reminisce,
but no one ever comes to read
or would know how.

                     — Dana Gioia

ORACLE BONES

Stretched out on the sofa, I watch the Cubs sink mid-inning —
runners at the corners, pitcher
ahead of the stiff-legged batter who lunges into his bunt;
the umpire checks the scoreboard.
The mailman brings a circular from Visa for pocket and desk
calendars in fake leather,
gold-tone corners, stamped initials; magazines expensive
to renew. Later I buy
a plastic fountain pen from Walgreen's to answer your letter —
two pages, single-spaced.
What do we remember of each other anyway? Ivy rings
my bedroom window
no matter how often I snap twigs, pull sticky nodes off brick.
Bitter payoff of green berries
lures flickers to the sill.

This much I can tell you: weekends I played cigarbox house
with Betsy McCall paper dolls,
saw Flash Gordon's squadron of Mixmasters chase Ming the Merciless
through piano-wire outer space;
followed my brother around Burrville playground, looking for coins,
Cracker Jacks prizes,
whatever could survive the hot water baptism Mother threatened.
From fruitcake tins
with village scenes — men sporting top hats, women ice skating
in ermine cloaks,
long skirts like those she hemmed for rich ladies — we stole
bobbins and spools
to build cities near her treadle machine. She caught grasshoppers,
fed them blades of grass
to make them "spit tobacco."

Before shadows drizzled mulberry at the brow of Harmony Hill,

Father bragged
that the heaviest thing he ever lifted was a pencil.
His idea of cooking:
eggs brown-laced in a cast-iron skillet; two dozen crabs
boiled in an aluminum pot,
lid weighted with brick. After Mother scalded the turkey
to swell its pores,
we tweezed out pinfeathers.

There were few things that mattered. At five I knew
sharks prowled
the Anacostia, waited for girls who stayed in the tub
while water swirled
down the drain. Under white sand, Seagull Beach,
boys buried
jellyfish whose damp sting never died. I gathered shells
I could not name,
whose frail edges snagged my pockets; sat in the kitchen,
traced around them
on drawing paper with red crayon. Darwinian footprints
ambled across the page.
O'Keeffe found stone clumps of mussels steeped
in million-year-old blue.
Before she knew the sea, she heard its rush trapped
in conch crowns,
as blood pulsed its echo in her ears.
Waves of grey sage
swept Taos bluffs.

New Year's Day, a man as first visitor brought good luck.
My neighbor's son
made his rounds to single women who welcomed with a sandwich;
widows, with scotch.
Mother doubted "stupidstitions," placed a filled shot glass
on the dining room table,
listened for his knock.

With no such guarantees, we should pierce tortoise shells
with glowing iron
like a Shang Dynasty scholar who ordered dragon's bones,
medicine from an Anyang apothecary;
instead got oracle bones whose crack pointed "auspicious"
or "inauspicious,"
which forecast when Earth believed in technicolor dreams:
"Three flames ate the sun

and big stars were seen." Total eclipse: coronal streamers,
stars tore
twice-told daytime sky.

It is enough that I begin in the middle of the page
away from margins.
About stark shapes in "Black and White," O'Keeffe wrote:
"This was a message
to a friend — if he saw it he didn't know it was to him
and wouldn't have known
what it said. And neither do I." Fireflies mark our palms
with pheromones;
we glow in the dark.

In the Medici, I start to write to you between the lines.
The bug-eyed man, again,
sits before me so he can sketch my portrait on his napkin
which he insists deserves
a three-dollar frame from Woolworth's. His thick hands,
rough like a farmer's,
like my uncle's, only much less kind. Meanwhile
the busboy sets afire
rows of saffron candles.

                                        — Martha M. Vertreace

SATAN

Satan is a name we use
for darkness in the world,
a goat on which we load
our most horrific sins,
to carry off our guilt.
But all the evil I have seen
was done by human beings.
It isn't a dark angel
who rigs a car into a bomb,
or steals money meant for others' food.
And it wasn't any alien spirit
that chained me to this wall.
One of those who kidnapped me
said once: "No man believes he's evil."
A penetrating and subtle thought
in these circumstances, and from him.
And that's the mystery:
He's not stupid, and doesn't seem insane.
He knows I've done no harm to him or his.

He's looked into my face
each day for years, and
heard me crying in the night.
Still he daily checks my chain,
makes sure my blindfold is secure,
then kneels outside my cell
and prays to Allah, merciful, compassionate.
I know too well the darker urges in myself,
the violence and selfishness.
I've seen little in him I can't recognize.
I also know my mind would shatter,
my soul would die if I did the things he does.
I'm tempted to believe there really is
a devil in him, some malefic,
independent force that makes him
less or other than a man.
That's too easy and too dangerous an answer;
it's how so many evils come to be.
I must reject, abhor and fight against
these acts, and acknowledge that
they're not inhuman—just the opposite.
We can't separate the things
we do from what we are;
Hate the sin and love the sinner is not
a concept I'll ever really understand.
I'll never love him—I'm not Christ.
But I'll try to achieve forgiveness
because I know that in the end,
as always, Christ was right.

—Terry Anderson

Notebook

LEVEL ONE

1. Look at my list of highs, lows and turning points—the one with specific incidents and epiphanies/peak experiences (on pages 7-8)—and come up with a similar list. Now you will have ten ideas for poems based on life experience and expressing specific truths. Put these in your journal and write a passage about what you hope your poem conveys. Try to envision key elements and list them. You'll use these ideas in notebook exercises in later chapters.

2. Review ways to research ideas using encyclopedias, quotation references, biographies, collections of letters and published diaries,

journals and autobiographies (as explained on pages 10-11). Visit the library and conceive ten more ideas for poems.

LEVELS TWO AND THREE

1. Look at the list of highs, lows and turning points that you created in the previous exercise when you last went through this text. Has any new experience happened that should appear in a revised list? If so, update. Then go through the list again and come up with new incidents for new entries and other incidents for old ones. You'll have at least ten more ideas. Record them as before.

2. Do the library exercise again, coming up with ten more ideas based on research of new listings in reference books.

Chapter Two

Love Poetry

Y ou may think that love poetry needs no introduction. After
all, chances are that sometime during your life you have
composed or received such verse. But as you'll learn by
reviewing the various genres of verse, the best poems often
cross borders, borrowing images from nature or politics to enhance a
love poem (or vice versa).

How, then, to categorize such work?

For instance, is this lyric by Ruth Daigon, editor of the literary
magazine *Poets On*, a love poem or a nature poem?

ALL THE LEAVES SAY YES
In the other, the sunken life,
in the world of green feedings,
all the leaves say yes, meadows
of curved stems say yes and warmth
flows from the depth of this yes
out toward horizons where hills
are still transparent and the ground
white with drippings from the moon.
Waking from this memory of green,
we'll face the skirmish of each day,
with hostages retrieved from the night.
This time will be different, new patterns
for the feet, wings for the eye,
rhythms for the heart, and our names
everywhere like grass.

One possible interpretation is that Daigon's poem belongs in the
nature category, because it uses images from nature. Another interpretation might emphasize the love theme suggested by the title and opening lines with the word "yes" and the romantic allusions in the final
six lines, in which the poet expresses heartfelt rhythms etched everywhere (as a person etches initials within a heart on a tree). In fact,

Daigon's work is *more* powerful because she crosses borders and borrows from the love and nature traditions, paying tribute to this unnamed "other" — the person for whom the poem was written or inspired. The bottom line is this: The only interpretation that matters is Daigon's at the time she conceived the idea for the poem.

You categorize poems on one criterion: intent. In other words, if you want to compose a love poem, feel free to borrow nature images (or whatever else) to express that love without worrying about what type of verse it is. (Only literary critics have to worry about getting the interpretation right.) However, it *is* important that you become familiar with the traditional topics so you can study the basic models and base your own ideas on them.

In this and the next five chapters, you'll be reading summaries of various types of poems defining each genre. By "types," I mean poems containing enduring *ideas* about love, nature, afterlife, war, politics and special occasions. As this pertains to love, chances are you already have read or know some of these poems. Now, however, you should scan them again as a writer in search of ideas and approaches that also apply to your life.

Here are a dozen common types of love poems:

The Carpe Diem. In Latin, it means "seize the day." In love poetry, this idea has come to mean: "Act quickly on your romantic impulses, because life is short." The idea was best expressed by Robert Herrick in his immortal "To the Virgins, to Make Much of Time," whose first stanza reads:

Gather ye rosebuds while ye may,
    Old time is still a-flying;
And this same flower that smiles today
    Tomorrow will be dying. . . .

The Complaint. This type of poem addresses another person who denies or in some way refuses to return feelings of love or affection. Here's an excerpt from "Song. To My Inconstant Mistress" by Thomas Carew:

Then shalt thou weep, entreat, complain
    To Love, as I did once to thee;
When all thy tears shall be as vain
    As mine were then, for thou shalt be
    Damned for thy false apostasy. . . .

Love Tribute. A love tribute is, simply, a celebratory poem dedicated to a lover, as this excerpt from a poem by Anne Bradstreet illustrates:

TO MY DEAR AND LOVING HUSBAND

If ever two were one, then surely we.
If ever man were loved by wife, then thee;
If ever wife was happy in a man,
Compare with me, ye women, if you can. . . .

The Proposal. In a proposal poem, one lover solicits the favors, affections or hand of another, as in this excerpt from a famous song by Ben Jonson:

TO CELIA

Drink to me only with thine eyes,
And I will pledge with mine;
Or leave a kiss but in the cup,
And I'll not look for wine. . . .

Love Concept. Such verse treats a phase of love — anything from infatuation to commitment — philosophically. In this excerpt, Abraham Cowley deals with the ancient concept of spiritual affection:

PLATONIC LOVE

Can that for true love pass
When a fair woman courts her glass?
Something unlike must in love's likeness be:
His wonder is one and variety.
For he whose soul nought but a soul can move
Does a new Narcissus prove,
And his own image love. . . .

The Obstacle. A poem about any person, object or thing that prevents one lover from reaching another. In Richard Lovelace's case, the obstacle was a jail cell, as stated in the title and last stanza from "To Althea, from Prison":

Stone walls do not a prison make,
Nor iron bars a cage;
Minds innocent and quiet take
That for an hermitage.
If I have freedom in my love,
And in my soul am free,
Angels alone, that soar above,
Enjoy such liberty.

Absent Love. This brand of verse bemoans (or cheers) the fact that one lover has left another. An example by Shelley:

TO MARY SHELLEY

My dearest Mary, wherefore hast thou gone,
And left me in this dreary world alone!
Thy form is here indeed — a lovely one —
But thou art fled, gone down the dreary road,
That leads to Sorrow's most obscure abode;
Thou sittest on the hearth of pale despair,

                                          where
For thine own sake I cannot follow thee.

Love Moment. This type recaptures the instant one person falls in (or out of) love with another, as in this lyric composed by Leigh Hunt, a friend of Shelley:

JENNY KISSED ME

Jenny kissed me when we met,
    Jumping from the chair she sat in;
Time, you thief, who love to get
    Sweets into your list, put that in;
Say I'm weary, say I'm sad,
    Say that health and wealth have missed me,
Say I'm growing old, but add,
    Jenny kissed me.

The Reconciliation. A reconciliation poem marks the end of an estrangement or a spat between lovers, as this excerpt from a poem by Robert Browning illustrates:

A WOMAN'S LAST WORD

Let's contend no more, Love,
    Strive nor weep;
All be as before, Love,
    — Only sleep!

Love Token. This type accompanies a token of affection or a gift, as this poem accompanied a lock of hair from Browning's wife Elizabeth Barrett Browning:

I never gave a lock of hair away
To a man, Dearest, except this to thee,
Which now upon my fingers thoughtfully,
I ring out to the full brown length and say
"Take it". . . .

Illicit Love. This type concerns an affair or tryst, as in this excerpt from a work by D.H. Lawrence:

TEASE

I will give you all my keys,
   You shall be my châtelaine,
You shall enter as you please,
   As you please shall go again. . . .

Future Love. A future love lyric imagines young lovers in the future and speculates about the quality of their relationship when they grow old, as Thomas Hardy did when he wrote this poem in 1909:

1967

In five-score summers! All new eyes,
New minds, new modes, new fools, new wise;
New woes to weep, new joys to prize;

With nothing left of me and you
In that live century's vivid view
Beyond a pinch of dust or two;

A century which, if not sublime,
Will show, I doubt not, at its prime,
A scope above this blinkered time.

—Yet what to me how far above?
For I would only ask thereof
That thy worm should be my worm, Love!

There are other ways lovers express feelings in verse, of course, and you can combine types to suit your circumstances. For instance, it is possible to meld a "love moment" with a "reconciliation" in a poem about forgiveness, depicting an estranged couple renewing their vows. Or "future love" and a "reconciliation" in a poem about hope, depicting an estranged lover who longs one day for forgiveness. The combinations and shades of meaning are seemingly endless. That's why you should study the basic types first so that you can vary and combine them later.

Keep in mind that you are contemplating the *ideas* behind these types rather than the voices or words used by poets who composed in other eras. As noted in the first chapter, ideas often outlive the language that poets have used to express them. The language of love evolves continually.

Finally, you can also generate ideas for love poems as you did in chapter one by classifying your romantic experiences in a list of highs, turning points and lows, as we'll soon see.

LOVE PRIMER

Using the right tone of voice to express love is an important aspect of mastering the genre. You'll become more familiar with the mechanical aspects of voice in chapter eight, but for now, think of it simply as the "sound" you hear on the page when you read a poem. According to Ruth Daigon, who has published and edited dozens of love poems, "For beginning poets, love poetry is synonymous with a passionate outpouring, a singing, a saying, a surrender to the emotion. They feel that to restrain or modify such language would in some way betray the depth of feeling. However, the greater the extent of passion, the more appropriate it is to harness and control such energy."

Daigon says Wordsworth's advice about poetry in general applies to love poetry in particular. "Wordsworth talked about poetry as being 'a spontaneous overflow of emotion recollected in tranquility.' Young poets too often emphasize the 'overflow' rather than the 'recollection.' Recollection implies a disciplinary process that is essential when composing love poetry."

As editor of a small-press magazine, Daigon says she sees plenty of undisciplined submissions. I can verify that fact. When I edited poetry for a literary journal, I read thousands of bad love poems (the most popular type of submission). These poems had two things in common: The subject matter was safe, usually a tribute to a lover, and the voice was either antiquated or raw. It seemed poets were mimicking voices of love poems that sounded contemporary in other centuries, as this example illustrates:

Let me love thee evermore,
For time knows not "yesterday"
    or "when,"
Nor will it honor deeds of yore
Or heed the heart again. . . .

Or they were failing to control their voices, as this example illustrates:

I want you so much I think about you every
hour and waking minute of the day hoping
that time slips away so I can be with you again.

Let's make some observations about antiquated language and safe subject matter in love poems.

Poets who try to sound like the Elizabethan and Victorian masters make two mistakes. First, they sound pompous or silly. Second, they forget that the ideas behind the poems of, say, Shakespeare and Dickinson are what fascinates contemporary readers. Surely the language of master poets is still beautiful and musical, but it is not *your* language anymore; you can't use it as well as your own contemporary tongue whose beauty and music should come to you more naturally.

As for the need to shun "safe" love poems, think about the nature of romance. Fact: People take all sorts of risks in real life when they feel love for or desire another person. Fact: Some people jeopardize or split up their families, others commit their lives forever to the wrong people, and a few even suffer physically and mentally from love's scars. Fact: Some couples overcome huge obstacles in life, others marry the right people and abandon destructive lifestyles, and a few even heal the physical and mental scars caused by past experience — all because of love.

But when many of these people sit down to compose love poems, for some reason they jettison what they know and write little ditties like this:

> I like to think of sunset nights
> and mornings full of dew,
> and all the moments in between
> I spend in love with you.

Perhaps they write such poems in part because they can identify them as love poems. They want their lovers or would-be lovers who receive them to acknowledge the gesture as much as the genre. But the fact is that they are not being truthful about the essence of love. Sure, it's a wonderful feeling when reciprocated, but it tends to mess up or reorganize your life.

Contemplate how love has reorganized your life goals and/or priorities. What happened? Refer to that list of highs, lows and turning points of your life (which you wrote in the chapter one notebook exercise) and make another more specialized list related to your love life or relationships. A high point can be as subtle as a glance across the room from someone you would like to know, or as heady as a marriage proposal. A turning point can be the realization that you love (or do not love) another person. A low can be telling that person that you have fallen out of love or listening to someone tell you. Moreover, if you truly care or have cared about a person, you should be able to generate dozens of ideas based on dozens of highs, lows and turning points, because the phases of each relationship — meeting and courting a loved one, consummating or ending the union — resemble peaks and valleys on a chart.

Once you have identified and classified your experiences, decide how you want to convey them. Do you want to direct your poem at a lover or at a reader or both? You would be surprised how such a determination can change an idea for a poem and serve almost as a check to see if your idea entails an element of risk. For instance, I find it helpful when brainstorming for ideas to imagine the person(s) I want to address in a particular setting.

I ask myself:

- How would I tell this idea to my lover?
- How would I tell it to a friend (reader)?
- How would I tell it to my lover, if I knew that my friend was behind a curtain in the room, overhearing the conversation?
- How would I tell it to my friend, if I knew that my lover was behind that curtain, overhearing the conversation?
- How would I tell it if I was speaking to my friend with my lover sitting with us at the kitchen table?
- How would I tell it if I was speaking to my lover with my friend sitting with us at the kitchen table?

What these questions accomplish, of course, is a preview of the type of voice you will choose for your poem. As Ruth Daigon stated earlier, voice is paramount in a love poem. It shapes content and indicates risk (a situation in which it would be uncomfortable to speak in the presence of another). To illustrate, I have taken a stanza from one of my love poems and altered the voice (whose sound is described by adjectives) according to each of the above questions:

1. How would I tell this idea to my lover?

   What is it that wants as the body never has, with every corpuscle of being, the system immune to shocks of blame and embarrass-
                                                                              ment,
   to all checks and balances that keep custody of the self?

   Voice: passionate, rhetorical, irritated

2. How would I tell it to a friend (reader)?

   Why does the heart yearn more than the body
   with every corpuscle of being,
   as if the system were immune to shocks
   of blame or embarrassment, to checks
   and balances of the self?

   Voice: philosophical, reflective, introspective

3. How would I tell it to my lover, if I knew my friend was behind a curtain in the room, overhearing the conversation?

   Why does the heart want you more than the body,
   with every corpuscle of being,
   my system immune now to blame and embarrassment,
   whatever keeps custody of the self?

Voice: bold, rhetorical, irritated

4. How would I tell it to my friend, if I knew my lover was behind
   a curtain in the room, overhearing the conversation?

It's not the body, but the heart
wants her with every corpuscle of being,
as if I'm immune now to shocks
of blame and embarrassment,
to all checks and balances of the self.

Voice: plaintive, introspective, candid

5. How would I tell it if I was speaking to my friend with my lover
   sitting with us at the kitchen table?

I want her more with my heart than my body,
though she doesn't believe this. No matter.
Every corpuscle of my being is immune now
to blame and embarrassment,
to all checks and balances of the self.

Voice: plaintive, resigned, candid

6. How would I tell it if I was speaking to my lover with my friend
   sitting with us at the kitchen table?

It's the heart, not the body, wants you
with every corpuscle of being. Say what you will—
I'm immune now to blame and embarrassment
to whatever it is that imprisons the self.

Voice: candid, defensive, imploring

As you can see, depending on the voice, the subject matter changes
somewhat in each setting. That's because the poem takes a risk. If the
voice doesn't change in each setting, then your topic is so mundane
or ordinary that no person would sneak behind a curtain to overhear.
No lover at the kitchen table would mind another person being present.
In fact, take the earlier examples of "bad" love poetry (employing
antiquated, undisciplined and sugary voices) and run them through
each scenario above. Nothing will change because nothing is at stake.

LOVE PERSPECTIVES

Stephen Corey, who has published several collections of verse and
helps edit *The Georgia Review*, is known for his varied and sustained
voice, particularly in love poems. The two reprinted here underscore
important points about the genre. One is a love poem and the other

an erotic one. Erotic poetry falls under the category of love with the emphasis, of course, on the physical act rather than the concept or felt emotion. In Corey's love poem, words exchanged between lovers have enhanced meaning; in his erotic one, words are muted because they need to show or describe.

Here's the love poem:

WHAT WE DID, WHAT YOU WILL KNOW

We invented a language
you will never speak,
but you will hear its diction
in all I can write.
Any scholar of my work
will know, for every word,
one less thing than you.
You will know a candle means
a tall gray bookcase,
any small wound is a rug,
and orange shirts are ropes
that can pull us to places
different from those we have known.

Says Corey, "Every poem is an attempt to get past the barriers of silence and isolation that necessarily form around all of our lives as we live them. This particular poem happens to announce that effort quite blatantly — and then to undercut itself by recognizing, explicitly and implicitly, that it is erecting barriers at the same time it is trying to remove them." With this poem, Corey says, he wanted to discover ways to show *and* tell, to make statements and associate those statements with images.

In his erotic poem, however, showing rather than telling takes precedence:

REDUNDANCIES

So we move to moisten
what is already damp,
to wet what is already moist.

Shadows in hand,
we trace the traced.

What is hot we heat —
what is open, open wide —
what filled fill again,
spill over, and fill.

The risen we raise,
the plumbed we sound.

Already posed,
the positions hold —
what was there
is there once more.

"In this poem," he says, "I was hoping to be as erotic and arousing as possible without using any statements, or even any words, that are directly or exclusively sexual. I wanted, simultaneously, clarity and mystery . . . specificity and abstractions once essential and removable.

"But, of course, the preceding explanation is all after the fact. At the time I was writing the poem, I wanted to capture, somehow and however vaguely, the experience of sex in the experience of words — so that I could give those words to the woman who was in my thoughts as I wrote."

Once again, Corey's love and erotic poems illustrate the importance of language in this category of verse. He tries to enhance meaning by commenting about love or showing the act; each entails a measure of risk (particularly in erotic poetry whose images are meant to arouse without lapsing into the crude or profane).

But poet Ann Townsend, whose work appears regularly in top literary journals, takes another view about risk in love, saying, "I want, in a compressed fashion, to explore moments of danger in human relationships." Here is a representative poem by Townsend:

MODERN LOVE

The rain streams past the gutters, overflowing
    a drain clogged with leaves. From inside
the sound is cool and precise, and though
    the door lies open and the light
spills out, the kitchen keeps its warmth.
    The refrigerator hums, the girl works on
beneath the pools of light, and the man
    outside her window sees her pull
on a cigarette; his eyes follow
    the orange-bright tip; he flicks water
from his eyes and wonders what to do next,
    how to proceed, whether to use the knife
or his hands to open the latched, screen door.
    He has never been so wet.

She studies the list on the table, decorum
    of crossed-out items — the few that remain.

The rain slows, and the last crickets begin
  a feeble song from the pond next door.
So far away, each thinks. He watches her mouth open
  in concentration. He must make her
hear him as he meant to be heard:
  what they have done has not been wrong.
His hands know their way past the buttons of her dress.
  She lifts her eyes to the window and catches
sight of her own likeness in the glass.
  She can never stop herself: smiling
at the ghost reflection before her.
  He believes she is looking at him.

Says Townsend, " 'Modern Love' is concerned with exploring love as an obsession. On the one hand the man in the poem wants the woman so badly he is willing to do violence to get her; the woman is concerned with the way the glass of the window reflects her and so never sees who waits for her outside the glass. I want the poem to be a little frightening, to show how easily what seems like love can turn dangerous. When I was writing 'Modern Love,' " she recalls, "I drew from a sense of danger, something that probably many women feel, about who might be waiting outside, whether lover or stranger."

Not only does Townsend take a risk in the poem, she also adjusts her voice to enhance the tension of the situation. Her descriptive, ominous tones are controlled throughout the work, adding suspense to the theme of obsession. Even if we have never experienced such an encounter, we will read her poem because at its heart is some important truth about the consequences of obsession, or "modern love."

Let's close our discussion about love poetry with a preview of contemporary examples in the mini anthology:

- In "Speaking of Love," Dana Gioia does just that—discusses the importance of words and the truths they evoke universally in all of us.
- In "One Dream," another poem by Ann Townsend, Townsend focuses on her lover as he sleeps next to her in bed. "It's a moment of stillness, a time when one lover steps back and looks at the other, knowing that some kinds of intimacy are not possible," she says.

"I don't think the poem thinks that's a bad thing, though, because the speaker can imagine all sorts of wonderful possibilities for the dreams the lover might be having. I think the poem finds a virtue in the solitude we keep at our center, even as the speaker wonders at her lover's thoughts and dreams."

- In "Sentimental: An Epithalamium," dedicated to Ann Townsend by her husband David Baker, Baker mixes nature and love imagery into a symphony of emotion celebrating their relationship.

Mini Anthology of Love Poems

SPEAKING OF LOVE

Speaking of love was difficult at first.
We groped for those lost, untarnished words
That parents never traded casually at home,
The radio had not devalued.
How little there seemed left to us.

So, speaking of love, we chose
The harsh and level language of denial
Knowing only what we did not wish to say,
Choosing silence in our terror of a lie.
For surely love existed before words.

But silence can become its own cliché,
And bodies lie as skillfully as words,
So one by one we spoke the easy lines
The other had resisted but desired,
Trusting that love renewed their innocence.

Was it then that words became unstuck?
That star no longer seemed enough for star?
Our borrowed speech demanded love so pure
And so beyond our power that we saw
How words were only forms of our regret.

And so at last we speak again of love,
Now that there is nothing left unsaid,
Surrendering our voices to the past,
Which has betrayed us. Each of us alone,
Obsessed by memory, befriended by desire,

With no words left to summon back our love.
                                        — Dana Gioia

ONE DREAM

You are unaware I spy like this
every morning, that I wake before you
to watch your eyes tremble and awkwardly
blossom. The casual remoteness of your body
still startles me in the grainy light
that lies between us. How your dreams must
hold you, their amorous and fascinating figures:
the populations inside your vast cities,
the quiet voices spinning kisses to keep you.

These must be, because you sleep and dream
alone, you smile like a conspirator
in a lovely game. Only your eyes are telling,
their lids pressing out a Morse code
at uncertain intervals, cautious even in sleep,
speaking out of great distance, from a place
neither of us will ever see. Everything is still
as these movements spread out, outlining
the yellow light, the quilt thrown back from our bodies,
the soft weight of our limbs. Inside this silence,
your breath is held tightly, and let go.
        —Ann Townsend

SENTIMENTAL: AN EPITHALAMIUM
for Ann

  Our willow lets its limbs down
almost to the water, almost so they brush
  the surface sheen, lightly,

  leaf-shadows
the shape of perch, palm-sized, blue-black,
  finning themselves still

  near the shoreline;
and when I touch my heel to the cool
  water and come in,

  you are there, as if always
we have waited for this moment
  when we enter

  each other's outstretched arms,
wade together to the center of the small pond
  which has become, now,

  somehow, as we drift together
in the clear sky of water, as perfect as any
  world we could desire—

  insects spin in the air,
redwings loosen from the limbs
  of willows, flying

  in small flocks to nowhere
and always returning—shy, miraculous
  acts of grace,

wind rocking barely
in the blue-black leaves — all
    of this, for hours, clear on the pond

    until, eyes closed,
shaken in and out of the water's own
    arms, we sense these finally

    no longer, feeling
only the pulse of the pond's deepest
    currents, fern

    and water-weeds sweeping
our legs, the soft, prescient muds bearing us
    toward each other, then away;

    so when, at last,
we open our eyes and sunlight has slipped
    from the surface, the redwings

    vanished as minnows
in the low leaf-shadow, we let ourselves,
    lazy with love, float

    beneath our willow
once again, whose thin limbs seem always
    to have been waiting for this,

    reaching its tender arms
down to us who are reaching up
    out of the last
                    swirling light.
                              — David Baker

Notebook

LEVEL ONE

1. Review the basic types of love poems that were excerpted in the beginning of this chapter. Relate each to your romantic life. For instance, is someone you love absent? If so, base an idea on the "absent love" model. Is there an obstacle preventing you from achieving love? If so, base an idea on the "obstacle" model. By now you should have designed a journal to suit your needs. Explore these ideas for love poems and conceive at least five of them.

2. Make a list of lovers, would-be lovers, pursuers or people you pursued. Under each name, make a "love list" of highs, lows and

turning points concerning each of those relationships. Try to remember specific incidents, moments, complaints and occasions in which strong feelings or situations arose. Base at least five ideas for poems on your lists.

LEVEL TWO

1. Analyze the lists you made of names and highs, lows and turning points from the Level One exercise. Reread your journal entries. Develop five more ideas based on any incidents left over from your first assignment.

2. Evaluate your love life since you did the Level One exercise and add to or revise your lists, citing new relationships or encounters. (If your love life has been static, write about reasons why or about would-be lovers.) Devote a passage in your journal to each new romance or encounter and base ideas for five more poems on them.

LEVEL THREE

1. Reread your journal entries from the Level One and Two exercises. Add new relationships and encounters as needed to your lists, recording what has occurred in your love life since you did the Level Two exercise. Look for patterns in the three lists — incidents of arguments, growth, loss, gain — anything entailing risk or enlightenment. Write about each pattern in a passage in your journal and base ideas for five poems on them.

2. Now evaluate the new entries to your lists of relationships and encounters — the people and/or events involved in your love life since you did the Level Two assignment. Write about each person or incident in a passage in your journal and base ideas for five more poems on them.

Chapter Three

Nature and Environmental Poetry

I f a poem is set in the world, it is in part a nature poem. But what qualifies verse to be included in this category so that the reader's first impulse is to identify it within a specific genre? Poems about the seasons, plants, animals — all these are common enough in the literary canon — but others, concerning humans, are more subtle. For instance, is this poem by Ann Townsend an example of love or nature poetry?

ON ALUM CREEK
Our boots slide on the solid creek,
frozen waist-deep water. A sycamore
is dying, its branches of white horn
fading in the sun. The roots trail
to the creek edge, where each day
ice gathers around the nubs,
surrounding and breaking and forming again.

We are one man and one woman.
It is the shortest day, the solstice,
and already we feel it passing on:
the flickering of sun, the colder
absorbing air disguised as breath, brushing
our faces, our ankles. You glide far
onto the ice, onto the deep shadow

of the sycamore, walking stick discarded
on the bank. Your breath follows you,
floating up as you shout, "Come on,
the water's fine!" I edge out, uncertain,
my stick tapping its tattoo before me.
Heavy yellow boots anchor your feet
as the sky presses down, the ice

trembling beneath you, water rushing through

the crust when the creek turns its corner.
Even when we came this way, a fading wind
washed over the fields. The bare crust of snow
broke beneath our boots, the numb earth
rose in tufts of brown grass and leaves
as we followed a dry gully down.

I stand ready to hear your cry,
to reach out when the ice divides
against you. I know you will fall.
I can see it in the slow ripple of the crust
each time you turn, push off, slide;
even as the ice cracks you drift away
smiling, daring me to follow.

One can argue that nature is mere background in this poem, that
the man and woman are testing their wills along with the frozen waters
and as such symbolize the implied dynamics of a relationship: commitment. That is one interpretation. If you only identify nature poems as
ones that contemplate or celebrate the outdoors, then Townsend's
poem belongs in the love category.

But take a closer look. Her poem is as much about nature as human
nature. The setting features a sycamore tree along Alum Creek, whose
waist-deep water appears frozen. The time is winter. The exact day is
the solstice — the shortest day in December — and the snow plays a
leading role in the drama's theme that not only pits man against woman
but both against nature. Thus, Townsend's poem also involves four
traditional elements of nature poetry: the setting, the season, the solstice and the theme.

In the end, Townsend's poem is a nature poem *broadly defined.*
Let's attempt such a definition:

*A poem in which nature plays an integral role, emphasizing ter-
rain and life (including humans) in a natural setting, season,
metaphor, symbol, situation or theme.*

Here are a dozen basic types:

Tribute to the Season. The nature poem also is the oldest in the
canon. Verses have been offered up to nature for millennia, usually
welcoming the season or asking the season to be gentle, joyous or
fruitful. Consider this excerpt by an unknown poet from one of the
oldest lyrics (circa thirteenth century) in English:

THE CUCKOO SONG

Sumer is i-cumen in —
  Lhude sing, cuccu!

Groweth sed and bloweth med
And springth the wude nu.
　　Sing, cuccu!

Nature Against Human. This type of poem casts a man or woman in a perilous situation, as this excerpt from William Cowper illustrates:

THE CASTAWAY

Obscurest night involved the sky,
　　The Atlantic billows roared,
When such a destined wretch as I,
　　Washed headlong from on board.
Of friends, of hope, of all bereft,
His floating home forever left. . . .

Human Against Nature. This type of poem reverses the situation, casting a man or woman overcoming a perilous situation or destroying some aspect of nature. Here's an excerpt from such a poem by Henry Vaughan:

THE TIMBER

Sure thou didst flourish once! and many springs,
Many bright mornings, much dew, many showers
Passed o'er thy head; many light hearts and wings,
Which now are dead, lodged in thy living bowers. . . .

Human-Nature Relationship. Typically this poem concerns a person fixing himself or herself in the natural world or contemplating some aspect of nature, longing for its qualities, as illustrated in this excerpt from a work by John Keats:

BRIGHT STAR

Bright star, would I were steadfast as thou art—
　　Not in lone splendor hung aloft the night
And watching, with eternal lids apart,
　　Like nature's patient, sleepless Eremite,
The moving waters. . . .

Nature as Metaphor for the Human Condition. In this poem type, the poet uses some aspect or element of nature to express how it feels to be mortal. Here's an example by William Blake that treats anger as if it were a living thing:

A POISON TREE

I was angry with my friend:
I told my wrath, my wrath did end.

I was angry with my foe:
I told it not, my wrath did grow.

And I waterd it in fears,
Night & morning with my tears; . . .

Nature as Symbolic of the Human Condition. This type of poem closely resembles the one above, but instead of using a metaphor (an overt or implied comparison) it employs a symbol — some aspect or element of nature that automatically harkens a feeling about humanity. Here's an example by William Wordsworth:

MY HEART LEAPS UP
My heart leaps up when I behold
  A rainbow in the sky:
So was it when my life began;
So is it now I am a man;
So be it when I shall grow old,
  Or let me die!
The Child is father of the Man; . . .

Human Encountering Nature. Simply, the poet suddenly beholds an element or aspect of nature as if for the first time, with keen perception. Here's another excerpt from a famous Wordsworth poem:

I wandered lonely as a cloud
That floats on high o'er vales and hills,
When all at once I saw a crowd,
A host, of golden daffodils;
Beside the lake, beneath the trees,
Fluttering and dancing in the breeze. . . .

Nature as Reflection of Mood. In this type of poem, the setting is outdoors and the poet describes a personal feeling, not in context with what is seen in nature, but as a backdrop for mood. Here's an excerpt from such a poem titled "Stanzas Written in Dejection, Near Naples" by Shelley:

I see the Deep's untrampled floor
  With green and purple seaweeds strown;
I see the waves upon the shore,
  Like light dissolved in star-showers, thrown:
  I sit upon the sands alone —
The lightning of the noontide ocean
  Is flashing round me, and a tone
Arises from its measured motion;
How sweet! did any heart now share in my emotion. . . .

Nature-Human Celebration. The poet celebrates himself or herself as part of nature, as does Walt Whitman in this excerpt:

SPONTANEOUS ME

Spontaneous me, Nature,
The loving day, the mounting sun, the friend I am happy with,
The arm of my friend hanging idly over my shoulder,
The hillside whiten'd with blossoms of the mountain ash,
The same late in autumn, the hues of red, yellow, drab, purple,
    and light and dark green, . . .

Essence of Nature. Such verse focuses on some element of nature and describes its beauty or essence, as H.D. does in this excerpt from a poem titled "Sea Violet":

Violet
your grasp is frail
on the edge of the sand-hill,
but you catch the light—
frost, a star edges with its fire.

Isolation From Nature. This type of verse describes how a person feels apart from the natural world, excluded somehow from its essence or beauty, as this excerpt from a poem titled "Blight" by Emerson illustrates:

Our eyes
Are armed, but we are strangers to the stars,
And strangers to the mystic beast and bird,
And strangers to the plant and to the mine. . . .

Nature as Reflection of God. One of the most common types of nature poems, this calls on some aspect or element of nature to harken images of the Creator. An example by Edna St. Vincent Millay:

GOD'S WORLD

O world, I cannot hold thee close enough!
    Thy winds, thy wide grey skies!
    Thy mists, that roll and rise!
Thy woods, this autumn day, that ache and sag
And all but cry with colour!

If you scan major anthologies, you'll find plenty of examples of nature verse. The best all have one common element: They do not gild the lily, as it were, attempting to improve nature. Nature cannot be improved—only observed.

POET AS OBSERVER

Nature *is*. If nature appears sullied, perhaps you are only viewing it as "sullied" or perhaps someone or something has caused it to appear so in your eyes. The nature poet is, in part, a chronicler of the outdoors and, in part, an interpreter of what is sensed or experienced. The poet uses *perception* to chronicle nature and *perspective* to interpret it (more on both concepts later). For now, let's focus on a basic requirement to write keen nature poetry: concentration.

When I began writing poetry, I did not ponder nature much. I felt cheated because, living so close to New York City, I had never seen great natural vistas or even national parks. My rivers and wetlands were polluted. Consequently, I *imagined* what nature would be like in pristine settings and then placed myself in that fiction. Of course, nature abounds in cities, even in cracks of sidewalks, vacant lots and abandoned buildings. But I disregarded these. The result was impure verse that lacked authority, vision and truth.

Later in life I moved to the Midwest and the South and learned that all those natural vistas and national parks weren't so pristine after all. I became more patient, simply recording what I saw in my journal and then evaluating what it meant or implied about me. In sum, I sharpened my concentration — of nature and myself!

Tom Andrews, whose second book won the Piper Award at the University of Iowa, puts the experience into context. "The first poems I ever wrote focused on the natural world, and they did so, I suppose, for the same reason that many other beginning poets turn to the natural world for content." That reason, he says, is to get in touch with "inner states of feeling, inner meditations." Andrews adds that after many unsatisfying poems, "I discovered that to be precise, I needed to develop greater powers of concentration and attention, powers I would have perhaps never found a desire for otherwise. Eventually, writing about the natural world offered me a desperately needed discipline: the struggle to be precise, not for the sake of my inner life, but because the images I was trying to create demanded precision."

Andrews notes that the natural world became interesting in a way he had never before experienced: "It was teaching me about curiosity and patience and awe."

Andrews points out that studying nature is just one way to develop these traits. "I don't mean to suggest that only nature poems can teach a poet about concentration and attention. William Carlos Williams, for example, showed us that *anything* — broken bottles, rumpled sheets of paper, vacant lots — looked at carefully enough can tell us about the essence of things." But when it comes to nature poetry, Andrews suggests that writers refrain from "using" nature and simply allow it to "present" itself without ornamentation.

Andrews illustrates with this poem:

AT BURT LAKE
To disappear into the right words
and to be their meanings . . .

October dusk.
Pink scraps of clouds, a plum-colored sky.
The sycamore tree spills a few leaves.
The cold focuses like a lens . . .

Now night falls, its hair
caught in the lake's eye.

Such clarity of things. Already
I've said too much . . .

                    Lord,
language must happen to you
the way this black pane of water,
chipped and blistered with stars,
happens to me.

Andrews is allowing nature to present itself in a context he can understand. He doesn't overburden the poem with comment or flowery words in an attempt to depict nature on the page. He easily could, because the lake holds many memories for him.

"Burt Lake is in northern Michigan," Andrews says, "about a half-hour drive from Mackinaw City. My wife's family has lived by the lake for many years. 'At Burt Lake' tries to embody the wonder that the particular landscape has always provoked in me. Central to such experiences, for me, is the strange sense of coming up against the limits of language to adequately communicate wonder and mystery." Andrews adds that he wanted those limits to be an explicit part of the poem. Thus, in part, "At Burt Lake" is a statement about nature poetry. "Perhaps, as one of the Upanishads [Hindu treatises] tells us, all we can say at such moments is 'Ah.' . . ."

PERCEPTION AND PERSPECTIVE
Understanding the idea of poets as observers is critical if you want to compose nature poetry. For centuries people have looked to the genre to help them appreciate the beauty and design of the natural world. Hence, a poet is expected to behold a tree or a place and see something the casual observer would miss. Again, all this has to do with perception (what we observe) and perspective (how we observe it).

Bad poems about nature abound and share two common traits:

1. The images from nature are either vague, lacking detail, or ordinary. The poet observes what anybody would observe when contemplating an object or living thing.
2. The truth of the natural world is overlooked, leaving the poem without an epiphany or the poet without a peak experience. The poet interprets nature in an inconsequential or clichéd manner.

Let's illustrate both shortcomings — ordinary images and lack of epiphany or peak experience — in a poem about Norfolk, a county in eastern England that boasts several rivers draining into the sea. I'll compose a poor nature poem. Then I'll reprint a nature lyric about the same topic by British artist, editor, publisher and poet Rupert M. Loydell.

Here's mine:

NORFOLK

The sun shines
on your face
as waves splash
on the beach.
People use rope
to pull sailboats in,
standing on the sand.
You can hear
birds in the sky,
even in the rain.

I've done my best to compose the above poem in a good form, but with poor imagery, to emphasize that weakness. The sun "shines." People pull "rope." They stand on "sand." You can hear "birds in the sky." I also included an interesting last line — "even in the rain" — to hint at an epiphany. But when one thinks about that statement, its "truth" is empty and does not move the reader emotionally.

Now let's read Rupert M. Loydell's poem:

NORFOLK

I miss your silent stare,
harsh glint of dawning sun
reflected in your murky face.

I miss your rhythmic slap,
drumming through the night,
quiet splash and ripple.

I miss the pull of wet rope
through chilled fingers,

the tautness of the sail.

I miss reeds and grasses, muddy shores.
strange calls of unknown birds,
the casual launchings of ducks.

I miss the smell of evening mist,
swallowing your beauty until tomorrow;
the sudden damp and clammy cold.

I seek your rivers Norfolk,
carry me in your wind again,
white sail against your green.

The first thing to note is how Loydell uses images that appeal to or suggest the five senses: "harsh glint" (sight), "rhythmic slap" (sound), "pull of wet rope" (touch), "smell of evening mist" (smell), and "swallowing your beauty" (taste). Notice the detail or allure of certain images: "quiet splash and ripple," "reeds and grasses," "the tautness of the sail," and "the casual launchings of ducks." Mark the repetition of "I miss" that generates each memory, a cadence like the breaking waves that conveys symbols of Norfolk like a sea chant. Finally, consider the final stanza in which the poet realizes that he, too, is part of the landscape: "I seek your rivers Norfolk,/carry me in your wind again,/white sail against your green."

Let's analyze a poem set on the other side of the Atlantic.

Stan Rubin teaches poetry at the university in Brockport, New York, organizes writer's conferences there, and vacations on the Maine coast. "From a house on the bluffs, looking out at the wind-blown sea, one can see five islands and, beyond them, the open Atlantic," he says. "It's a landscape of cliffs, and wind, and fog, which can cover everything so that the ocean pounding the rocks can only be heard, far below, and the fire burning in the stone fireplace is reflected in fog. . . . It's a place where more than one ship — like the 'Caledonia' in my poem — has come to grief."

He adds, "On a clear night, the lights of three different lighthouses come, in alternating rhythms, into the dark room, into your dreams."

Here is his poem, a contemporary gothic, featuring sharp images and eerie truths:

HIGH SEA, COW POINT
                    i
The first thing to think of,
and maybe the last,
is the continual, high whine of the sea
ruining its edges, crashing on the rocks

the way memory meets desire,
or lightning strokes an entire
forest to ash, leaving "Burnt Lands,"
as Thoreau found them (in his *Ktaadn*),
"no man's garden," but "Matter, vast,
terrific," not "mother Earth
that we have heard of" —
nor mother Sea, either, that
the poets wrote, but this
cold continent of drift.

ii
What is the thing you fear most in a storm?
Whose death would haunt you
moonless in the warm chair, fire
spraying on your face from a split spruce,
the roundwood rapture of fire on your breath,
whose name would you call lonely as a flame
left burning in the ashes when ashes dry
and every remembered touch is like a storm?

iii
The Libby Island light
flashes through the mist
every twenty seconds.
Can it be seen
above the Fundy fog
when its horn is lost
inside the relentless roar,
lost, forever lost
as certainly *forever* as the ship
"Caledonia" and her crew,
as certainly forever as I thought
the past was before this fire
which turned out to be
the fire of memory
whose storm you can't outlast.

As you can see, Rubin's familiarity with the landscape helps him
transcend mere description. On a piece of scratch paper, you might
want to list the natural images that Rubin has observed. He knows
those images so intimately that he can address readers directly, move
them emotionally, and state universal truths about nature and memory — replete with an epiphany in the final line.

According to Rubin, "Landscape means far more than a physical description, however vivid. I call those 'postcard' poems. Landscape really exists for us only in the human presence, the human consciousness. It includes everyone who ever lived in it, or ever viewed it with real attention. Landscape includes what *happened* there. It embodies human memory and desire."

Now that you are familiar with the concepts of perception and perspective, we can discuss another ingredient in the making of nature poetry: culture.

CULTURAL FILTERS

At this point it is important to note that each of us views nature differently, however hard we try to depict it in verse. Each of us carries the filters of culture and experience that influence how we perceive and interpret the world. Rather than attempt to explain the myriad types of possible interpretations — an exercise that could fill an encyclopedia! — I'll contrast the poems of two women from different cultures and regions.

Poet Sharon Klander came north to earn a doctorate in creative writing at Ohio University. "In August 1987," she recalls, "I moved from Houston — an hour's drive from the Gulf of Mexico, where, except for a five-year stint as an undergraduate in Austin, Texas, I'd lived my entire life — to the small town of Athens, Ohio, in the foothills of the Appalachians.

"I was suddenly surrounded by hills covered with full, brilliant trees that blocked the sunset before the sun could reach the horizon. And while this particular landscape may have felt comforting to natives of the area, while they may have felt as safe and secure within these natural boundaries as in the shadow of the Almighty, I felt claustrophobic and more apprehensive than ever about the upcoming winter. There were no bold western vistas, no suns dipped slowly in water, no faceted, fascinating light tipping the waves. I was left to exchange all my cotton for wool, to burrow in with books, and — thank God — to write poems."

For Klander, writing nature poetry was the means to acquaint herself with Ohio. Slowly her perception and perspective began to change, and she was able to produce several poems, including this one, which melds the two different landscapes:

WEST TEXAS, OHIO

There was no rain, no relief; no wind but dust.
The sun like a burning bush pointing *back*.
Small wonder we fought blind in that constant
glare, lost every kind word in sand and heat,
in a closed hand.

For the first time we each live far
from home, starting over in landscapes so different
we'd believe their succulent beauty blasphemous
if it weren't for the nights, this autumn sky
filled with hieroglyphics of desert awe,

desert faith. I've missed you.
In the east the moon makes lace of what clouds are left.
I go inside, read your letters come up by accident
with the blankets for an early cold season.

"In 'West Texas, Ohio,' " Klander explains, "the desert landscape of El Paso, Texas, is more than mere backdrop of the problems in the relationship between the speaker of the poem and the 'you' [the man]." In part, she says, the speaker's grief is triggered by remembering a relationship and the old landscape: "her search for something — anything — in the nature of her new home." As such, when the poet leaves West Texas and ends up in Ohio, fusing the two regions in her title, she settles in for a hard winter with letters from her "unforgettable other." Her epiphany — "I've missed you" — leads to an emotional chill, which corresponds to the season, requiring blankets.

Klander advises, "An early poet and mentor once instructed me to 'look out the window and write what you see.' And I do, as I believe most poets do, most of the time."

At the heart of Klander's poem is acclimation — how she adapts to a new environment — and how that causes her to see the world in different light. Klander's cultural influences and experiences force her to come to terms with nature in a new region. Initially, at least, she does not feel comfortable in her new environs.

Native American culture treats nature much differently.

Charlene Blue Horse is a published poet, speaker and teacher whose heritage is Ogalala Lakota (Pine Ridge Sioux). Says Blue Horse, "I suppose I had never thought about 'the role of nature in Native American verse.' When I think of the way Native Americans use nature, I first think *Mi Takuye Oysin* (All My Relations). *Mi Takuye Oysin* is what we say at the beginning and end of all ceremonies and at the end of all prayers. It's sort of like saying Amen, but rather than signifying the end of a prayer, or an agreement, it is a respectful reminder that we are related to all that lives and has a spirit. We are reminded that we depend on all our relations and they depend on us, for survival. When we refer to all our relations, we do not mean just immediate family, we mean all that were created by the same God."

Consequently, nature appears in the poems of Charlene Blue Horse without ornament, as part of her psyche, as this poem illustrates:

SINCE COLUMBUS

Grandmothers, Grandfathers —
Ancestors spread over deserts, across plains.
We watch the flight of the Spotted Eagle
Listen to the mingling of blood.

Red pain deeper than skin, we swim
Back through blood this morning moment.
Brothers, Sisters in Four Directions
Look to Father Sky, Mother Earth.

We know our histories as well as desert winds.
Centuries of pain and prisons pierce this
Dawn like a swift river that runs through us.

These few close moments are like the spreading
Of sweetgrass, running water and trees.
They are the fragrance of ancient stirrings
Throbbing, sharp, insistent as the song
Of the Eagle Bone Whistle.

Grandfathers, Grandmothers —
The Spirit Drums are silent.
Tonight, when the hot moon cries
We will know that it rains
In Four Directions.

As the title indicates, Blue Horse's poem is in part a chronicle about what has happened to Native Americans since the arrival of Columbus in the so-called New World. If nature imagery is central to her poem, perhaps the non-Native American interpretation of such imagery is tainted by European culture.

Here's how Blue Horse describes it: "When I use the words 'Four Directions' I capitalize them. I am referring to relatives. In western thought, this is not so; if you look at directions, you would call them perhaps, nature. (I always tell my students, 'I know you guys believe that everything has a spirit, too, even machines, because I see you kicking and cursing the pop and food machines when they eat your money.')"

"In the Old Testament," Blue Horse observes, "it says that there are four angels that sit on the four corners of the earth. Such is Native American thought. The Four Directions are spirits (angels) of the four winds. Each wind comes from a different direction and each has one or more Nations that 'sit' in that direction" (i.e., creatures with two legs, four legs or winds, etc.). She adds, "Each direction has a color — red, black, yellow and white, which stands for the four colors of people created by the same God. This reminds us that the earth is our mother, and we are related to all four colors of people and all the Nations that live and grow within those Four Directions.

"So when I think about the way Native Americans use nature in verse, I think: *Mi Takuye Oysin*. All My Relations."

As you can see by comparing and contrasting the views and approaches to nature by Sharon Klander and Charlene Blue Horse, it would be wrong for anyone to suggest how *you* should view your habitat. On the other hand, every nature poet from every culture or region has to observe nature through his or her own perspective and represent it through that filter as authentically as possible.

Now that we have reviewed the basics of nature poetry, let's consider the related genre of environmental verse.

ENVIRONMENTAL POETRY

Some people might argue that if you crossbred nature poetry with political poetry, you would end up with a mutant — environmental verse. I think the genre is much richer than that. The problem, however, is that any poetry that becomes too didactic, or moralizing, tends to be better suited to the essay, which processes instruction more easily than verse does. We look to poetry to feel ennobled, or inspired, or to understand the essence of truth — not the facts of it, or the consequences. Yet poems about the state of the planet and our impact on it also convey the essence of our ever-changing relationship with nature.

Although I believe that environmental verse belongs in the nature poetry category, I have set aside a separate section for it for these reasons:

1. For centuries, too many poems about nature have de-emphasized the relationship between the planet and humanity.
2. For centuries, poems about nature have celebrated the seasons or the outdoors.
3. For centuries, themes in noncelebratory poems have emphasized conflict (i.e., man against nature/nature against man) with nature usually depicted as invincible.

Environmental poetry seems to run against the grain of these long-standing conventions. Neither does it seem appropriate to include the category under political verse. Although ecological issues may concern government and its policies (or culture and its values), they deal primarily with a narrower view: policies and values that affect the human-planet relationship.

The human part of that dual relationship is world population; the planet part is other living things (including, of course, Earth as a living entity). Thus, this type of poetry does not celebrate the seasons or

outdoors, chiefly because each has been endangered in the last decades of the twentieth century. (Perhaps one day environmental poetry
will be celebratory, chronicling the accomplishments of ecologists or
nature as triumphant, after all.) Finally, the conflict in such poetry
highlights human capacity to destroy the world as we know it.

This topic is becoming more popular as we become more ecologi-
cally aware. Although poetry is the natural place to express our cur-
rent-day concerns about the planet, environmental verse has a tendency to teach, preach at or even insult its readers.

Here's a quick example:

YOUR PLANET, MINE

You consume my dreams with paper cups!
   I have watched you drive your van
      everywhere except the dump.
      The remains of your planet
      are on display, incinerating mine.

All that is expressed, alas, is anger. As with all genres of poetry,
the best environmental verse shares an epiphany or experience that
unifies our convictions or emotions. The above poem doesn't do either.
It notes a few truths, one can argue, but it is too self-serving and
predictable to interest readers.

The best way to characterize good environmental poetry is to analyze examples of it. I have chosen ones by authors who have varying
interpretations of the subgenre. Though their definitions may differ,
their poems have one thing in common: They deflect the impulse to
preach or teach.

Poet Roger Jones, who teaches creative writing in Texas, fell in
love with nature poetry after reading the canon of Robert Frost. He
says he is wary of the political overtones associated with environmental
verse: "In a sense, almost all poetry is nature poetry in that it deals
with something in the world, and nature in a large sense encompasses
all that is in the world. On the other hand, what these days is designated as 'environmental poetry' to me is marked either by didacticism
[the virtuous 'natural' attitude versus the 'corrupt' city attitude] or by
a conscious attempt on the author's part to dramatize nature as an
entity profoundly nonhuman in its essence."

Jones questions motives of poets who also label themselves environmentalists. But he admits that he is torn between resisting stereo-
typical poems — "Save the Yellow Banded Warbler! Preserve the
Ozone!" — and admiring ones that he calls "quiet poems of ecological
commitment." Here is an example of the latter by Jones:

MAKING MY PEACE

The owner left his gate wide open —
a dare — so I crossed onto his land
and met for the first time a dozen or so
pine saplings clustered in a ring,

their arms up, their thin
copper wrists showing. At once
I heaved my impossible prayers
to the slight weight of their

top limbs. They swayed and bent.
Far away a woodpecker drummed and paused.
I waited for the wind to hum
betrayal, but the small needles

trilled hymnlike and all my secrets
held fast in the gnarled eyes of wood.

Were it not for the title, "Making My Peace," Jones's poem could
pass for pure nature verse. But in the shadow of such a title, we can
read the "impossible prayers" and his "secrets" in different light,
particularly in combination with the ending: The gnarled eyes of wood
seem to behold the speaker's sins against nature.

The idea behind the poem, as the title also suggests, calls for a
quiet ecological commitment. Finally, Jones speaks with a hushed,
plaintive voice in keeping with his understated epiphany.

The approach avoids preaching at all costs.

Like Jones, Neal Bowers doesn't write overtly environmental poems,
although nature figures prominently in his work. Bowers, author of
several poetry collections and a top literary editor, says he likes to
explore the connection, or lack thereof, between humankind and the
surrounding natural world. "My own vision of nature is, I hope, characterized by humility and even awe," he says. "Humans have a tendency
to think they are the supreme beings on the planet and that everything
lives (and dies) at their pleasure. Personally, I side more with the
earlier cosmologists who viewed humankind in the context of nature
and less with my contemporaries who think the surrounding world is
nothing more than a projection of one's own fictive imagination.

"When I die," he adds, "I fully expect the world to go on, without
my perceptions of it. The fact that it will stop for me, individually, is
of no great consequence on the large scale." Thus, he observes, the
concepts of man over nature or nature over man misrepresent the
ecological realities of our lives — "not just our human lives but all
lives.

"We're all part of the same, lovely, breathing thing." This poem by Bowers best represents this view:

ONE FOR THE ROAD

The lone petunia growing
in a driveway crack
is an illustration of nothing
but itself, a weak domestic hybrid
planted by the wind and chance.
The fact that it survives
hardier mums and marigolds
and holds to the blown landscape of November
is no testament to will or strength,
because the car stands over it at night,
heat from the engine block
keeping frost away, upper leaves dark
where they brush the black transmission.

No reason to make anything of this —
I park where I've always parked.
Anyway, what would be the point
in playing such a game,
with winter holding trump?
If I idle the motor for a while
before turning in,
it's for an easier start in the morning.
I don't kid myself
about what I can do
to help this dumb, green life
waving goodbye when I leave,
goodbye when I come home again.

In "One for the Road," we have man over nature — literally, while idling his car. But the stubborn petunia that found life in the crack of a driveway, and whose growing was an act of chance, not only survives the exhaust from the poet's car, but seems to thrive. What will kill the flower is not the car but the approaching winter. For now, the plant waves "goodbye" when the poet leaves and "goodbye" when he comes home — not "hello" — because the second "goodbye" is an allusion to what will outlast the writer: nature.

It is perfectly allowable to take such a pronature stance when writing poems about the environment. The point is to avoid a didactic tone. In sum, environmental verse can be as celebratory as traditional nature poetry; but it also should allude to ecological arguments and contemplate the essence of what some would label "a sullied world."

By *alluding* to arguments and *showing* how nature endures, the poet deflects preachiness.

Ideas About Nature and the Environment

Ideas for nature and environmental poems surround you — literally — no matter where you live. The first step is to concentrate on objects and images that you normally overlook in your everyday activities. Once your perception has sharpened, your perspective — how you opt to view nature and the environment — should develop and help you generate ideas. Try these exercises:

1. Go outdoors to your favorite spot or just wander until you arrive at a place. Stop and observe all its natural characteristics — weeds, insects, flowers, animals, trees — whatever you see that has not been made by a person. Now look for the manufactured objects — sidewalk, house, skyscraper, garden, pop can. Contemplate the relationship between human and nature in that setting.

2. Wander to your least favorite spot outdoors and do the same exercise.

3. Return to your dwelling and look out the window. Describe what you see that is natural — not manufactured by a person. Now go outdoors to the scene that you viewed through your window. Describe what you see that is natural and manufactured. Contemplate how, if at all, your perspective changed between viewing the scene from your window and from the outdoors.

4. Conduct a tour of your dwelling. Inspect it closely for rocks, plants, insects, animals (not pets) — anything ordinarily found outdoors that hasn't been touched by a person. Describe those objects or living things. If viewing an object, touch and contemplate it. If viewing a plant, inspect it closely. If viewing another living thing, imagine touching it and contemplate how you or it would feel or react. Interpret the experience.

5. Walk out of your house and look at the largest and the smallest living thing. If you live in a suburban area, that may be a tall tree and an ant. If you live on a farm, it could be a cornstalk and an ant. If you live in a city, it could be a blade of grass and an ant. Imagine how the tallest and smallest would view each other if they could. Imagine how each would view you. Assess how you viewed each of these entities, if at all, before the exercise and how you view them now.

To inspire your muse, let's preview nature and environmental poems in the mini anthology:

• In "Vespers," poet and professor R.T. Smith focuses on the lone image of a bird. "One of my students once asked me why I write so much about birds," he says, "and the answer is threefold. As a former countryman now moved to town, the birds are the only features of the old landscape that I've been able to stay in touch with. Secondly, birds fly and sing, the two gifts I've spent a life trying to approximate. Finally, the old practice of augury haunts me, the belief that somehow the secret of things is contained in birds."

Smith has this to say about nature poetry: "The natural is, for me, Yeats's 'whatever is begotten, born, and dies.' That passage, in all its beauty, pathos and instructive radiance, is the nature that insists on occupying my imagination."

• In "On the edge," Charlene Blue Horse depicts nature in the tradition passed along to her by Elders, who in this poem, make an appearance.

• In "Sand and Blue-Green Algae," Seattle poet Michael Spence got his environmental idea from a documentary. "I'd been watching some nature film about reefs and blue-green algae, and how the algae made not only the reefs but a good deal of the very air we breathe. And I got to thinking how important so many small things are to our basic existence on this planet, and how most often we pay no attention or denigrate such things. And it seemed to me then that the only time we acknowledge something is when it's so huge, so physically overpowering or unignorable, that even the most arrogant of us has to confront it on its own terms."

• In "Redwings," William Heyen writes about the experience of seeing a flock of these birds burst in flight. He calls this "witnessing a primal act of the natural world," underscoring our ecological relationship. Heyen notes that when he saw the redwings "there was a surprising moment when they flared into essence and vanished. The speaker seems to hold to this as truth and perhaps as prophecy."

• In "Reflections on the Sherwin Williams Can," Debra Kaufman uses an urgent voice — "environmental poetry has a nitty-gritty edge," she says — to express her concerns about Earth's future.

• In "The End of Science Fiction" by Lisel Mueller, a poem written in the 1970s, aspects of the human-planet relationship are no longer prophecy but fact.

Mini Anthology of Nature and Environmental Poems

VESPERS

A cedar waxwing gray
on the gatepost holds
a wet seed in his beak,

surveys the lawn, blue
spruce fringe shaking.
A parasite burrowing
in his wing feathers is
working, a cyst
in his belly thickens.
He drops the seed
to recite his two notes,
and the twilit yard,
chilly as it darkens,
becomes the green
church of his yearning,
the parish of his
sweetest dying need.

— R.T. Smith

ON THE EDGE

Yes, I lived on the edge of Mother Earth
Then, but ran my toes through her green hair.
Still, my heart lives within her heart and beats
With a similar yet quicker music.

And I too, remember that spring of laughter.
The music of love that fell like water from a
Cliff, spread like a child's perfect hoop.
My heart a gold and black polka dotted skirt
Flared over toes in spiked heels that brushed
That precarious edge.

Remember that hot, humid afternoon that honored
Elders at Ghost Hawk Park, and the Thunders drummed
Us home, sang and danced against the sky, let down
Skirts of water while I danced drenched in warm rain
And laughter? You watched from the safety of the
Dry worried house.

I lived on the edge, then. Now, I walk quiet
On moccasined feet, feed birds, not lions.
Sometimes, I lift my voice in song, borrow words
From the young one, long ago, who stepped back
Over the edge. "There was a man I loved so dearly
I will see my man again." How we laughed
When the buck sprang from woods below.

— Charlene Blue Horse

SAND AND BLUE-GREEN ALGAE

Size impresses a man.
Fact. A man is much
Larger than grains of sand.
Correct. His foot can kick
The crest of a sand dune
To myriad particles.
Right. He's much larger
Than blue-green algae.
True. His foot can crush
Thousands, millions of them.
Yes.
          The algae grow
Sticky coats which grains
Of sand, over time,
Cling to; a man hates
To touch sticky things.
Fact. Underwater,
The algae climb closer
To the sun, slowly building
Layers of sand. Correct.
A man doesn't see them
Harden to reef.
                    A man
Can build faster than reefs.
True. Inside them are paths
Twisted as convolutions
In his brain: they build
The air he breathes, bigger
Than any reef. This
Impresses the man.
And if he kicks what sand
And blue-green algae make —
Yes — his foot can break.
                         — Michael Spence

REDWINGS

Maybe you've noticed that around here
red-winged blackbirds aren't rare,
but aren't seen often, either, and then, at distance,
banking away from roads as we pass.

But one morning, I saw a hundred,
more, feeding on seed I'd scattered

under a line of pines planted
more than a hundred years before.

Almost at rest, their feathers folded close,
only yellow wingbars
break their black bodies. But when, as they did,
all at once, they lifted, that *red* . . .

I've tried for a long time, and maybe should,
to tell you how the disembodied redwings
flared and vanished.
I've lost them in every telling.

So much for me. I could die now, anyway.
Could you? We will close our eyes
and rest, in case the blackbirds, in slow motion,
assume again the flames they are, and rise.

—William Heyen

REFLECTIONS ON THE SHERWIN-WILLIAMS CAN

The Master Painter, weary of sending rainbows,
gets pissed off for the last time
and pours a giant can of paint
over the globe: sludge-grey
oozing down
first over the frozen desert;
then like lava down Sequoias and skyscrapers,
the wings of birds thick with it, plummeting;
it coats our mouths
and the mouths of our children,
slogs the panic of city rats,
gums up anthills, seeps down
to where the mole chews a beet root,
deeper, slowing now,
mingling with the squid's
last black ink jet;
freezing into a dirty sleet
over the iced graves of Byrd's men.

You half-believe it could end like this,
so why not keep driving your sleek white Jag,
wrap your lover in pelts of cheetahs,
order that baby grand with its cool ivory keys?
And more! Think of it:
to be as opulent as Diamond Jim Brady

(pass the chocolate hummingbird tongues),
to wallow in your just desserts
until your fingers tingle,
your arm goes numb,
your fat heart hammers down for the last time,
and you stagger and grab onto
the velvet drapes and pull them
and your world down around you.

— Debra Kaufman

THE END OF SCIENCE FICTION

This is not fantasy, this is our life.
We are the characters
who have invaded the moon,
who cannot stop their computers.
We are the gods who can unmake
the world in seven days.

Both hands are stopped at noon.
We are beginning to live forever,
in lightweight, aluminum bodies
with numbers stamped on our backs.
We dial our words like muzak.
We hear each other through water.

The genre is dead. Invent something new.
Invent a man and a woman
naked in a garden,
invent a child that will save the world,
a man who carries his father
out of a burning city.
Invent a spool of thread
that leads a hero to safety;
invent an island on which he abandons
the woman who saved his life
with no loss of sleep over his betrayal.

Invent us as we were
before our bodies glittered
and we stopped bleeding:
invent a shepherd who kills a giant,
a girl who grows into a tree,
a woman who refuses to turn
her back on the past and is changed to salt,
a boy who steals his brother's birthright

and becomes the head of a nation.

Invent real tears, hard love,
slow-spoken, ancient words,
difficult as a child's
first steps across a room.

                              —Lisel Mueller

Notebook

LEVEL ONE

1. Review the twelve basic types of nature poems presented in the beginning of this chapter and base ideas on ten of them, using your own environment and perspective to observe and interpret the outdoors. In other words, don't feel the need to look elsewhere for nature but depict it as it is where you can find it easily.

2. Do the five exercises for generating "nature" ideas as found on page 59 and outline five more ideas in your journal.

3. Make three lists in your journal. First, think about your household and how environmental issues have affected it, from recycling to product labels. Think about your workplace and how environmental issues have affected it, from smoking bans to safety regulations. Generate five ideas for poems.

Next, study a week's worth of daily newspaper articles (if possible, buy the *New York Times*). Look for articles in which environmental issues are discussed. Generate five ideas for poems.

Finally, visit the library and scan back issues of environmental magazines and newsletters. Generate five ideas for poems.

LEVELS TWO AND THREE

1. Do the second part of the Level One assignment again, noting any change in perception or interpretation of your natural surroundings. Base at least five ideas for poems on those changes (or lack thereof) and include insight about why they did (or did not) occur.

2. Invent five of your own exercises (similar to ones described in the second part of the Level One assignment above) and contemplate nature. Base at least five ideas for poems on your own exercises.

3. Do the third part of the Level One exercise again, noting new ideas based on your household and workplace, the daily newspaper and environmental publications. What has changed in the interim? Generate at least five more ideas for poems related to your lists.

Chapter Four

Extranatural Poetry

W e began the chapter on nature poetry by noting that, at least in part, poems set in the real world are about nature. What about poems set somewhere else: in heaven, on Mars, in the mind? What to call these? For centuries, critics have labeled such categories of verse *religious, metaphysical* and *sublime*. The religious poem usually was devotional; the metaphysical, metaphoric; and the sublime, intellectual. More recently, however, religious verse has become associated with churches or movements (e.g., Catholicism or Fundamentalism); the metaphysical, with the supernatural; and the sublime, with psychology. Clearly, another nomenclature is needed: hence, the term *extranatural* (or beyond the natural world).

The term is broad, encompassing many types of poems. For example, is this one by Kevin Bezner (a poet-essayist who teaches writing in North Carolina) an extranatural or an environmental poem?

GOD EXPLAINS EARTH TO HIS ANGELS
They would watch the colors of the sun, birds
all around them, animals and insects
of all kinds. They would watch the stars
and when they came out they would sit
with them for hours. Then

they began to make things.
They began to clear the land,
the green earth, the grasses, the trees.
They forgot about the sun, the stars,
and thought only of what their work

could bring. The animals
and the birds left them. The insects
became angry. I asked about this.
They cleared more trees.

They said leave, old man, go away.

One can argue that the poem is environmental in that it addresses ecological issues such as cutting trees and endangering species. Making things could be an allusion to the industrial era that has sullied the air and green earth. Moreover, Bezner's poem concerns the changing relationship between humans and the planet.

On the other hand, the poem is not set on earth but *beyond* it. The voice is that of God speaking to supernatural beings about human ones. Finally, allusions about how people "began to make things" may or may not be associated with the industrial era, but they *are* associated with the Book of Genesis in the Bible (God as Maker). Thus Bezner's poem contains two critical aspects of extranatural poetry: divine or supernatural beings and a setting other than earth.

Poems set in the mind may also fall under this category. For instance, is the lyric below by Mary Martin (a dance instructor and English teacher) an erotic/love poem or an extranatural one?

MIRAGE

Suddenly there is motion in the desert.
Arms like scarves
signal me over out of the sun,
under the tent strewn with pillows,
plates of fruit and wine. As I stare
at the billowing walls I'm grabbed
by a man in armor who doesn't speak
but stretches his tongue out beyond
the grid of his helmet licking
each crevice, each turn my body takes.

He drapes me in white silk,
and I float from cushion to cushion
afraid to know where I am.
The billows become halls,
a continuous sway of space
where I wander, always the clatter
of his steps close by. I'm allowed to touch
nothing but him, feel nothing but him,
his silver hands, the chalice
from which I must drink.

Again, you can make a case for calling this an erotic poem—one that focuses on physical rather than emotional love. Certainly the images are overt. The setting is a desert, an allusion to all those erotic Arabian (k)nights. But also notice the fantastic element of Martin's

piece, combining Medieval images with Middle Eastern ones, coupled
with her title: "Mirage." The knight is imagined — extraterrestrial, almost, given the setting — a desert *in the mind.*

As such, her poem falls under the extranatural category.

Let's attempt to define it: "Any poem addressing or involving divine, supernatural or extraterrestrial entities and/or human beings in
a setting that exists beyond earth or only in the mind."

Certainly, this type of poem can be found in the literary canon. In
some sense, *Beowulf* — that old English epic featuring a fire-breathing
dragon — is extranatural. And poets throughout time have offered up
their prayers to deities, from sun-gods to Zeus, from Jupiter to Jesus.

Here's a brief summary of common types:

The Metaphysical Poem. Typically, a metaphysical poem employs a "conceit" or an extended metaphor or other comparison to
convey its theme. Here is an excerpt from a sonnet by John Donne
who uses a lovelike conceit of submission to God:

Yet dearly'I love You,'and would be lovéd fain,
But am betrothed unto Your enemy.
Divorce me,'untie or break that knot again;
Take me to You, imprison me, for I,
Except You'enthrall me, never shall be free,
Nor ever chaste, except You ravish me.

The Theological Poem. This type deals with a concept of religion
(sin, goodness, penance, etc.). Here is an excerpt from such a poem
by George Herbert, a seventeenth-century contemporary of Donne:

DENIAL

When my devotions could not pierce
        Thy silent ears,
Then was my heart broken, as was my verse;
        My breast was full of fears
                and disorder. . . .

The Mystic Poem. Such verse deals with supernatural realms.
Henry Vaughan, who gave his life over to God after reading poems by
George Herbert, composed this excerpt that contains what we would
now call a "near-death experience" vision:

THE WORLD

I saw Eternity the other night
Like a great Ring of pure and endless light,
        All calm as it was bright;
And round beneath it, Time, in hours, days, years,

Driven by the spheres,
Like a vast shadow moved, in which the world
And all her train were hurled. . . .

The Intercession Poem. This type calls on a deity to intercede
in events on earth, as illustrated by this excerpt from Milton's "On
the Late Massacre in Piedmont" (about an attack on Protestants):

Avenge, O Lord, thy slaughtered saints, whose bones
　　Lie scattered on the Alpine mountains cold,
　　Even them who kept thy truth so pure of old
When all our fathers worshiped stocks and stones,
Forget not: . . .

The Doomsday Poem. Doomsday poems echo the destruction of
all humanity at the hand of a deity, as in this example from "The Day
of Judgment" by the eighteenth-century poet Isaac Watts:

Such shall the noise be and the wild disorder,
(If things eternal may be like these earthly)
Such the dire terror, when the great Archangel
　　　　　Shakes the creation, . . .

The Canonization Poem. This type elevates the men, women and
children who have given over their lives to a deity or have died because
of persecution. Here is a short poem by Richard Crashaw about the
innocents slain by Herod:

TO THE INFANT MARTYRS

Go, smiling souls, your new-built cages break,
In heaven you'll learn to sing, ere here to speak,
Nor let the milky fonts that bathe your thirst
　　　　　Be your delay;
The place that calls you hence is, at the worst,
　　　　　Milk all the way.

The Demon Poem. This type addresses the devil or other demonic
figure, as illustrated by this example from William Blake:

TO THE ACCUSER WHO IS
THE GOD OF THIS WORLD

Truly My Satan thou art but a Dunce,
And dost not know the Garment from the Man;
Every Harlot was a Virgin once,
Nor canst thou ever change Kate into Nan. . . .

The Prayer. One of the oldest forms of religious verse, this one by Emerson is almost an antiprayer in that it addresses how words cannot capture the essence of God:

THE BOHEMIAN HYMN

In many forms we try
To utter God's infinity,
But the boundless hath no form,
And the Universal Friend
Doth as far transcend
An angel as a worm.

The great Idea baffles wit,
Language falters under it,
It leaves the learned in the lurch,
Nor art, nor power, nor toil can find
The measure of the eternal Mind,
Nor hymn, nor prayer, nor church.

The Supernatural Poem. Emily Dickinson, who wrote devotional verse, spoke of other entities — disembodied spirits — in this excerpt set in the mind:

GHOSTS

One need not be a chamber to be haunted,
One need not be a house;
The brain has corridors surpassing
Material place. . . .

The Devotional Poem. A Jesuit priest, the Victorian poet Gerard Manley Hopkins, is known for his tributes to God. In this excerpt from "God's Grandeur," he uses modern images to express his faith:

The world is charged with the grandeur of God.
    It will flame out, like shining from shook foil;
    It gathers to a greatness, like the ooze of oil
Crushed. . . .

The Dramatic Rendering. This type employs a first-person voice ("I") of a deity or supernatural entity, as in this poem by Edgar Lee Masters:

THE VILLAGE ATHEIST

Ye young debaters over the doctrine
Of the soul's immortality,
I who lie here was the village atheist,
Talkative, contentious, versed in the arguments

Of the infidels.
But through a long sickness
Coughing myself to death
I read the *Upanishads* and the poetry of Jesus.
And they lighted a torch of hope and intuition
And desire which the Shadow,
Leading me swiftly through the caverns of darkness,
Could not extinguish.
Listen to me, ye who live in the senses
And think through the senses only:
Immortality is not a gift,
Immortality is an achievement;
And only those who strive mightily
Shall possess it.

The Surreal Poem. Such verse contains dreamlike or hallucinatory images. To illustrate, here is the fourth and last section of "Preludes" by T.S. Eliot:

His soul stretched tight across the skies
That fade behind a city block,
Or trampled by insistent feet
At four and five and six o'clock;
And short square fingers stuffing pipes,
And evening newspapers, and eyes
Assured of certain certainties,
The conscience of a blackened street
Impatient to assume the world.
I am moved by fancies that are curled
Around these images, and cling:
The notion of some infinitely gentle
Infinitely suffering thing.
Wipe your hand across your mouth, and laugh;
The worlds revolve like ancient women
Gathering fuel in vacant lots.

Now, a disclaimer: Although these examples and others mentioned later in this chapter concern aspects of Judeo-Christian mythology, the ideas behind the various types apply to all religions or beliefs. And, while poems may be set in the occidental mind in some examples, you certainly should not attempt to mimic that mind if you hail from another culture. In sum, the beliefs, entities and settings described herein are important because of the methods that poets employed to compose their poems.

Let's see what those methods involve, by way of craft.

APPROACH AND PERSPECTIVE

Simply defined, *approach* means how a poet articulates beliefs or de-picts entities or settings within and beyond the natural world. An ap-proach is a strategy and usually involves a device that a poet uses to discuss and/or describe the extranatural. It might be a lecture (device) delivered in heaven (setting), or it might be a religious or supernatural figure (device) through whom the poet speaks in a real place like a cafeteria or a surreal one like a wormhole in space (setting). The possibilities and combinations are endless, but the goal is the same: to convey beliefs in vivid or surprising ways.

Those beliefs are products of *perspective*, a concept explained in the previous chapter. You may recall that the poet observes nature (perception) and then interprets it (perspective). Perspective also is influenced by cultural filters, as we saw in the poems of Sharon Klander and Charlene Blue Horse.

Keeping all that in mind, consider the prefix *extra* in the term *extranatural poetry* (something beyond nature). You could argue that perspective is more difficult to fathom when it is not necessarily based on perception in the real world. Moreover, if any human sense is vital in extranatural verse, it may be the *sixth* sense: intuition. If you prefer another word, substitute *faith* or *fantasy*.

Now you are beginning to understand the challenges associated with composing poems that are, literally, out of this world.

Anyone who has edited a literary magazine will tell you that each year poets submit reams of extranatural poetry, often in the form of religious, surreal or fantasy verse. Much of it is bad. The chief reason is that the work lacks an authentic or vivid setting and tends to com-pensate for that shortcoming by using empty words, as this quick poem illustrates:

THE REUNION
The day I lay me down to sleep,
Never again to wake,
I hope to see no loved ones weep
With heavy hearts that break,

For I will dwell in heaven's land
And sit with God above,
A willing servant at His hand,
Commanding all His love.

Now there's nothing wrong with the idea behind the poem. The speaker wants to comfort loved ones so they do not grieve but celebrate faith in the afterlife. However, the work has serious flaws. For one, the speaker seems to lack vision — what heaven might look like, for example, or how a soul might feel in eternity. Moreover, there is no real setting other than the usual implied symbolic chairs in which the speaker and deity sit. In other words, the approach is ordinary. Consequently, the poem is expository — it tells rather than shows, emphasizing a noble idea, perhaps, but one that has been expressed already by millions of people. In other words, the perspective is ordinary.

Extranatural poetry stands little chance of interesting many readers with ordinary approaches and perspectives.

Typically when editors reject such poetry, the writer feels the rejection more deeply because of personal belief. But the problem transcends that. Editors would be doing a disservice to readers by lowering standards and accepting a poem simply because it uses the word *God* or *Jesus* or a similar counterpart.

That is not to say that traditional religious figures or extranatural settings should be avoided. Just the opposite. Such figures or settings appeal to millions around the world; thus, if you use them in new or imaginative ways, you will appeal to a vast audience. That's why approach and perspective are so important and why you should take time to contemplate how you will articulate faith or depict fantastic situations. Let's look at the approaches and perspectives of other poets to help you formulate your own.

EXTRANATURAL IDEAS

"All true poetry is religious poetry — all poems are prayers — but not in the sense of a belief in or worship of a god or a supernatural power," says Kevin Bezner. He adds that true or sincere poems, by their very nature, always reflect a poet's faith, commitment, desire to commune, conscientiousness and devotion "in both the language and the experience that must be expressed."

This does not have to involve a belief in the afterlife. "Some poets I admire believe in a god, others don't," Bezner says. "Blake, Dickinson and Donne are Christian poets whose writing is always informed by their faith no matter what they are writing about. Donne's poems of reverence, for instance, are matched by his wonderfully sensual, erotic and just-as-religious love poems, among the best in English. All three of these poets transcend their Christianity to take their readers to a place that is essentially nameless, but which seems full of light, the only way I can describe it."

Bezner says he has found the same light in the secular Chinese Confucian poet Tu Fu and the Japanese Buddhist haiku master Basho. He also cites masters of other arts, including the composer Mozart and the painter Van Gogh.

"What all of these great artists have found," he observes, "is something that is most human while connecting human beings to all things."

Describing his perspective, Bezner says that he hopes his poems show "reverence for the world in which we live, those things many of us, including me at a different time and when I am not mindful, over-look." Bezner adds that he tries to express reverence without overstate-ment as concisely as possible, as in this minipoem:

PRAYER

All steps, all moves, each spoon lifted
to the mouth, every said word, all thought.

You might note that even in a two-line work, Bezner has a clear approach. He uses vivid words like "steps," "moves" and "spoon," which gradually lead to "mouth" — from whence prayer emanates and thought is conveyed. Thus, we realize Bezner's perspective or view about prayer includes every human gesture, however insignificant, as tribute to a higher power.

Says Bezner, "Most of the poems I write serve as a bow of thanks to those things that give me life, and a recognition that we inhabit the same world with many others."

If Bezner's views appeal to you, ask yourself these questions to fathom your own perspective:

• In what ways am I isolated from other human beings in particular and life in general?
• How can I overcome that isolation and connect with others?
• How can I best express reverence and gratitude for the aspects of life that mean most to me?

Once you have the answers, decide on an approach you can use to convey them. The approach is always a variable, but in this case strategies might include settings or situations that somehow overcome isolation and result in awe or thanksgiving.

Martha Whitmore Hickman, a widely published poet and freelance writer, has found that in some poems her perspective is best conveyed through the device of a traditional religious figure, as this dramatic rendering illustrates:

MEDITATION OF MARY,
MOTHER OF GOD

I've quite a flair for turning clay,
Among the women I'm known to be a seer,
I've studied field grass and the roots of herbs.
In the village I hear whispers — "There's Mary —
she's his mother."

Sometimes I want to scream. "Wait! I'm something
  else, too!"
Of course when he died I felt guilty—
You wanted something for yourself? Well, he's gone
  now. Take it.

This is hardly the view of Mary depicted in typical devotional verse.
Moreover, to convey her perspective, Hickman uses modern speech
and focuses on Mary as a woman and as the holy mother. This approach
relies on the reader's familiarity with a figure associated with a Catholic world view—"people rather than abstractions," she says. In addition, in the above poem, Hickman uses vivid images ("field grass"
and "roots of herbs") and a common setting ("village").

In the following work, the approach is deceptively simple:

FOR THOSE WHO HAVE DIED AT BIRTH

What do they say, the souls of the newborn dead
When, lolling about in the long afternoons of heaven,
The conversation turns to reminiscing—
  "Remember how it was . . .
    The feel of silk
    The taste of strawberries
    The smell of a mother's hair?"

Her perspective can be reduced to a few words, Hickman says:
"the ultimate triumph of love." To convey that, she imagines lazy
afternoons in heaven (setting) in which images associated with touch,
taste and smell—important senses to newborns—are recalled in easy
talk (device). As you can see, to compose good extranatural poems,
you do not have to design complex, flowery or ornate methods.

If Hickman's method intrigues you, ask yourself these questions to
understand your perspective:

* What figures from holy books of my faith most intrigue me?
* What aspects of or incidents from their lives still have meaning
  today?
* What concept of my religion is symbolized in this figure or associated with a certain aspect of his or her life, and how can I tap
  this to express my own beliefs?

Once you have the answers, consider taking an approach that
grounds your perspective with vivid or sensory images. As Hickman's
poems show, those images don't necessarily have to come from the
Bible or other holy book. That's where your intuition, faith or fantasy
comes into play.

"It's sometimes difficult to separate what we've come to call 'religious poetry' from other kinds," says David Citino, author of several collections. Citino notes that the poet is often concerned with "the reality behind appearances, with the shimmer of the nonmaterial, with the pristine other (perhaps even spiritual) world, with ethics, with first things and last things, with miracles." Citino adds that anyone who reads the Bible, for whatever reason, realizes that certain aspects of religious experience — prophesy, heroic stories, songs and psalms — "seem to require poetry in their expression."

Verse, he says, is the natural vehicle to convey the extranatural. "It is a heightened, pure, vatic mode of speech and writing whereby the poet attempts to express his or her sense of the inexpressible." At the same time, he adds, religious poetry, which uses religious metaphors and themes, "can entertain, enliven, make us laugh, or suppose, or conjecture, or even pretend."

That comment best describes a device that Citino created to express some of his best extranatural poetry. He created a complex character: Sister Mary Appassionata, a comic, wise and sometimes tragic figure who dominates a few of his books. Citino's approach is simple; typically, the good sister delivers a lecture or sermon, as in this example:

SISTER MARY APPASSIONATA LECTURES
THE THEOLOGY CLASS
ON THE LIFE AND DEATH OF ST. TERESA

She's become a journey.

Her left arm's at Lisbon,
fingers of the right hand at Seville, Avila, Paris,
Brussels, Rome.
Right foot in Rome, a slice of flesh.
One tooth in Venice.
Piacenza boasts of a napkin stained with her blood.
Milan keeps a piece of the heart, another tooth.
Lump of her flesh in Naples, scapular.
Her slippers at Avila,
most of the torso at Alva,
at Cagliari her veil.
The wooden cross she used to beat the demons
sent to try her, at Rome. Also Brussels.
Two very large slices of flesh in Krakow.

She lived to keep herself intact.
At the instant of death love tore her to pieces.

The invention of a character like Sister Mary Appassionata lets Citino speak about the present through the filters of history and tradition. " 'Catholicism is form,' T.S. Eliot claimed," he says. "I'd want to change that to 'is history.' I'm concerned — often obsessed — with the limitations of our sense of the past. How do we come to believe a thing to be true or untrue? What has taken the place of all the belief we've lost? Can we know any more of what is than we know of what was? Who were we, before we became our parents? When (and how) did we come to love or rail at love in these human ways? What I believe or don't believe today is dependent in great part on what, as a child, I thought possible."

If Citino's perspective is similar to your own, ask yourself these questions:

- What do images or objects associated with my faith symbolize in terms of religious experience?
- How have these symbols influenced my beliefs in the past and how, if at all, do they do so today?
- Do these symbols and what they represent apply only to me or to a group or congregation? (If the former, why do I feel this way about them? If the latter, how have they influenced others or culture?)

Once you have answers to these questions, invent a character to deliver your ideas in an everyday setting. You could reinvent yourself as a child or re-create a person from your past, with whom you associate your spiritual beliefs.

The perspective of Karen Joy Fowler is not associated with commonly held religious beliefs. Fowler, a nationally known science fiction and fantasy writer and poet, says, "I use supernatural or extranatural elements in most of my work, fiction and poetry. I find in the work of many writers the use of extranatural elements to suggest a belief in destiny, or at the very least, a belief in cause and effect." Although such use of the extranatural can result in "a sort of cold justice," Fowler notes, "I feel it has a comfortable rationality to it.

"I have no such beliefs. I see the world as frighteningly random and the extranatural elements in my work are expressions of irrationality, of chance and luck. The world is full of people who mean you ill, or people who mean you well but do you ill, or people who don't give you a thought but harm or save you inadvertently as a part of living their lives. And that's just the people. And that's just you. The world is also full of rocks and trees and bacteria, any one of which may collide with you, or worse, your children unexpectedly."

In this poem, Fowler uses an extranatural theme to explain a scar to her son:

MY SON ASKS ABOUT HIS SURGERY

After a shower, the scar surprises you in the mirror,
curving from your left armpit to your spine.
You were born with one wing—I answer—
shaped like a football pennant, covered in fine
white feathers. Half an angel. We had it
removed, your father and I, afraid it would
prove difficult later to fit into t-shirts, to fit
in with peers. And, after all, what good
is one wing? An appendage so numinous
might one day have tempted you beyond yourself.
Where is it now? With a hundred other superfluous
parts, pickled on some laboratory shelf.
The feathers we saved for your pillow. They bring
those not-quite-human dreams. Kiss me. I see despite
all my persuasion, you would like to have a wing.
You think you might have gained a modest height,
a little lateral control, done just a bit of hovering.

Though her voice is at times gentle, humorous and witty, at the center of this poem is the perspective of a harsh world requiring surgery for a son and leaving scars (emotional and physical). Her approach is to set the poem in the bathroom after a shower and to expand the angel metaphor to explain, as lovingly as possible, what she calls "irrational" aspects of life.

She notes, however, "This same irrationality adds delight to the world as well as peril. It pleases me that fish occasionally fall from the sky, that the Loch Ness monster continues to be sighted, that a man in India is going into the record books with the world's longest fingernails. As a writer this is the world that attracts me the most. If this is what you write about you can hardly call yourself a realist. You are so barely real. Real, but irrational. And the best way I know to express the irrational in our lives is through the extranatural."

If Fowler's perspective appeals to you, ask yourself these questions to put your own views into context:

• What aspects of life continue to enchant, intrigue or worry me?
• Why do they do so? Did some incident happen to me in the past or did they affect people I care about, dislike or love?

Once you have answers, concentrate on an effective approach. You might want to employ a setting or figure from the extranatural who explains or illustrates the unpredictable aspects of life and/or the emotions they evoke. To help inspire you, I've included a mix of extranatural poems dealing with traditional, nontraditional, sublime, extraterrestrial and fantastic themes:

• In "The Papal Saw in a Roman Blind," Colette Inez shows compassion for her Catholic-priest father whose specter has wreaked havoc in her life. Moreover, she sets the scene in her mind and uses symbols to dispatch her father to the afterlife, two elements of the extranatural in a poem that also concerns traditional religious beliefs.

• In "Assuming All Goes Well God Will Say," Eve Shelnutt uses the extranatural to deal with, understand and ultimately accept the dynamics of a relationship.

• In "When Angels Came to Zimmer," Paul Zimmer uses these supernatural beings in a delightful way, proving that extranatural poems can have a sense of humor, too, as they enlighten us about ourselves and our world.

• In "For Roland, Presumed Taken," Jim Barnes alludes to alien abduction. "For a long time I wanted to write a poem with flying saucers in it," he says, "but finally decided I couldn't. This is my 'couldn't' poem." The work also contains images from "The Song of Roland" — (a French epic poem c. 1000) — "the horn, the rocking horse, toy swords, perhaps the setting and certainly the name," he adds. The literary symbols combine with UFO images in a modern-day metaphysical poem.

• In "Miss Intensity Meets the Holy Ghost," Katherine Murphy creates a dream-vision to convey an encounter with a divine entity. "The date in the poem is the date of the actual dream of what I like to believe was a religious experience. I take heat from the feminists when I read this poem because the Holy Ghost is a very male patriarchal figure. The poem is also criticized by the religious for being too sexual, but I think of Miss Intensity as a modern-day Mary Magdelene." Murphy concludes, "Men have always had female muses. The Holy Ghost is mine."

Mini Anthology of Extranatural Poems

THE PAPAL SAW IN A ROMAN BLIND

I can almost hear the bells
rung by the priest who sired a child.
Nuncio, let that father rise
to sit at my right touch. One last
kiss to ease his grief in the afterlife.

I, his bastard, bid for calm
like a Papal See in a murmur of signs.
Confessor, hear my doubts of the Seven
Dolors of Mary, Elevation of the Host.

I can see the church walking

on its knees and offer my alms
to a ghost who cannot see the weight
of years, blood-soaked stones and
the orphanage drilling its wards
on the telling of beads.

My father, does he hear the lambs
bleating the hundredth psalm
of man's praise to God? Vicar of Christ,
here is a silver monstrance, here is
a chasuble of gold to pay for his release.

All our wrongs take refuge in the hospice
of time. I make this offering to lift up
my father's heart out of his remains,
mysterious as particles of light
flooding the earth from the sun.

— Colette Inez

ASSUMING ALL GOES WELL GOD WILL SAY

How do you know he loved you
when he touched you, what?
a dozen times? And
you didn't think he loved you
only then. It was as if
you'd been struck for all
of what you call time. But
women can watch a world
they never made
and estimate forces of which
they've only heard. Why
did he write to you so
infrequently? Since he loved you
it is interesting to consider.
One day (you wouldn't know this)
he bent mysteriously
over the ground for minutes
as if to be bent double
was what he had expected.
He went on quietly afterwards.
Well let it be. When you confess
I may or may not pity you.

— Eve Shelnutt

WHEN ANGELS CAME TO ZIMMER

One morning a great gaggle slid
Down through holes in clouds,
Twirling like maple seeds
Through trees to the windowscreen.
Fervent as new tussock moths,
They flapped and dashed themselves,
Smearing their heavenly dust,
Until Zimmer, in pity and alarm,
Opened to let them into his study.
They flew in with smiles and sighs,
Making him bashful, as if a dozen
Gorgeous chorus girls had suddenly
Pranced into the room.
                    They perched on
Bookshelves, cigar stubs and beer cans;
One even tried to sit on Zimmer's lap.
All day they danced the Lindy,
And some, not knowing better, dabbled
Their darling toes in the toilet bowl.
They sang chorus after chorus of
"Stardust" and "Moonlight In Vermont,"
Constantly touching and stroking Zimmer.
Then at day's end, as if someone
Had rung a bell, they stood to sing
A final chorus of "Deep Purple."
With a whoosh of air and expensive perfume,
They fluttered from the room and ascended.
Zimmer stepped out to watch them rise
And flapped his dirty hankie at the stars.
                              —Paul Zimmer

FOR ROLAND, PRESUMED TAKEN

By the time we missed you dusk was settling in.
The first reaction was to think
of drowning, the deep hole just north of the house
that the spring flows into
out from under the sycamore.
You had played there earlier in the day
and had wanted to wade the still water
after minnows schooling the shadows.

We tracked you back to the spring, and I died
with fear that you would be floating

among the lilies, white as the ghost of fish.
But your tracks veered left
toward the valley where the cattle grazed,
then vanished in the flowing grass.
I blew the horn that called the cattle in.
You knew the sound and loved the way
the cattle came loping up at feeding time.

Roland, still, today, you cannot hear the sound of the horn,
cannot holler back up the mountainside
to let us know in your wee voice you are safe and found.
Why you walked off into the green of that day
we can never know, except the valley
and the mountain beyond must have yielded a sudden
sound or flash of light that took your eyes away.
And you were gone. It is as if

eagles swooped you up, leaving
not one trace to tell us the way you went away.
Nights I imagine the beat of drums,
the clanging of toy swords,
rocking horses neighing
on their tracks.
In another age
I would offer
up my glove
to God
to have you back.

Now, we have packed away your life
in boxes we store
in case the memory
we hold is swept away
by chance
or the slow years.

—Jim Barnes

MISS INTENSITY MEETS THE HOLY GHOST

It was January 11, 1988 (because I thought
I want to remember this, even though I didn't
tell a soul, they'd think I was like those crazy
UFO people in *The National Enquirer*), and I was wandering
around the edge of one of my winning-the-lottery dreams,

(the one where I would get the money to fix
my teeth and get the calluses off my heels, some
Elizabeth Taylor-violet lenses
and a Thallium stress test because my heart
beats too fast and I'd postpone my trip to Paris

for six months so I could have plastic
surgery at a spa in California where they serve this
arugula salad for lunch) when I heard that voice,
the most fascinating voice I ever heard, call
my name and I recognized Him—I did—and I thought

Wow a mission, now my life will have purpose
and we talked and talked (as if we were at the
greatest party and on the verge of a torrid
last-for-ever affair, oblivious of everybody
in the room) and talked about me writing—He said

"*good* poetry: sestinas, pantoums, barzelettas, decent
free verse not going to workshops unless you want to,"
(the kind of party where I'd wear my black taffeta
with spaghetti straps, Chantilly lace like a little apron
and my high heels with the tiny rhinestone hearts

and I'd have lost thirty pounds to test if I'm old
enough yet to stop ending up in the beds of strangers
the way I always do when I'm thin, and where
I'm afraid I'll be murdered some night) and I thought
He probably wants me to be a feminist

and wear Denim skirts and Docksiders and turtleneck
shirts with little strawberries on them and teach
poetry at a women's prison or a cancer ward
or Hungary, where it's colder than Cleveland
(I could wear my muskrat cape and boots), but He said

"No, Darlin', just anything to make you happy,"
and "I love you—no matter what" and I said
"I feel a little funny" (mind you, this was after
He had taken me in his arms and flown me around Venus,
Mars, and across the Milky Way and back—after I begged him,

and He said "Not you too"—and I sang my scat
Swing Low Sweet Chariot and *Stars Fell on Alabama*)
and He said "It's not wrong to feel a little funny,"
and I, forgetting everything I had learned in English 303
about the omniscient point of view and suddenly thinking

this is the Holy Ghost, Girl! averted my eyes
and said "Well, it's a cross between a warm Jacuzzi
with those good Lily of the Valley bath salts
and the dippiest roller coaster ever," (I swear
this is true) and His voice smiling in the dark said, "So?"
                                                        —Katherine Murphy

Notebook

LEVEL ONE

1. Reread the sections titled "Approach and Perspective" and "Extranatural Ideas" and generate five ideas for poems, at least one based on each of the methods of Kevin Bezner, Martha Whitmore Hickman, David Citino and Karen Joy Fowler. Don't feel compelled to agree with the perspectives. Simply conceive your own and note the various approaches. Afterward, return to the poet whose methods have intrigued you most and generate another five ideas for extranatural poems.

2. After you have generated your ideas, return to your journal and describe your beliefs about religion, the supernatural, the extraterrestrial, the fantastic or any other aspect that qualifies as extranatural according to the definition at the beginning of this chapter.

LEVEL TWO

1. Come up with at least five more ideas based on the methods described in the sections titled "Approach and Perspective" and "Extranatural Ideas."

2. Go over the journal entries you made doing the Level One, Exercise Two. How have your ideas changed, if at all? Describe this in a journal passage and base at least five new ideas for poems on those changes (or lack of changes).

LEVEL THREE

1. Reread your journal entries from the Level One and Two assignments. In another passage, describe how your ideas have changed, if at all, about religion, the supernatural, the extraterrestrial and the fantastic. Base at least five new ideas for poems on these changes (or lack thereof).

2. Analyze each journal entry from Level One, Two and Three, charting any patterns of growth and recalling the incidents or experiences that might have prompted those patterns. Base at least five ideas for poems on them.

Chapter Five

War Poetry

T he combination of poetry and war seems oxymoronic, a type of water and oil mix. When we think of poetry, we think of beauty — images so lovely or stunning they take our breath away. When we think of war, other images come to mind — destruction, sacrifice. Death. And yet war poetry remains one of the earliest categories of verse in Western literature. Perhaps only poetry about nature and love — two aspects of humanity that war often consumes — are more popular in the annals. Our greatest poetic masterpieces — from Homer's *Iliad* to several of Shakespeare's plays — are, essentially, war poems.

War poetry is universal. War is war, pain is pain, loss is loss; the topics and themes seldom change — only the names of battles, casualties and weapons do. Consider the essence of this excerpt translated by Michael Alexander from *Beowulf* (c. 1000), whose content deals with historical battles of the sixth century (along with a few fire-breathing dragons):

There were melting heads

and bursting wounds, as the blood sprang out
from weapon-bitten bodies. Blazing fire,
most insatiable of spirits, swallowed the remains
of the victims of both nations. Their valour was no more.

Those lines could apply to any war, Anglo-Saxon to Gulf.

Nonetheless, defining what constitutes war poetry is not as simple as it may seem. The category is broad because war affects so many people: the combatants, of course, but also their families, loved ones, civilians, activists, clerics, medical personnel, and peace- and policy-makers.

"Most war poetry deals with the extremes of human behavior," says Bruce Weigl, author of the collection *Song of Napalm* (Atlantic Monthly Press, 1988). "In a war writers are/were able to see their fellow human beings at their very best and at their worst. War poetry has a tendency to be more politically based than poetry in general (though I see this as a mixed blessing, depending on the poet). And war poetry has a tendency to define and describe a historical period, which I see as a major and important characteristic."

Kevin Bowen, poet and codirector of the William Joiner Center for the Study of War and Social Consequences at the University of Massachusetts, says war poetry (like other kinds of poetry) focuses on conflict, pain and suffering. "The experience of war is so far outside the range of normal experience that the heart and spirit feel split and betrayed—no one is a victor, there are only survivors. So in many ways such poetry is a reaffirmation of the physical and spiritual horrors of war and a commitment to the act of bearing witness."

Lady Borton, a nationally known author and columnist whose poems appear in the anthology *Visions of War, Dreams of Peace: Writings of Women in the Vietnam War* (Warner, 1991), observes, "War is the *world* gone insane: explosions and wailing, rubble and the smell of burnt flesh. Soldiers—often emotionally mallable teenagers—are forced to break immutable commandments ('Thou shall not kill'). In the process, they fracture their own souls. Forgetting becomes impossible; hiding, a delusion. There rises an urgency to speak, but what must be said is unspeakable. And to comfortable listeners expecting tales of glory, the unspeakable becomes heresy.

"As a poet," she concludes, "what greater challenge could you greet?"

Let's see how poets through the ages have greeted that challenge.

OVERVIEW

The literary canon contains many war poems because war is part of the human condition. And the voices that sing of war not only span the centuries but employ a variety of verse forms and approaches.

Here are some basic types:

The Prayer. A popular type of war poem, this seventeenth-century example by Robert Herrick—known ironically for his love poetry—qualifies as one of the best:

A VOW TO MARS

Store of courage to me grant,
Now I'm turn'd a combatant:
Helpe me so, that I my *shield*,
(Fighting) lose not in the field.
That's the greatest shame of all,
That in warfare can befall.
Do but this; and there shall be
Offer'd up a Wolfe to thee.

The Farewell. When soldiers leave for war, some of them also leave poems to loved ones. This one by Richard Lovelace, who fought the Spaniards in the seventeenth century, is typical:

TO LUCASTA, GOING TO THE WARS

Tell me not, sweet, I am unkind
That from the nunnery
Of thy chaste breast and quiet mind,
To war and arms I fly.

True, a new mistress now I chase,
The first foe in the field;
And with a stronger faith embrace
A sword, a horse, a shield.

Yet this inconstancy is such
As you too shall adore;
I could not love thee, dear, so much,
Loved I not honor more.

The Tribute. Tribute poems honor a leader or commander, as illustrated by this 1652 Milton lyric which pays tribute to Oliver Cromwell, who took over Parlimentary armies after Charles I was dethroned and executed:

TO THE LORD GENERAL CROMWELL

Cromwell, our chief of men, who through a cloud,
    Not of war only, but detractions rude,
    Guided by faith and matchless fortitude,
    To peace and truth thy glorious way hast ploughed,
And on the neck of crownéd Fortune proud
    Hast reared God's trophies, and His work pursued,
    While Darwen stream, with blood of Scots imbrued,
    And Dunbar field, resounds thy praises loud,
And Worcester's laureate wreath: yet much remains
    To conquer still; peace hath her victories
    No less renowned than war: new foes arise,
Threatening to bind our souls with secular chains.
    Help us to save free conscience from the paw
    Of hireling wolves, whose gospel is their maw.

The Invective. This type of poem is a verbal attack, and Jonathan Swift, satirist and political journalist, excelled in making them. The following excerpt was composed in 1722 to mark and mock the death of John Churchill, decorated general and first Duke of Marlborough:

A SATIRICAL ELEGY ON THE DEATH OF A LATE
FAMOUS GENERAL

His Grace! impossible! what dead!
Of old age too, and in his bed!
And could that mighty warrior fall?
And so inglorious, after all!
Well, since he's gone, no matter how,
The last loud trump must wake him now:
And, trust me, as the noise grows stronger,
He'd wish to sleep a little longer.
And could he be indeed so old
As by the newspapers we're told?
Threescore, I think, is pretty high;
'Twas time in conscience he should die.
This world he cumbered long enough;
He burnt his candle to the snuff;
And that's the reason, some folks think,
He left behind so great a s---k.

The Historical. Lord Byron, English poet and Greek national hero
(he fought with Greeks in their war of independence against the
Turks), penned this immortal work about an invading king whose armies met with the plague during a 701 B.C. seige of Jerusalem:

THE DESTRUCTION OF SENNACHERIB

1

The Assyrian came down like the wolf on the fold,
And his cohorts were gleaming in purple and gold;
And the sheen of their spears was like stars on the sea,
When the blue wave rolls nightly on deep Galilee.

2

Like the leaves of the forest when summer is green,
That host with their banners at sunset were seen:
Like the leaves of the forest when autumn hath blown,
That host on the morrow lay withered and strown.

3

For the Angel of Death spread his wings on the blast,
And breathed in the face of the foe as he passed;
And the eyes of the sleepers waxed deadly and chill
And their hearts but once heaved, and forever grew still!

4

And there lay the steed with his nostril all wide,
But through it there rolled not the breath of his pride;
And the foam of his gasping lay white on the turf,

And cold as the spray of the rock-beating surf.
    5
And there lay the rider distorted and pale,
With the dew on his brow, and the rust on his mail:
And the tents were all silent, the banners alone,
The lances unlifted, the trumpet unblown.
    6
And the widows of Ashur are loud in their wail,
And the idols are broke in the temple of Baal;
And the might of the Gentile, unsmote by the sword,
Hath melted like snow in the glance of the Lord!

The Memorial. Herman Melville, who volunteered for service in the Navy during the Civil War (but was rejected), commemorated the battle at Shiloh Church in Tennessee in which about ten thousand soldiers on each side perished:

SHILOH
A Requiem (APRIL 1862)

Skimming lightly, wheeling still,
    The swallows fly low
Over the field in clouded days,
    The forest-field of Shiloh—
Over the field where April rain
Solaced the parched one stretched in pain
Through the pause of night
That followed the Sunday fight
    Around the church of Shiloh—
The church so lone, the log-built one,
That echoed to many a parting groan
        And natural prayer
Of dying foemen mingled there—
Foemen at morn, but friends at eve—
    Fame or country least their care:
(What like a bullet can undeceive!)
    But now they lie low,
While over them the swallows skim,
    And all is hushed at Shiloh.

The Character Study. Walt Whitman, who tended to and cheered the wounded on both sides during the Civil War, characterized a soldier who suffered post-traumatic stress syndrome in this haunting excerpt:

THE ARTILLERYMAN'S VISION

While my wife at my side lies slumbering, and the wars are
                                                    over long,
And my head on the pillow rests at home, and the vacant
                                              midnight passes,
And through the stillness, through the dark, I hear, just hear,
                                        the breath of my infant,
There in the room as I wake from sleep this vision presses
                                                    upon me;
The engagement opens there and then in fantasy unreal,
The skirmishers begin, they crawl cautiously ahead, I hear the
                                              irregular snap! snap!
I hear the sounds of the different missiles, the short t-h-t! t-h-t!
                                          of the rifle balls. . . .

The Chronicle. Edward Thomas, English poet and private soldier, wrote this 1917 account, describing the scene and his thoughts on a typical day during war shortly before he was killed in France:

FEBRUARY AFTERNOON

Men heard this roar of parleying starlings, saw,
    A thousand years ago even as now,
    Black rooks with white gulls following the plough
So that the first are last until a caw
Commands that last are first again, — a law
    Which was of old when one, like me, dreamed how
    A thousand years might dust lie on his brow
Yet thus would birds do between hedge and shaw.

Time swims before me, making as a day
    A thousand years, while the broad ploughland oak
    Roars mill-like and men strike and bear the stroke
    Of war as ever, audacious or resigned,
And God still sits aloft in the array
    That we have wrought him, stone-deaf and stone-blind.

The Elegy. Canadian physician, soldier and poet John McCrae, who died in 1918, eulogized the dead with this famous poem written while under fire:

IN FLANDERS FIELDS

In Flanders fields the poppies blow
Between the crosses, row on row,
    That mark our place; and in the sky
    The larks, still bravely singing, fly

Scarce heard amid the guns below.

We are the Dead. Short days ago
We lived, felt dawn, saw sunset glow,
  Loved and were loved, and now we lie
  In Flanders fields.

Take up our quarrel with the foe:
To you from failing hands we throw
  The torch; be yours to hold it high.
  If ye break faith with us who die
We shall not sleep, though poppies grow
  In Flanders fields.

The Protest. Social activist and populist Carl Sandburg composed this piercing antiwar poem that still echoes through the ages:

READY TO KILL

Ten minutes now I have been looking at this.
I have gone by here before and wondered about it.
This is a bronze memorial of a famous general
Riding horseback with a flag and a sword and a revolver on him.
I want to smash the whole thing into a pile of junk to be hauled
                    away to the scrap yard.
I put it straight to you,
After the farmer, the miner, the shop man, the factory hand,
                    the fireman and the teamster,
Have all been remembered with bronze memorials,
Shaping them on the job of getting all of us
Something to eat and something to wear,
When they stack a few silhouettes
          Against the sky
          Here in the park,
And show the real huskies that are doing the work of the
          world, and feeding people instead of butchering them,
Then maybe I will stand here
And look easy at this general of the army holding a flag in the air,
And riding like hell on horseback
Ready to kill anybody that gets in his way,
Ready to run the red blood and slush the bowels of men all
                    over the sweet new grass of the prairie.

Perhaps by scanning the above examples you can see that, except for the farewell and the chronicle, you don't have to be in a war to write about one. In fact, although the various types outlined here will help you come up with ideas for poems, you might want to simplify the genre of war poetry by thinking of it in these terms:

• *Poet as Visionary.* The poet can be a veteran of a war — someone who has fought in or witnessed one — or someone who hasn't. The poet gives his or her overview of events; praises, scorns or memorializes combatants; studies combatants or civilians affected by war; imagines what it would have been like to have fought in a war; or makes political statements about war.

• *Poet as Eyewitness.* The poet should be a veteran — someone who has fought in or witnessed a war (military or civilian). Content can be about any aspect of such an experience viewed or felt firsthand by the participant.

Basically, the visionary method puts the emphasis on the poet and his perspectives or opinions. The eyewitness method emphasizes the impact on or experiences of a veteran, conveying to readers firsthand the felt emotion of participating in or being affected by combat.

THE VISIONARY METHOD

One of my favorite war poems is by Wayne Dodd, esteemed poet and longtime editor of *The Ohio Review.* In this example, Dodd taps part of his heritage to recapture a scene from the Plains War against Native Americans:

OF SITTING BEAR
(from *The General Mule Poems*)

Hoka hey, Lakotas, Sioux warriors used to shout
before riding into battle: *It's a good day
to die.* Comanche braves must have said it
every morning before breakfast.
Now the Comanches I don't miss much,
and the Plains Indian may not have been
the noblest human ever to walk
or ride the surface of the earth, but I say
it does take something fine
to make a man, old and sick and huddled
beneath a blanket, patiently, mile
after mile in an open wagon, strip
the flesh away from his wrists
with his teeth, until at last the manacles slide
from his hands and he attacks
and attacks and attacks the guarding soldiers
till they shoot him finally
to death, there on the road
to prison, because it was,

he knew, a bad day for Sitting Bear
to be captured, but a good day to die.

First of all, the above account is true. In 1871 Sitting Bear, a member of an elite Kiowa military group, had been captured and was handcuffed in an open wagon on his way to prison in Texas when the scene that Dodd recounts occurred. During the trip Sitting Bear was guarded by soldiers with carbines as cavalrymen rode alongside. Periodically on the trip Sitting Bear would hide beneath a blanket and rip the flesh of his hands so he could slide off the cuffs. Somehow he had managed to procure a knife, and suddenly he sprang on his captors who shot him as he slashed.

Now if you had read such an account in a history book, and in part it spoke of your heritage, you might be moved as Dodd was to compose such a lyric. What makes Dodd's so special is that he relates history and re-creates the moment personally, as if you were listening to him across the room — "Comanche braves must have said it/every morning before breakfast./Now the Comanches I don't miss much. . . ." All the while he presents his research in clear, accessible lines — "*Hoka hey*, *Lakotas*, Sioux warriors used to shout." Moreover, while the poet obviously could not have witnessed the scene, he can compose a good war poem because he has a genuine interest in its story.

In everyone's family tree, someone has fought in or has been affected/afflicted by war. To generate an idea for a war poem, conduct research into your own background and heritage. If one of your relatives has documents from a war, ask to borrow them. In your journal, record how you feel about or relate to specific battles or events. If the veteran is still alive, interview him or her. Look up significant episodes in reference books or military history collections at the library. Get a sense of historical fact to shape your perspective. Remember, the real topic is not the war but your feelings or comments about it.

If you still believe that your perspective is lacking, keep the following in mind: Sooner or later everyone's life is touched by armed conflict. Even my son Shane, two years old at the time, experienced the televised Gulf War in 1991 and now identifies combat with flashing anti-aircraft lights on an illuminated green background: "War," he says. In my own life, of course, I (and many of you) have been affected by the Vietnam War. I didn't serve in the military, but that hasn't stopped me from writing about war.

If you have little experience thinking about war, or no feeling associated with it, contemplate why in your journal. (That can be the basis for a poem itself.) Or visit a veteran's club or hospital and do some volunteer service and question members. Eventually specific topics, perspectives, truths and lessons will be aroused.

Let's consider another way to generate ideas for war poems.

As human beings, we can sympathize with veterans or loved ones who have suffered in a war (even if we haven't). While this type of poem has an implied political theme, its focus is on emotion. True, you may not be able to convey emotion firsthand, but if you empathize with a person who has felt intense experience, you really will be writing about compassion — what we feel for our hurting friends or loved ones.

This poem is based on an anecdote a woman shared with me about her husband, officially declared "missing in action":

MISSING

They mean more than the medals,
The spit-shined Marine portraits
Dotting her mantel: letters,

Undated and timeless in their talk
About love and coming home. She forges
On the envelope her name and address

As he would write it, in a font
Slanted toward future. His letters arrive
Like poems, the lines saying nothing

New, save *I am alive*
          the heart behind this sentence
          beats another day. Again

She will send off his last, the paper
Dog-eared by sorters and caught
Once in rain that bled his words blue.

She takes it to the post office. For him
Alone she has rented a box:
The carrier, a veteran, knows. She knows

Her number has mail today, another envelope
Pushed in the slot, eyes of the sorter
Momentarily distorted through plexiglass,

Melding with hers like a sad lover.
She unlocks the box, pulls its toy door
Open to grope for that slip of face —

Gone, among the missing, her fingers
Retreating for the mail, for word
That once more he's made it home.

Essentially, this is a kind of character study in which I had a personal stake—I knew the woman upon whom the poem is based. I could empathize with her pain although I could not imagine her loss. Thus, if my poem has a ring of truth, it is the result of compassion rather than experience.

If this type of poem appeals to you, try these methods to generate ideas:

• *Focus on an individual with whom you share a bond.* The person should have experienced war or the pain of war firsthand. He or she should be a relative or friend so you have a fix on his or her feelings and a stake in the outcome of the poem. Talk to that person. Such people are closer than you think. In my own life, for instance, my mother lost her first husband (not my father) in Germany during World War II when she was only twenty-two and a newlywed. While writing this chapter, I realized that I have never spoken to her about Lou Pfaff and her feelings for him, particularly on the day she received her telegram.

• *Base an idea on an incident or anecdote concerning that person.* The topic will depend on what he or she tells you, but the theme is yours. Emphasize the compassion we have for people who have suffered in war and convey that compassion by imagining appropriate tones of voice. The epiphany in such a poem should be implied or stated but always based on what you as a visionary poet have learned from your source about the consequences of war.

In any visionary-based war poem, being truthful is essential. While veterans can write about all aspects of war, the nonveteran should think twice about pretending to be a combatant or victim of combat. There are ways to accomplish that feeling—by depicting it in others as I did in "Missing," by sharing your political views, or by taking a historical approach as Wayne Dodd did in "Of Sitting Bear." The bottom line is clear: To compose powerful poems about war, when you haven't been in one, you should have a personal stake in the topic or outcome of your poem. Otherwise it will smack of pretense or worse, falsehood.

THE EYEWITNESS METHOD

For those who have experienced war firsthand, composing poems about it can be a catharsis. Initially at least, it can bring back suppressed memories that cause veterans pain — and writer's block. In some sense, the eyewitness method is much easier than the visionary one, when it comes to subject matter. Poets who have never been in a war have to understand how war has nevertheless affected them. However, those who have been in a war only have to recount their experiences to purge them, but that, of course, is the catch.

"The images — scenes, sights, sounds, smells — are all there, waiting," says Lady Borton. "Reaching their depths requires the endurance to dig through slag, the commitment to apply adult compassion to youth's anguish, and the courage to weep."

"Unfortunately," says Bruce Weigl, "suffering a trauma like war does not necessarily guarantee that one will be able to turn all that suffering and the effects of that trauma into art. My advice to vets has always been the same: You have a story to tell so tell it; write it down exactly the way you would tell it to a friend, a fellow vet, a spouse. Once one has told one's story and gotten the word on the page, the struggle becomes manageable."

Weigl adds that vets should be willing to do "revision after revision" until their accounts are true to the experience. Only then may they find some poetry. "Nothing will be lost in the process," he notes, "and you will only learn more about yourselves and your experiences."

One way to tell a war story is, ironically, to write a vignette — a self-contained prose passage — instead of a poem. Your challenge, simply, is to get the words on the page, as Weigl recommends, without worrying about the mechanical aspects of verse — line, stanza, title (and other tools covered later in this book).

Here is an example of a vignette by Bruce Weigl:

SHORT

There's a bar girl on Trung Hung Do who has half a ten
piaster note I tore in my drunken relief to be leaving
the country. She has half and I have half, if I can find
it. If I lost it, it wasn't on purpose, it's all I have to
remember her. She has a wet sheet, a PX fan, PX radio,
and half a ten piaster note, as if she cared to remember
me. She thought it was stupid to tear money and when I
handed it to her she turned to another soldier, new in
her country, who needed a girl. I hope I burn in hell.

As you can see, the passage has many of the elements of a good poem — including epiphany — and as such is self-contained. It lacks the added meaning and power of poetry attained via line break and stanza, perhaps, but it simplifies the creative process. It also can be argued that, depending on the anecdote, a vignette may be the best vehicle for the work. For instance, Weigl's vignette succeeds because it resembles a journal entry — as if he is showing us something personal and painful, a private moment of sharing.

Sharing, of course, is the goal. If you have trouble expressing your idea on paper, even in your journal, try tape-recording yourself speaking to another veteran or friend and then transcribe what you said.

This will represent an idea for a poem, and you will have gotten it down on paper.

Getting the poem on the page may be painful, but there are payoffs, too. Says Weigl, "I do know that for me the war was an enormous paradox. On one hand it practically ruined my life; it took away my innocence and gave me twenty years of nightmares in exchange. But on the other hand, I'm quite sure that given my background, if I hadn't been in the war, I would have never become a writer."

Experience, of course, is the backbone of the best poetry. But when experience approaches the traumatic, the best way to express it is to tell your story image by image, scene by scene without commenting on it. The more traumatic the episode of war, the less need you have to put it into perspective.

The episode will speak for itself.

Here is an example by Weigl that transports the reader to the scene of war without delving into the horror of aftermath:

TEMPLE NEAR QUANG TRI, NOT ON THE MAP

Dusk, the ivy thick with sparrows
Squawking for more room
Is all we hear; we see
Birds move on the walls of the temple
Shaping their calligraphy of wings.
Ivy is thick in the grottos,
On the moon-watching platform
And ivy keeps the door from fully closing.

The point man leads us and we are
Inside, lifting
The white washbowl, the smaller bowl
For rice, the stone lanterns
And carved stone heads that open
Above the carved faces for incense.
But even the bamboo sleeping mat
Rolled in the corner,
Even the place of prayer is clean.
And a small man

Sits legs askew in the shadow
The farthest wall casts
halfway across the room.
He is bent over, his head
Rests on the floor and he is speaking something
As though to us and not to us.
The CO wants to ignore him;

He locks and loads and fires a clip into the walls
Which are not packed with rice this time
And tells us to move out.

But one of us moves towards the man,
Curious about what he is saying.
We bend him to sit straight
And when he's nearly peaked
At the top of his slow uncurling
His face becomes visible, his eyes
Roll down to the charge
Wired between his teeth and the floor.
The sparrows
Burst off the walls into the jungle.

Weigl does not have to illustrate the violence that accompanied the explosion. All he has to show are sparrows bursting in flight into the jungle. We know that the charge has been triggered and now soldiers are dead or suffering, as the memory may evoke. But Weigl resists that scenario by leaving the reader with a visual, suggestive ending, eliminating the impulse to elaborate on horrific events.

Poetry has that power.

"I wish I could say I believe that poetry can stop war," Weigl says. "It can't, but it may be able to jar a few people out of their complacency and encourage them to at least think for themselves more and to not be so willing to accept the 'official' versions of what happens in war and afterward to veterans."

To illustrate Weigl's remark, I've included these firsthand accounts of war in the mini anthology section:

• In "A Boom, a Billow," Lady Borton describes the devastating effects of napalm in a before/after format. Moreover, she emphasizes the unique view of women who have experienced war. Borton, who served with the American Friends Service Committee, a Quaker group, says of her Vietnam tour: "American men in ground combat fought and then moved on. In contrast, most American women hovered over the mangled, living a horror (and seeing futility) that the men who kept moving on kept moving past." She observes that for Vietnamese women, the mangled included their own children. "For the Vietnamese, there was no end of tour."

• In "Playing Basketball With the Viet Cong" by Kevin Bowen, the initial image "comes from a very vivid memory of watching a gunship stalk an old couple and their water buffalo in a free fire zone," he says. "I carried that image for years in my head. It seemed to hold some truths about the war. But I had nothing to connect it with until the day I was teaching Nguyen Quang Sang (a Vietnamese writer) how to play basketball in my backyard. Standing back I could see both images — events — merging to somehow complete each other and say something together." Bowen says he often unlocks war memories by linking them to the present.

• In "The Last Lie," Bruce Weigl harkens one of his most intense memories, writing about the rage of American soldiers and the desperation of Vietnamese children.

Mini Anthology of War Poems

A BOOM, A BILLOW

While waiting for a plane to DaNang
I watched American bombers a mile away.
The uninvolved objectivity with which I stared at the sleek jets,
their wings sloping back in fiercely powerful lines,
confused and disturbed me.
The jets swooped down,
then up quickly,
to circle and swoop once more.
A boom.
A billow of dark gray smoke.
Napalm.

That afternoon I met a boy at the Helgoland hospital ship.
He sought me out because I came from Quang Ngai,
his ancestral home.
He had no nose,
only two holes in the middle of his face.
His mouth was off to the side.
One eye was gone;
there was a hollow in his forehead above the other.
All his face was shiny red scar tissue.
Most of the rest of his body was the same.
One hand was partly usable,
the fingers of the other,
soldered to his wrist.
Napalm.

— Lady Borton

PLAYING BASKETBALL WITH THE VIET CONG
for Nguyen Quang Sang

You never thought it would come to this,
that afternoon in the war

when you leaned so hard into the controls
you almost became part of the landscape:
just you, the old man, old women, and their buffalo.
You never thought then,
that this grey-haired man in sandals
smoking gauloises on your back porch,
drinking your beer, his rough cough
punctuating tales of how he fooled
the French in fifty-four,
would arrive at your back door
to call you out to shoot some baskets, friend.
If at first he seems awkward,
before long he's got it down,
his left leg lifts from the ground,
his arms arch back then forward
again from the waist to release the ball
in a perfect arc to the hoop, one, two, three . . .
ten straight times. You stare at him,
in his tee shirt, sandals and shorts.
Oh yes, he smiles. It is a gift —
good in the war for bringing down gunships —
as he did most proudly in the Delta
and other places from where, he whispers,
there may be other scores to settle.

— Kevin Bowen

THE LAST LIE

Some guy in the miserable convoy
Raised up in the back of our open truck
And threw a can of c-rations at a child
Who called into the rumble for food.
He didn't toss the can, he wound up and hung it
On the child's forehead and she was stunned
Backwards into the dust of our trucks.

Across the sudden angle of the road's curving
I could still see her when she rose
Waving one hand across her swollen, bleeding head,
Wildly swinging her other hand
At the children who mobbed her,
Who tried to take her food.

I grit my teeth to myself to remember that girl
Smiling as she fought off her brothers and sisters.
She laughed

As if she thought it were a joke
And the guy with me laughed
And fingered the edge of another can
Like it was the seam of a baseball
Until his rage ripped
Again into the faces of children
Who called to us for food.

— Bruce Weigl

Notebook

ALL LEVELS

For Poets Using the Visionary Method

Review the basic types of war poems included in the introduction, excluding "The Farewell" and "The Chronicle." In other words, since you have not experienced leaving loved ones to go to war, or experienced war itself, you will focus on:

A War Prayer. (Unlike Herrick's example, make yours *related* to war — perhaps a prayer for *peace*, instead of for victory.)

A Tribute. (Praise a warrior or leader, living or dead, or someone who tried to intervene or end a war.)

An Invective. (Mock a warrior or leader, living or dead, or someone who tried to intervene or end a war.)

A Historical Poem. (Re-create a battle or event in which you have a vested or personal interest.)

A Memorial. (Commemorate the dead in a particular battle based on a researched account in which you have a vested or personal interest.)

A Character Study. (Imagine yourself in a warrior's boots or as someone who has to tend to the mangled.)

An Elegy. (Eulogize the fallen by setting your poem in a cemetery or national monument.)

A Protest. (Express your intense political views in an anti- or pro-war poem.)

Base at least ten ideas on any or all of the above categories.

For Poets Using the Eyewitness Method

Generate at least seven ideas for poems based on any of the examples above except the first (a war prayer). Draw on research instead of your war experience. Then tap that experience by basing at least three more ideas on:

The Prayer. (Come up with ideas for prayers you would have made before, during and after your war experience.)

The Farewell. (Describe how it felt to leave a person, town, loved one, etc., as you went off to war . . . and then how it felt to leave a person, town or loved one behind in the war zone when you returned home.)

The Chronicle. (Base ideas on combat or the results of combat or some other incident that happened during the war.)

Chapter Six

Political Poetry

A s I write, poets in other lands are in prison because they composed verse with political content that angered or frightened their leaders. These are brave men and women, willing to risk their lives to express their political beliefs. In most countries in Europe and North America, the right to compose political poetry is protected by laws and constitutions, so we tend to take this freedom for granted. Few, if any of us, will ever write a political poem that prompts the FBI to investigate our backgrounds or tap our phones, although we know this happened (in my era, during the turbulent Vietnam War). Few, if any of us, will ever write a political poem that captures the essence of an entire generation (although you will read such a poem in this chapter). Few, if any of us, will compose revolutionary verse so powerful that the media in America carries its message to millions (although you will also find such a poem here).

It can happen. Political poetry, more than any other kind of verse, has the power to change society or our notions about society. It combines a volatile subject with the most powerful vehicle of expression: verse. That's why many dictators have banned political poetry and why you should consider writing it because you enjoy free speech. However, if you are like most poets, you will tend to ignore public issues and write about intensely private ones.

Certainly I've composed my share of personal poems, especially when I was just starting out as a writer. Although I had strong political beliefs, I suppressed them because I thought poets should discuss love or nature. Eventually, I learned to balance that impulse by expressing my political concerns and discovering how effective poetry was in its ability to convey candid opinion.

In sum, I learned that political verse:

• *Catches a reader's eye.* Political poems are relatively rare. When I edited poetry for a literary magazine, I received about a dozen love/nature lyrics for every political counterpart. When a political poem came in, I read it more closely simply because the submission stood out from the others in the pile of manuscripts on my desk.

• *Catches a reader's ear.* Political verse contains strong opinion, and opinion, by its very nature, affects voice — the sound or pitch of the poet's voice. For instance, too many love lyrics sound too sentimental or sweet, but a political poem may contain an angry, passionate or direct tone. This, too, distinguishes it from other submissions.

• *Catches a reader's attention.* Readers have political beliefs and opinions, too. They may embrace your poem as divine truth . . . or dismiss it as propaganda. Moreover, if you send such poetry to editors, you also may get a personal response. Either they will encourage you to send more poems or tell you they disliked your work, depending on their agendas.

Political poetry underscores the fact that message is as important as language in verse. Even a mediocre political poem, composed in a weak voice or poor form, has the power to arouse readers because of controversial or patriotic content. But the best poems in the genre also rely on elements of craft to hone, shape or otherwise enhance content.

Before we see how, let's review the three basic types of political poetry:

The Revolutionary Poem. This type advocates the overthrow of a specific government or culture, as in this excerpt from Ralph Waldo Emerson's "Concord Hymn":

By the rude bridge that arched the flood,
    Their flag to April's breeze unfurled,
Here once the embattled farmers stood
    And fired the shot heard round the world.

The Patriotic Poem. This type celebrates a country, culture or form of government, illustrated by Sir Walter Scott in this passage from "Patriotism":

Breathes there the man with soul so dead,
Who never to himself hath said,
    'This is my own, my native land!'

The Protest Poem. Here the poet protests certain acts or systems of a government. For example, this excerpt from "America" by Allen Ginsberg refers to labor, political and racial trials during the so-called McCarthy era of the mid-1950s:

America free Tom Mooney
America save the Spanish Loyalists
America Sacco & Vanzetti must not die
America I am the Scottsboro boys.

Each type of political poem has benefits and drawbacks. The more you become acquainted with them, the better equipped you'll be to discover your own political agenda and to generate ideas for such verse.

THE REVOLUTIONARY POEM

Revolutionary poems advocating the overthrow of a government or a culture are protected by the First Amendment. You can burn the flag in the United States because of free speech . . . or write a lyric like the one below, composed to make a point:

COUP D'ÉTAT

If everyone threw a brick
through a window
at the White House,

If everyone cast a stone
instead of a vote,
a rock instead of a telegram,

Maybe then
we would have a government
for, by, and of the people.

Perhaps you share the same opinion. Chances are, however, that you don't. If you're like me (or most readers of poetry), you're not interested in the overthrow of the U.S. government. So the risk of writing revolutionary poems lies in the fact that relatively few people may want to hear your message — unless your message arrives at a propitious moment in history.

Revolutionary poems live or die by the clock. For instance, when Ishmael Reed wrote revolutionary work in the 1970s, the literary world took note as he sang about black power. But in the more conservative 1980s, such verse had little appeal.

On the other hand, during the 1980s, I was able to publish dozens of revolutionary poems that advocated the overthrow of a culture. The reason, as this poem illustrates, is because the poem was set abroad and the culture was not American:

WE PLOT
WHILE MY LAME UNCLE PRAYS

Outside the cathedral Aunt Lena makes the sign
to carry in protest against the British
governor, at mass. It is a good sign,
the wood handle ripped from her rabbit hutch,

our Sunday dinner last seen
hopping seaward, a kind of sacrifice.

She colors her slogan in red: *Limey*
Set Sail! The choir inside chants Amen.

My uncle is among the first
to see the protest. He leads the charge
against us, his walking stick held like a sword.

I don't move when he spots me, my rump ready
for the cane. Auntie cuts
in front — her sign a shield — wood against wood,
over my head
for a moment, almost a cross.

This poem wouldn't rile the staunchest conservative. The riot happens outside a cathedral in a foreign land, advocating the overthrow of another culture and using the church to symbolize another echelon of power. Even though violence ensues, in which the narrator is caught between warring sides of his family — the rebel aunt and the royalist uncle — one can argue that the anti-British/anti-Catholic stance almost qualifies as patriotic in that America was founded on similar political and religious notions. Thus, this type of revolutionary verse was acceptable even during a conservative era.

Overtones of conservatism were extant in 1992. So revolutionary verse was still regarded as untimely because of conventional politics. But racial issues were about to loom large over the horizon. A year earlier Rodney King, an African-American, was videotaped being beaten by Los Angeles police officers. A trial against the officers ensued, and when the verdict was announced, riots erupted in that and in other cities. At the time, Harry Johnson — manager of corporate communications at Polaroid — became so upset by the verdict that he took the morning off and composed this poem:

DAMN YOU, AMERICA!

News item: Four white Los Angeles police officers,
following a three-month trial and seven days of jury
deliberations, were found not guilty of using excessive
force on the evening of March 3, 1991, when they subdued
Rodney King, a black man, by shooting him with a stun gun
and striking him 56 times with their police batons.

Damn! Damn!
Damn! Damn! Damn!

No, I wasn't in the courtroom.
No, I wasn't privy to all the evidence.
No, I didn't see everything the jury saw.
No, I didn't hear everything the jury heard.
No, I am not in a position to second-guess their decision.

Yes, I try to believe the promise of America.
Yes, I try to believe that the rules are fair, that justice is blind.
Yes, I try to believe — God knows, I try to believe —
    that America works nearly all the time,
    for nearly all the people.

But, don't ask me to believe today.
Today, I believe something different.
Today, I believe that America lies.
Today, I am disappointed. Shocked. Angry. Enraged.
Today, I am a skeptic. A cynic. An unbeliever.
Today, I am not an American.
Today, I am a black man.

Today, I know what the black man has always known.
Today, I know that America — deep in its heart —
    doesn't know what to do with me,
    doesn't know how to deal with my audacious blackness.
Today, I know that for many white Americans,
    slaves forever to the emotional apartheid
    that infects their very souls,
    I am not different from Rodney King.

Today, I know that nothing that I do —
    not the way I dress, not the way I talk,
    not the way I comport myself, not the way I invest my life —
    will ever make me any different from Rodney King
    in their eyes.
Today, I know that nothing I have ever done,
    nothing I will ever do —
    not the tears that I cry, not the blood that I shed —
    will ever make any real difference.
Today, I know that the bruises to my black man's ego,
    the pain in my black man's heart,
    the scars on my black man's soul
    will never heal completely.

Today, I know that I am not an American.
Today I know that I am a black man,
    living at the margin

of a place called
America.

Damn! Damn!
Damn! Damn! Damn you, America!
Once more, you have lied to me!

More than any political poem I have read, this one proves how timely and powerful revolutionary verse can be. For starters, an excerpt of this poem was picked up by *The Wall Street Journal* and appeared in that nationally distributed newspaper on May 1, 1992. Soon after, National Public Radio and other media outlets were reciting or reprinting the poem. It went out over fax machines across the country. (In fact, that's how I received my copy of the work.) Thereafter, it was recited in churches and in small groups whose members wanted to experience what Harry Johnson did on that fateful day. In the space of a few days, Johnson reached millions of people with his one political poem — more people than Pulitzer Prize-winning poets reach during the span of their careers.

Three factors were involved:

1. *Timeliness.* The nation was ready to hear Johnson's poem because it occurred after the Los Angeles riots, coinciding with the public's outcry against treatment of African-Americans.

2. *Message.* Johnson expressed his political views with strong words that literally seethed on the page.

3. *Media.* If Johnson wrote a letter to the editor expressing similar views in similar tones, his piece likely would have appeared in one or only a few publications. But he combined elements of timeliness and message with the powerful medium of poetry, and mass media carried his voice across the country.

These, of course, are elements that make for publishable revolutionary work: a voice that speaks when others are prepared to listen and one whose message is funneled through the enduring medium of verse.

THE PATRIOTIC POEM

While revolutionary poetry is written only by a handful of poets and succeeds only at propitious moments, patriotic poetry appeals to many writers and is timeless. Those are drawbacks. At any given moment, poets are writing this type of verse and doing so in similar or antiquated ways.

Consider this rather typical lyric:

WHY I LOVE THEE, AMERICA

Thou art as rich as proud,
from snow cap to gulf stream,
panhandle to prairie,

I sing my hope aloud,
the American dream:
May all who hear it love thee.

Chances are, you've seen poems like this or even written a few. Indeed, *anyone* could have written the above work, with its safe ideas and outdated language. Essentially, however, the risk of writing patriotic poems lies in the fact that so many people have felt the same emotion and expressed it in the same way. As Sir Walter Scott implies in the lines quoted earlier from "Patriotism," who hasn't felt a surge of pride at the mention of his or her native land—throughout time?

Love of country, for many people, is eternal. So patriotic poets tend to preach their causes using clichés and addressing readers who already are converted. Patriotic verse should aspire to greater goals. An example of a good patriotic poem is this lyric by Walt Whitman whose form (free verse) was new, whose diction (passionate) was exciting, and whose cause (freedom for all races) was controversial in the Civil War era:

FOR YOU O DEMOCRACY

Come, I will make the continent indissoluble,
I will make the most splendid race the sun ever shone upon,
I will make divine magnetic lands,
    With the love of comrades,
    With the life-long love of comrades.
I will plant companionship thick as trees along all the rivers
    of America, and along the shores of the great lakes, and all
                                over the prairies,
I will make inseparable cities with their arms about each other's
                                    necks,
    By the love of comrades,
    By the manly love of comrades.

For you these from me, O Democracy, to serve you ma femme!
For you, for you I am trilling these songs.

The lines above evoke Martin Luther King's "I Have a Dream" speech. A century later Americans are still trying to live up to Whitman's dream of "the most splendid race the sun ever shone upon." As the Whitman poem also illustrates, good patriotic poetry often encourages us to foresee a more glorious future rather than the one most of us envision.

The patriot knows that freedom, if taken for granted, often is taken away.

Hilary Tham, a native of Kelang, Malaysia, and author of two collections published in America, embraces that notion. Her patriotic poem below also rises above the norm by (a) creating a fictive persona who has emigrated to America, (b) providing an outsider's view of what we take for granted, and (c) employing a passionate voice to articulate opinions about free expression:

MRS. WEI ON PATRIOTISM

Here many people over-exercise
their right to free speech. Everywhere
bumper stickers shout at me: Have you
hugged your child today? I brake
for animals, Honk if you love
Jesus! We support our troops! Say No
to drugs! I am for America!
But when they want us all
to chant slogans and tie yellow
ribbons to our houses, I plant
my feet and say No.

Loyalty to one's land should be
as natural as sap in the tree
whose roots know the earth which gives
it sustenance. It is not a hair ribbon
to run to the store to buy
when it becomes fashionable.

Poems like Whitman's "For You O Democracy" are based on visions of what a country will become because of its politics, government, law or culture. Poems like Tham's "Mrs. Wei on Patriotism" are based on visions of what a country has stood for or symbolized because of its politics, government, law or culture. These represent atypical approaches to composing good patriotic verse — ones that bring us forward as a people, and ones that take us back to our roots.

THE PROTEST POEM

Like the patriotic poet, the protest poet knows that freedom taken for granted is apt to be taken away. But the protest poet expresses that notion differently. Instead of praising a nation's potential, or taking a nation back to the principles on which it was founded, the protest poet criticizes policy so our leaders do not become complacent. Such poets believe that debate is good in a democracy—the more controversy, the better—because truth thrives when people have access to all manner of ideas.

It is often easy for the masses to dismiss revolutionary poetry. In general, people feel confident that their government or way of life will continue. But protest poetry threatens the masses because it challenges basic concepts about such issues as equality or justice. Moreover, it doesn't seek to overthrow government or to disavow culture but to *change* it.

That's why practitioners of protest verse often are called unpatriotic. The label means that protesters lack faith in their country or culture or are too quick to abandon principles about freedom or government. As proof, critics often maintain that protest poetry emphasizes only the cynical or negative.

And to some extent, this is true. The idea was best put forth by the late Robert Penn Warren in his Jefferson Lecture of 1974, which appears in book form as *Democracy & Poetry* (Harvard University Press, 1975). Warren observed that "we are driving toward the destruction of the very assumption on which our nation is presumably founded. A bearer of ill tidings—and that is what our poetry, in one dimension, is—generally gets regarded as the guilty perpetrator of the disaster reported."

In other words, the protest poet often reminds us what the government stands for and what, at times, it stoops to in carrying out policy. The poet is deemed traitorous because he or she delivers a message of bad news.

News is the operative word in a country that embraces free speech. This freedom sets a high standard for protest poetry, for not only must it enlighten or challenge us, it must compete with other messages in the media—a cacophony of opinion! Unlike revolutionary verse, whose message lives or dies by the clock, protest poetry contributes to an ongoing debate and has to rise above other messages to be heard. So while your first impulse may be to express your opinion in a protest poem, you'll have to use all your skills as a poet to interest readers in your topic or agenda.

Let's illustrate. This poem protests commercialism, comparing dissident lists compiled in Russia by the KGB (security force) with direct-mail lists compiled in the United States by corporations:

VOICE OF AMERICA

You heard our propaganda,
Now you visit us and see:
We keep lists, too, like
The KGB. Your name is in

The computer and the offer
Is in the mail with free
Coupons. Eat your fill!
You'll grow fat on freedom,
So we'll sell you fat-free
Entrees while you exercise
Free speech, singing new
Anthems with your Sony.

The poem tries to work a metaphor, but beyond that, relies solely on message to discuss an agenda: our economic addictions. Thus, the poem is mediocre. It preaches to the converted, like patriotic poetry often does. In general, a good political poem should contain as many images as a typical nature poem. It should move us emotionally as the best love lyrics do, emphasizing song, and challenge or stimulate us with its aesthetics (or style).

Here's a rewrite of that poem containing more images and using more emotionally charged words, to enhance message:

VOICE OF AMERICA

This is a plea to preserve the word
Free. Synonym of liberty
When you let it loll off the tongue,
Milk and honey on the other side of
The Atlantic. Come visit us, see
Cereal boxes with trinkets inside,
Sort our sacks of junk mail
Generated by the same traitorous
Chip of KGB silicon. We have lists
Too. Soon your name will appear on
Embossed letterhead of informants
Bearing gifts of fine plastic:
Free! You'll grow fat on freedom
As a boar on feed before the slaughter.
So we'll sell you a slew of fat-
Free items, aisles of ware and woe,
Lines as short as lifespans.
You'll exercise free speech,
Learn the language of double meaning,
Misspell the ad word "lite." In time,
Dictionaries will prove you right.
Then you will master the oxymoron
Free with proof of purchase and sing

Our anthem by flickerlight of Sony,
Remembering the rocket's red glare.

The work reads more like a poem now instead of a piece of propaganda. The result may be that more people will listen, even those who would debate its politics.

"The thing to bear in mind when writing any kind of political or sociopolitical poetry," says Hilary Tham, "is to focus on the personal, the felt experience, or the poem quickly becomes demagogic and unpoetic."

THE UNIVERSAL POLITICAL POEM

One of the first poets to balance the public message with the felt experience is Carolyn Forché whose book *The Country Between Us* (Harper and Row, 1981) remains a touchstone for the contemporary political poet. Her politics occasionally disturb readers but her poetry always stirs them to the quick. In the 1980s, when many of her contemporaries were writing about shopping malls and love at honky-tonks, Forché was writing about America and Latin America. Her verse was so accomplished that it will echo for decades to come. The poet Denise Levertov wrote about Forché: "Here's a poet who's doing what I want to do, what I want to see all of us doing in this time without any close parallels or precedents in history: she is creating poems in which there is no seam between personal and political. . . ."

To illustrate, let's read one of Forché's best political works:

SELECTIVE SERVICE

We rise from the snow where we've
lain on our backs and flown like children,
from the imprint of perfect wings and cold gowns,
and we stagger together wine-breathed into town
where our people are building
their armies again, short years after
body bags, after burnings. There is a man
I've come to love after thirty, and we have
our rituals of coffee, of airports, regret.
After love we smoke and sleep
with magazines, two shot glasses
and the black and white collapse of hours.
In what time do we live that it is too late
to have children? In what place
that we consider the various ways to leave?
There is no list long enough
for a selective service card shriveling

under a match, the prison that comes of it,
a flag in the wind eaten from its pole
and boys sent back in trash bags.
We'll tell you. You were at that time
learning fractions. We'll tell you
about fractions. Half of us are dead or quiet
or lost. Let them speak for themselves
We lie down in the fields and leave behind
the corpses of angels.

As you can see, Forché weaves the personal—"There is a man /
I've come to love"—with the political—"a selective service card
shriveling /under a match." What seems to start out as a love poem
ends with the poet as bearer of bad news: the loss of yet another
American generation.

Future citizens are forewarned.

Unlike Allen Ginsberg, for example, in the passionate but sometimes profane voice of "America," Forché knows that tone is as important as her message. Moreover, it might be said that Ginsberg's diction—the words he used—articulated the rage of his generation in
certain poems (he also can be as open and celebratory as Whitman);
but he turned off some listeners who otherwise could have learned
from his wisdom.

Not so with Forché. Take a pencil and circle the nouns of "Selective
Service" to see how her images help shape her inviting voice. Isolate
her symbols such as "match" and "angels" and see how she juxta-
poses these with others like "trash bags" and "fractions." Note, too,
how she welcomes all citizens into the work, even those who might
disagree with her agenda. Forché knows that poems *endure* and thus
have a key role in preserving our freedoms.

Now that you are familiar with the three types of political poems,
and the craft involved in making them, you should be able to envision
your own political ideas.

GENERATING IDEAS FOR POLITICAL POEMS

You may claim that you don't have a political bone in your body, but
if you have bones, some of them are political. You might not care for
protest poetry and might shrug at the mention of revolutionary or patriotic verse. Perhaps you are quite content with the status quo. If so,
imagine an issue that would send you into the streets with a sign and
a slogan.

Surely, there's one. For instance, millions of Americans are content
to watch spectator sports every weekend or consume hours of soap
operas during the week. Some of these people might claim they have

no interest in politics, but they would soon become irate if somehow their televisions or their favorite shows were banned. True, that probably won't happen. But it also proves that there is something in everyone's life that he or she takes for granted but, actually, values quite highly.

Make a list. Cite issues that you would be willing to fight for:

- Dolphin-free tuna
- Credit cards
- Your privacy
- Your land
- Your family's security
- Equal pay
- The right to bear arms
- Communism, capitalism, socialism
- Medical care
- Day care

Depending on your values and agendas, these topics can generate ideas for revolutionary, patriotic or protest poems. For instance, the person who would fight for land might be a Native American who wants to reclaim her ancient territory or culture (revolutionary), a rancher who wants to protect his homestead rights (patriotic), or an activist who wants to stop the leasing of federal lands (protest).

You'll be surprised at the feelings you have about things you take for granted. But life is far more political than that. In communities across the country, dozens of neighbors petition local governments about such issues as education or zoning. Churches and their governing boards often take controversial political views on issues like abortion or single parenthood. Unions have political views. So do corporations. Even families have political traditions, boasting several generations of Democrats, Republicans, Independents or other affiliations.

Make another list. Cite the organizations or institutions in your life:

- PTA
- Writer's Guild
- Neighborhood Watch
- Catholic Church
- Republican Party
- Optimist Club
- Literacy drive
- Recycling committee
- Alcoholics Anonymous
- Voter registration

These organizations can give you ideas for all sorts of political poems. A member of the local PTA might have strong opinions about school budget allocations. He or she can compose a poem about lack of quality education for minorities (revolutionary), praising the concept of free public education (patriotic), or damning taxes that support education (protest).

Each day the media bombards you with political messages, and not only at election time. The opinion page of a newspaper is highly political, and letters to the editor in response to those opinions often feature revolutionary, patriotic and protest-making voices.

Make one more list. Cite issues being debated in your newspaper:

• Abortion
• Smoking ban
• Animal rights
• Welfare cuts
• Sin tax
• Recession
• Teacher salaries
• New cancer drug
• Higher electric bills
• Threatened strikes

These topics can yield a wide range of political concepts. You can write a revolutionary poem about banning smoking in a tobacco-producing state like North Carolina, or a patriotic poem about your freedom to smoke, or a protest one about being fired for smoking in the privacy of your own home.

David Baker, whose poem we read in the chapter on love poetry, maintains that tapping into our personal politics can provide a sense of social awareness or public responsibility. "After all," he says, "language is itself a value-laden system. Our lives are greatly political, like it or not."

To underscore Baker's point, I have chosen three political poems that feature strong voices and opinions but that balance those with vivid images or scenes appealing to the emotions as much as to the intellect.

• Hilary Tham's "Mrs. Wei Wants to Believe the First Amendment" expresses a patriotic idea through the voice of an immigrant. Tham reminds us that we take for granted our right to speak out against the government, but she uses eerie images of repression from another country to emphasize her point.

• In "The Issues" by Sharon Olds, we encounter a protest poem against foreign policy. Although Olds is known for what she calls "apparently personal poems" about her life and family, her political verse excels because of the power of her voice and the preciseness of her images.

• "Patriotics" by David Baker is revolutionary not in its call for the overthrow of our government, but for its rejection of our violent culture (symbolized by Fourth of July celebrations). He says that the poem reprinted here is one of the "truest" he has ever written. "That is to say, its narrative is virtually a transcript of something my wife and I experienced one summer in a small river town of southeast Ohio. Our sense of irony, rage and guilt — to see the happy celebration of war and silly patriotism, and at the same time to discover the town's recent, small, terrible tragedy — gave impulse to the poem."

Mini Anthology of Political Poems

MRS. WEI WANTS TO BELIEVE THE FIRST AMENDMENT

That letter telling your President
he is wrong, please don't mail it!
I am so afraid for you. Back home, such

forthrightness will drag you to jail,
your family will have to hide their name.
Or worse, a noose on the raintree, only the wind

to keep your ghost company. Speaking out
is like flying a kite, a banner for police
to track you down.

In my country, we have learned
to fly kites under the bed.

— Hilary Tham

THE ISSUES
(Rhodesia, 1978)

Just don't tell me about the issues.
I can see the pale spider-belly head of the
newborn who lies on the lawn, the web of
veins at the surface of her scalp, her skin
grey and gleaming, the clean line of the
bayonet down the center of her chest.
I see her mother's face, beaten and
beaten into the shape of a plant,
a cactus with grey spines and broad
dark maroon blooms.
I see her arm stretched out across her baby,

wrist resting, heavily, still, across the
tiny ribs.
            Don't speak to me about
politics, I've got eyes, man.
                                    — Sharon Olds

PATRIOTICS

Yesterday a little girl got slapped to death by her daddy,
    out of work, alcoholic, and estranged two towns down river.
America, it's hard to get your attention politely.
    America, the beautiful night is about to blow up

and the cop who brought the man down with a shot to the chops
    is shaking hands, dribbling chaw across his sweaty shirt,
and pointing cars across the courthouse grass to park.
    It's the Big One one more time, July the 4th,

our country's perfect holiday, so direct a metaphor for war
    we shoot off bombs, launch rockets from Drano cans,
spray the streets and neighbors' yards with the machine-gun crack
    of fireworks, with rebel yells and beer. In short, we celebrate.

It's hard to believe. But so help the soul of Thomas Paine,
    the entire county must be here — the acned faces of neglect,
the halter-tops and ties, the bellies, badges, beehives,
    jacked-up cowboy boots, yes, the back-up singers of democracy

all gathered to brighten in unambiguous delight
    when we attack the calm and pointless sky. With terrifying vigor
the whistle-stop across the river will lob its smaller arsenal
    halfway back again. Some may be moved to tears.

We'll clean up fast, drive home slow, and tomorrow
    get back to work, those of us with jobs, convicting the others
in the back rooms of our courts and malls — yet what
    will be left of that one poor child, veteran of no war

but her family's own? The comfort of a welfare plot,
    a stalk of wilting prayers? Our fathers' dreams come true as nightmare.
So the first bomb blasts and echoes through the streets and shrubs:
    red, white, and blue sparks shower down, a plague

of patriotic bugs. Our thousand eyeballs burn aglow like punks.
    America, I'd swear I don't believe in you, but here I am,
and here you are, and here we stand again, agape.
                                    — David Baker

Notebook

LEVEL ONE

Make three entries in your journal. Discuss:

- Those things in your life that you take for granted and would be willing to fight or picket for. Explain why.
- The politics of organizations or institutions to which you belong. Describe their agendas and your beliefs.
- Political topics being debated in the newspaper. Defend your stance (or lack thereof) concerning these issues.

On a separate page, come up with ten ideas for poems based on each of these entries.

LEVEL TWO

Do the Level One exercise again, noting new things that you take for granted (or no longer do), new groups that you have joined (or quit), and new issues being debated in your newspaper. Read over your journal entries that describe how you felt politically about the various aspects of your life and note how you feel now. Have you changed politically since you last did the exercise? Discuss any changes in your journal. Finally, come up with ten more political ideas for future poems.

LEVEL THREE

1. Once again in your journal, note new items, groups, issues and/ or changes in your political views. Base at least five ideas on them.

2. Study your journal entries from the Level One and Two exercises and chart any patterns of growth or awareness as they pertain to your political perspectives. For instance, did you vote in a recent election for a candidate whose values or campaign promises would not have appealed to you when you did the previous assignments? Can you chart a deepening (or lessening) commitment to a cause or agenda? In what ways do you feel your political views will change (or remain the same) over the next five years? Ten? Write about this in your journal and base at least five more ideas on these entries.

Chapter Seven

Occasion Poetry

T his is the catchall category of the text. After reading chapters on love, nature, extranatural, war and political poetry, you should have read many poems that cross borders. For instance, a love poem may speak of the soul and be set in nature. War poetry can have an environmental theme while protesting government policies. However, behind *all* such poems was an occasion, an incident or a memory that inspired or angered the writer and that may or may not even be mentioned on the page.

When we speak of occasion poems, usually we mean ones that overtly note a date and are based on an event or a memory fixed in time. Such poetry often treats subject matter like birthdays, celebrations, weddings, anniversaries, state or academic functions, historic events, news items, and personal and public tragedies. But you certainly shouldn't limit your muse to those. Essentially you can compose an occasion poem if, at a certain date or time, you witnessed something extraordinary or experienced a turning point in your life.

It can be as simple as this moment depicted in a song by Robert Browning:

THE YEAR'S AT THE SPRING

The year's at the spring
And the day's at the morn;
Morning's at seven;
The hillside's dew-pearled;
The lark's on the wing;
The snail's on the thorn:
God's in his heaven —
All's right with the world!

Here is a sampling of the various types of occasional verse:

The Wedding Poem. An epithalamium, Greek for "at the bridal chamber," is any song or poem sung outside the lovers' bedroom on the wedding night, to augur a good life. This excerpt is from a 1596 poem by Edmund Spenser who describes a moment *"before* the bridal chamber" to mark the double wedding of daughters of an earl:

PROTHALAMION

With that, I saw two Swannes of goodly hewe,
Come softly swimming downe along the Lee;
Two fairer Birds I yet did never see:
The snow which doth the top of *Pindus* strew,
Did never whiter shew, . . .

The Historic Poem. This excerpt by John Donne chronicles the fall of an earl (in the court of King James) who was convicted of poisoning a man opposed to the earl's wedding:

UPON THE SUDDEN RESTRAINT OF THE EARL OF
SOMERSET, FALLING FROM FAVOR

Dazzled thus with height of place,
While our hopes our wits beguile,
No man marks the narrow space
'Twixt a prison and a smile. . . .

The Anniversary Poem. This excerpt by Donne, published after his death in 1631, commemorates another year with his wife Anne:

THE ANNIVERSARY

All kings, and all their favorites,
All glory 'of honors, beauties, wits,
The sun itself, which makes times, as they pass,
Is elder by a year, now, than it was
When thou and I first one another saw:
All other things to their destruction draw,
Only our love hath no decay; . . .

The Solstice Poem. This excerpt by Donne celebrates the "solstice" — days marking the change of seasons — or, in his example, the shortest day of the year in December, which happened to fall then on a holy day:

A NOCTURNAL UPON ST. LUCY'S DAY,
BEING THE SHORTEST DAY

'Tis the year's midnight, and it is the day's,
Lucy's, who scarce seven hours herself unmasks;
The sun is spent, and now his flasks
Send forth light squibs, no constant rays;
The world's whole sap is sunk; . . .

The Holy Day Poem. This excerpt is from John Dryden who wrote his lyric to commemorate another saint's day:

A SONG FOR ST. CECILIA'S DAY

From harmony, from heavenly harmony
  This universal frame began:
  When Nature underneath a heap
    Of jarring atoms lay,
  And could not heave her head,
The tuneful voice was heard from high:
"Arise, ye more than dead."

The Departure Poem. Richard Lovelace going abroad in the 1640s marked the occasion with a lyric to his lover. Here's an excerpt:

TO LUCASTA, ON GOING BEYOND THE SEAS

  If to be absent were to be
    Away from thee;
    Or that when I am gone
  You and I were alone;
  Then, my Lucasta, might I crave
Pity from blustering wind, or swallowing wave. . . .

The Personal Tragedy. In this excerpt, whose title explains all, Anne Bradstreet chronicles what happened to her household on a fateful day in early America:

HERE FOLLOWS SOME VERSES UPON THE BURNING OF OUR HOUSE JULY 10TH, 1666
Copied Out of a Loose Paper

In silent night when rest I took
For sorrow near I did not look
I wakened was with thund'ring noise
And piteous shrieks of dreadful voice.
That fearful sound of "Fire!" and "Fire!"

The Incident Poem. Incidents, of course, are too numerous to categorize, but also can involve petty occasions, as this excerpt by Matthew Prior proves:

TO A LADY: SHE REFUSING TO CONTINUE A DISPUTE WITH ME, AND LEAVING ME IN THE ARGUMENT

Spare, gen'rous victor, spare the slave,
  Who did unequal war pursue;

That more than triumph he might have
In being overcome by you. . . .

The Birthday Poem. Such poetry can celebrate the birth of a child or the birthday of an adult. This excerpt from a poem by Jonathan Swift celebrates the birthday of his companion Esther Johnson:

STELLA'S BIRTHDAY
March 13, 1727

This day, whate'er the fates decree,
Shall still be kept with joy by me:
This day then, let us not be told
That you are sick, and I grown old, . . .

The Momentary Poem. Like Browning's earlier, this type of occasion poem simply describes what a poet thinks, sees or feels at a particular instant in time. Here's an excerpt by William Wordsworth:

COMPOSED UPON WESTMINSTER BRIDGE,
SEPTEMBER 3, 1802

Earth has not anything to show more fair:
Dull would he be of soul who could pass by
A sight so touching in its majesty;
This City now doth, like a garment, wear
The beauty of the morning; silent, bare,
Ships, towers, domes, theaters, and temples lie
Open unto the fields, . . .

The End-of-State Poem. This type of verse chronicles the demise of a government, culture or reign. Again, an excerpt by Wordsworth:

ON THE EXTINCTION OF THE VENETIAN REPUBLIC

Once did She hold the gorgeous East in fee;
And was the safeguard of the west: the worth
Of Venice did not fall below her birth,
Venice, the eldest Child of Liberty. . . .

The Birth-of-State Poem. This brand of poem marks the birth of a government or reign. Here's an excerpt by an unknown author chronicling the birth of the United States:

INDEPENDENCE BELL—JULY 4, 1776

There was a tumult in the city
In the quaint old Quaker town,
And the streets were rife with people
Pacing restless up and down—

People gathering at corners,
Where they whispered each to each. . . .

The Tribute. Such poetry commemorates the contributions of a person, past or present. Here is an excerpt from one of the most famous examples by John Keats, praising a translation by George Chapman who had lived in the earlier Elizabethan era:

ON FIRST LOOKING INTO CHAPMAN'S HOMER

Much have I travell'd in the realms of gold,
  And many goodly states and kingdoms seen;
  Round many western islands have I been
Which bards in fealty to Apollo hold.
Oft of one wide expanse had I been told
  That deep-brow'd Homer ruled as his demesne;
  Yet did I never breathe its pure serene
Till I heard Chapman speak out loud and bold: . . .

The Animal Elegy. Poets through the ages have written verses for departed pets, as in this excerpt of a lyric by Thomas Gray:

ODE
ON THE DEATH OF A FAVOURITE CAT, DROWNED IN A
TUB OF GOLDFISHES

'Twas on a lofty vase's side,
Where China's gayest art had dyed
  The azure flowers that blow;
Demurest of the tabby kind,
The pensive Selima, reclined,
  Gazed on the lake below. . . .

The Banquet Poem. This type of verse celebrates a banquet honoring a person or group, as this excerpt by Charlotte Brontë illustrates:

WRITTEN UPON THE OCCASION OF THE DINNER
GIVEN TO THE LITERATI OF THE GLASSTOWN,

which was attended by all the Great Men
of the present time: Soldier, Sailor,
Poet and Painter, Architect, Politician,
Novelist, and Romancer.
The splendid Hall is blazing with many a glowing light,
And a spirit-like effulgence mild, a flood of glory bright,
Flows round the stately pillars, . . .

The Academic or Government Function Poem. This type of verse marks an act, gathering or other event in a university or government setting. Here is a sample from a poem by James Russell Lowell:

ODE RECITED AT THE HARVARD COMMEMORATION
July 21, 1865

To-day our Reverend Mother welcomes back
  Her wisest Scholars, those who understood
The deeper teaching of her mystic tome,
  And offered their fresh lives to make it good: . . .

The Public Tragedy Poem. This verse marks an event so catastrophic that its date will be remembered through time, illustrated by this excerpt from a famous poem by Thomas Hardy:

THE CONVERGENCE OF THE TWAIN
Lines on the loss of the Titanic

    In a solitude of the sea
    Deep from human vanity,
And the Pride of Life that planned her, stilly couches she. . . .

The Holiday Poem. This type chronicles events on a traditional holiday, as this excerpt does from a poem by Sara Teasdale:

NEW YEAR'S DAWN — BROADWAY
When the horns wear thin
And the noise, like a garment outworn,
Falls from the night,
The tattered and shivering night,
That thinks she is gay;
When the patient silence comes back,
And retires,
And returns,
Rebuffed by a ribald song,
Wounded by vehement cries,
Fleeing again to the stars. . . .

Again, these are types of occasion poems found most often in the literary canon. Identifying them can help you come up with ideas for such work. To inspire you, let's take a look at how a poet goes about the business of composing occasion poems and conceiving ideas for them.

CASE STUDY: THE PUBLIC TRAGEDY

Roger Jones, whose views on environmental poetry we read in chapter three, composed an occasion poem to mark one of the worst public tragedies in his part of eastern Texas. First we'll read the work — it contains an epigraph describing the event—and then analyze it for elements of craft. Then Jones will discuss his poem in detail and share how he develops an idea for occasional verse.

REMEMBERING NEW LONDON

On March 18, 1937, 293 children, teachers and visitors were killed as the "richest rural school in the world" at New London, Texas, exploded from the ignition of natural gas, which had seeped up from the ground and accumulated in the walls.

> Even as we sat
> in our third-wing last classroom peering out
> at the mantis-like structures plunging
> into the soil, gritty and black,
> rising again with jaws drenched
> in the thrilling crude,
> those fifteen minutes mattered to us more;
> then the bell would scatter us
> in our separate braids across the hills and town,
> by stores and the small graveyard,
> and other familiar paths we'd take
> to the shanties our parents held breath to burn
> when the oil coins came, when the Depression
> knots rode out on Spindletop.
>
> And crosslegged we sat, safe in our structure
> of concrete and steel, learning America's story,
> visions of capitol and chaos.
> And we were scattered, in a rapid Pentecost,
> a baptism of fire and sanding riding a ball
> that lifted us, snatching breath and sense,
> blending us in a symphony of screams,
> battered desks, rattling books and death
> riding the wave of its quickened harvest,
> dropping all back down, limbless and lifeless.
>
> Grimy roughnecks dropping ringing tools
> came running at the first rustle of the world,
> awakened by their loss, to prop up the night
> when parents would fight over unclaimed limbs,
> a night of mortal importance
> lasting with us all this time,
> who were lifted somehow, vague, unhurt,
> placed out from the wreck and left alone.

Who can deduce what we have learned
in the hundreds of pains that have transpired
since so many lives there were erased?
Even now I can see that blackboard,
blown a hundred yards
to rest against a tree:

Oil and natural gas are East Texas' greatest natural assets. Without them this school would not be here, and none of us would be here learning our lessons.

Let's summarize the elements of craft that go into an occasion poem:

- *An Appropriate Title.* In occasion poems, the title should help set the scene. You'll learn more about titles in chapter eleven, but for now you should think about the importance of describing the site of a public tragedy. By titling it "Remembering New London" instead of "New London," Jones also forebodes that he will recall this event through an invented persona — a person, not the poet, whose voice we hear on the page.
- *A Descriptive Epigraph.* In occasion poems, an epigraph also is important — even if only a date — to ground the reader in time or convey information that will overshadow, forebode or otherwise color the reader's perception of events. In occasion poems about public tragedy, this often is an excerpt from a history book or newspaper account.
- *Research.* Several types of occasion poems document historic events, end-of-state and birth-of-state proclamations, or public tragedies. Usually, research is required to set the scene or re-create it. Going through Jones's poem, you can see the fruits of his research in such images and phrases as "third-wing," "fifteen minutes," "bell," "hills," "shanties," "roughnecks" and "fight" (over unclaimed limbs). Research augments his personal knowledge about the terrain and helps him reconstruct the disaster.
- *An Appropriate Ending.* Perhaps more than any other category of verse, occasion poems require either a sense of resolution or a sense of milieu because the writer is marking a moment, incident or event in time. A sense of resolution produces a closed ending: The reader leaves the work feeling satisfied. A sense of milieu produces an open ending: The reader leaves the work feeling a lingering presence. In Jones's poem, which employs an open ending, the contents of the sign against the tree not only articulate the epiphany in an ironic way but serve as an epitaph for the children who lost their lives at New London. We're left with their presence, as if we were still at the scene. (A closed ending might have stated what the narrator learned upon viewing the sign, resolving our concern.)

In any case, you can sense that Jones had a personal stake in writing about such an occasion. "I used to pass through New London on my way home when my parents lived in Dekalb," he recalls. "There's a big monument now where the old school used to be." Eventually, Jones decided to write about the blast because it was so tragic. "Tragedy," he notes, "is a great occasion for poetry."

He spent hours researching the event before writing about it. "I found it was full of irony," he says. "For instance, right after the blast, Adolf Hitler sent a wire to President Roosevelt expressing profound condolences about the explosion — even as Hitler himself was planning to send millions of Jews to the gas chamber throughout Europe. It also was Walter Cronkite's first big story out of Houston. And there really were parents spotted in the schoolgrounds fighting over unclaimed limbs. The blackboard was spotted against a tree with that message on it. Another blackboard nearby read 'Good things come to those who wait.' "

Jones feels that, before you write occasional verse, it is essential to have some sort of personal stake in the topic. For example, in "Remembering New London," he had heard about the blast from people who lived in the area in which he grew up. Perhaps he could envision himself in that setting, as his invented persona implies. Certainly, he knew about the benefits and drawbacks of living in an area of Texas known for its natural resources. The personal element in conceiving ideas for such poems is important, but that didn't stop Jones from researching the incident. While the personal element ensures a measure of passion, interest or commitment to an occasion, added knowledge through research often enhances the work so the personal can appeal to the public.

When sketching ideas for occasion poems, ask yourself these basic questions:

1. Do I have a personal stake in the poem? (If not, consider another idea or research the original one until you do.)

2. How, if at all, can research enhance the personal so that my poem will have public appeal? (The amount of research will vary with the topic, with little involved in recalling a moment and more in recreating historic or public events.)

3. What is the theme? (To balance the personal impulse to write such a poem, make the theme — or underlying message of the piece — broad or universal so it appeals to a wider audience.)

4. What is the epiphany or peak experience? (Again, the more universal truth, the greater the appeal.)

5. What ending best marks the occasion in time? (Options: Fix the occasion with a closed ending that resolves issues, or suggest a milieu

with an open ending, leaving a lingering presence.)

By now, you may have noticed that one of the most popular types of occasion poems has been missing from our discussion of the genre. The human elegy, commemorating someone's life, is so important (and universal) that I have reserved a separate section to describe it.

LIVING LEGACIES

On the surface, an elegy seems to be composed to honor the deceased, speaking directly to that person. But in actuality the deceased will never get to hear or read it. The only people who will are those who may have *known* the deceased, as this powerful example by Chidiock Tichborne — put to death in 1586 — illustrates all too well:

TICHBORNE'S ELEGY
Written with his own hand in the tower before his execution

My prime of youth is but a frost of cares,
My feast of joy is but a dish of pain,
My crop of corn is but a field of tares,
And all my good is but vain hope of gain;
The day is past, and yet I saw no sun,
And now I live, and now my life is done.

My tale was heard and yet it was not told,
My fruit is fallen and yet my leaves are green,
My youth is spent and yet I am not old,
I saw the world and yet I was not seen;
My thread is cut and yet it is not spun,
And now I live, and now my life is done.

I sought my death and found it in my womb,
I looked for life and saw it was a shade,
I trod the earth and knew it was my tomb,
And now I die, and now I was but made;
My glass is full, and now my glass is run,
And now I live, and now my life is done.

Here are examples or excerpts from several types of elegies:
The Self Eulogy. As was the case with Tichborne's, such a poem is popular among prisoners who face execution, as this example by the great poet and adventurer Sir Walter Raleigh illustrates:

EVEN SUCH IS TIME
These Verses following were made by Sir Walter Raleigh
the night before he died and left at the Gate House

Even such is Time which takes in trust
Our youth, our joys, and all we have,
And pays us but with age and dust;
Who in the dark and silent grave
When we have wandered all our ways
Shuts up the story of our days.
And from which earth and grave and dust
The Lord shall raise me up I trust.

The Public Eulogy. Such a poem honors a literary or public figure, as do these excerpts from poems by Ben Jonson and A.E. Housman:

TO THE MEMORY OF MY BELOVED MR. WILLIAM SHAKESPEARE

I, therefore, will begin. Soul of the Age!
   The applause, delight, the wonder of our Stage!
My Shakespeare, rise; I will not lodge thee by
   Chaucer, or Spenser, or bid Beaumont lie
A little further, to make thee a room:
   Thou art a monument, without a tomb, . . .

TO AN ATHLETE DYING YOUNG

The time you won your town the race
We chaired you through the market-place;
Man and boy stood cheering by,
And home we brought you shoulder-high. . . .

The Private Eulogy. This honors a member of the family or a relative or friend. Here are excerpts from elegies by Jonson and Anne Bradstreet:

ON MY FIRST DAUGHTER

Here lies, to each her parents' ruth,
Mary, the daughter of their youth;
Yet all heaven's gifts being heaven's due,
It makes the father less to rue. . . .

ON MY DEAR GRANDCHILD SIMON BRADSTREET, WHO DIED ON 16 NOVEMBER, 1669, BEING BUT A MONTH, AND ONE DAY OLD

No sooner came, but gone, and fall'n asleep,
Acquaintance short, yet parting caused us weep;
Three flowers, two scarcely blown, the last i' th' bud,
Cropt by th' Almighty's hand; yet is He good.

With dreadful awe before Him let's be mute,
Such was His will, but why, let's not dispute, . . .

The Epitaph. An epitaph is based on an inscription of a memorial or tomb, as illustrated by this excerpt from a poem by Richard Crashaw:

AN EPITAPH UPON HUSBAND AND WIFE
WHO DIED AND WERE BURIED TOGETHER

To these whom death again did wed
This grave's the second marriage-bed.
For though the hand of Fate could force
'Twixt soul and body a divorce,
It could not sever man and wife,
Because they both lived but one life. . . .

The Graveyard Poem. This type is based on, set in or inspired by a cemetery. One of the most famous is this one by Thomas Gray:

ELEGY WRITTEN IN A COUNTRY CHURCHYARD

The curfew tolls the knell of parting day,
    The lowing herd wind slowly o'er the lea,
The plowman homeward plods his weary way,
    And leaves the world to darkness and to me. . . .

These are basic types of elegies found in the literary canon. By categorizing them, I hope to stimulate ideas based on personal, private and public eulogies or on inscriptions/experiences in cemeteries.

Now let's take a closer look at the universality of elegies and propose ways for you to sharpen ideas for them.

CASE STUDY: THE PRIVATE ELEGY

In early April two years ago, I wrote in my journal:

Last night I took my daughter Erin to Ann Howland's horse farm called "Windy Hills." Ann died during the weekend, and I saw her several times leading up to her final hours.

Anyway, Erin and I brought her family some bread last night, at twilight. Ann's daughter Andrea gave Erin her high school jacket and some "Black Beauty" books. Ann's son, Josh, took Erin up to a hilltop rink where he and she rode his prize-winning Paso Fino bareback as in "The Black Stallion." Only Josh's stallion was roan and beautiful as the two rode with a purple sky like a backlight. The moon was full and Venus shone in the far sky.

I can't believe Ann's gone.

Ann Howland, a local psychologist, was one of my best friends and confidant. She died of cancer and would cringe if I used the euphemism "after an extended illness." Ann believed in telling the truth. She loved words because she knew their power to heal pain and help us carve paths to each other.

That's what elegies do. The impulse to write one is at once human and humane. In Appalachia, where I live and where Ann had her horse farm in the hollows, people publish their elegies in the local newspapers. It's a tradition here. Coal miners — some of the toughest, most hard-bitten Americans you will ever meet — compose elegies when they suffer a loss. So do professors, loggers, farmers, social workers, merchants, doctors, pensioners and the unemployed. Their poems appear in the classified ads under the "In Memoriam" or "Card of Thanks" sections. On Sundays, when as many as a dozen elegies can be found in the classifieds, I always turn to that section first to scan the poems. They come in all forms — rhymed, free verse, even prose paragraphs — whose sole purpose is to soothe rather than impress.

One Sunday I opened the newspaper expecting to find the usual selections. Instead I came upon this elegy:

ANN HOWLAND

Now one complete cycle
beyond our vision.
Three trees are planted.
(more will follow)
Your horse delivered a
magnificent, independent foal
(Valour!) and survived a
terrible contest with old barbed
wire. Spring percolates,
hesitates. The records are
boxed, estates in order,
patients redirected.
Still . . . the winds blow thru
the hills and the brightly
colored wings are missed.

The poem was signed by her husband Gerry Hilferty and Ann's children Andrea and Josh. Later I learned that Hilferty, a designer of museums and exhibitions, had composed the piece, proving again that elegies are the most natural of poems (even for nonpoets). The form can bring out our best, often at our worst moments.

To emphasize that point, I quote Gerry Hilferty at length as he explains why he was inspired to eulogize Ann Howland in verse:

I thought I would first sit for awhile upon my trusty tractor, bright red, 65 horses—it cuts a mean swath in weeds and pasture. I spend a great deal of time on that tractor, trimming the Windy Hills. Ann used to say that mowing was my therapy, what kept me sane in a strange world.

And so my swath led me toward the knoll, highest point on Windy Hills, shaped like a prehistoric native mound. That's where Ann's best tree, a maple, is planted, dusted by her remains, commanding a distant view of horse paddock and cow pasture.

It was dusk. I unlatched the gate and checked the tree, mindlessly pruning leaves and branches.

At that point he felt Ann's energy around him—"the whole bit," he says, "all the memories, all the loss"—and was moved to write.

"I'm not sure Ann would have approved of what I put in the paper," he muses. "But I wrote an elegy not so much for Ann but for her friends. She cared so much about each one that I thought we might share the loss."

Let's stop here and consider what Gerry has said. He is struck by the muse, surrounded by images that inspire him to remember Ann. Sitting on his tractor and then tending her favorite tree, overlooking her farm, he is in a natural setting to remember his wife. The impulse kicks in. Moreover, he publishes the poem in the paper not for Ann but for friends of Ann like me, leaving a living legacy.

Read his poem aloud and listen to the voice. More than a year has passed since Ann's death, so Gerry remembers her in tranquility. The tone of his poem comes across unsentimentally on the page. He packs it with images and symbols that Ann's friends would associate with her: trees, horses, a foal, the barbed wire of her farm, the records of her patients, the wind and her "wings" of wit and wisdom. By doing so Gerry resists talking about his pain or grief and shares his poem like a gift with his audience.

When sketching ideas for elegies, ask yourself these basic questions:

1. Do I have a personal stake in the poem? (Obviously, if you are composing an elegy for someone you know, you are committed to the poem by that bond alone. But if you want to compose an elegy for a public or literary figure or base one on an inscription or experience in a cemetery, answering this question is a must.)

2. What images or objects are associated with the deceased? (We come to know people by what they keep, whether an heirloom or a lifestyle. Before you write your elegy, make a list of images that best depict the person or what the person stood for, believed in or loved.

These images will become symbols of the deceased, conveying meaning about a person's life.)

3. What principle of life do I want to convey? (This is your epiphany. Your truth can be as simple as Gerry Hilferty's, an affirmation of love "beyond our vision.")

4. What theme best accompanies that principle? (Once you know your epiphany, coming up with a theme — what your poem really is about under the surface — should be clear. Themes are related to feelings, an undercurrent running through the work. Decide what feeling best expresses your principle of life. For instance, in Hilferty's poem to his wife, his affirmation is best expressed through the feeling of trust, marking the occasion of another cycle or year but knowing that his wife can hear him.)

Although an elegy is about loss, it also should articulate a lesson that we learned, losing what we loved. Moreover, the elegy and other forms of occasional verse underscore a lesson about poetry. In ages past, it used to be a public activity. Occasional verse reminds us of that tradition and invites us to partake.

In closing, let's preview poems included in the mini anthology. I've tried to find ones that contain elements of the elegy and other kinds of occasional verse.

• Corrinne Hales, a poet and creative writing teacher, composed "For Mary Who Was Killed Here Before I Moved In" — a work that has elements of "the incident poem" and the elegy.

• Peter Makuck, an editor of a literary magazine and respected poet and teacher, composed "A Sense of the Other Side" — a work that combines elements of "the momentary poem" with a private eulogy.

• Neal Bowers's "Tenth-Year Elegy" combines elements of "the anniversary poem" with another private eulogy.

Perhaps Bowers's words are most apt in ending this chapter on occasion poems. "The most difficult thing to achieve in art is a profound simplicity — something that in an earlier time might have been called awe."

Mini Anthology of Occasion Poems

FOR MARY WHO WAS KILLED HERE
BEFORE I MOVED IN

I have tried on hands and knees
To find the dark stain
That must be
Blood in the hardwood.

Rubbing my fingers along the fabric
Of her curtains, I want something
To be missing—or torn.

They say it was violent, and happened
In this room. *A dancer,*
My neighbor tells me, nodding his head.

I think of my father
Killing a cat in the barn, a spot
Relentlessly left on the floor
That never came clean.

And the highway that killed
My brother glistens still
With broken glass suddenly imbedded
Under Montana sun.

But this is clean. No signs
No trace. And I long for a shadow
To relieve such perfect disappearance.

A clock should stop
At the instant of death. I need to know
That this woman lived.

So I stand here holding on
Hard to the windowsill as if it were
Her ballet barre, and dream

Of the floor, worn by her practicing,
Shining beneath my feet.
                              —Corrinne Hales

A SENSE OF THE OTHER SIDE

Back home at last
After seeing my mother
Lowered into frozen earth,
I couldn't find sleep
With wine or even pills,
When our calico, as if
Called, came to the sofa
And did something
Never repeated since—

One soft foot at a time,
She climbed on my chest,

Looked through the blank
Lid of my face, made
The faintest cry, then
Curled over my heart
And slept, so that I could,
For three nights in a row—
Visitations like belief,
Unreal, against all odds.

— Peter Makuck

TENTH-YEAR ELEGY

Careless man, my father,
always leaving me at rest-stops,
coffee shops, some wide spot in the road.
I come out, rubbing my hands on my pants
or levitating two foam cups of coffee,
and can't find him anywhere,
those banged-up fenders gone.

It's the trip itself that blinds him,
black highway like a chute
leading to the mesmerizing end,
his hands locked dead on the wheel
and following, until he misses me,
steers wide on the graveled shoulders,
turns around.

This time he's been gone so long
I've settled in here—married,
built a house, planted trees for shade,
stopped waiting to see him pull into the drive—
though the wind sometimes makes a highway roar
high up in the branches, and I stop
whatever I am doing and look up.

— Neal Bowers

Notebook

ALL LEVELS

Each time you go through this text at Level One, Two and Three,
review the eighteen types of occasional verse and five types of elegies
and select ones in which you have a personal stake. For some types,
like the public or personal tragedy, that may change from year to year.
Also, friends, relatives and loved ones—along with public figures—
may pass away in the interim and can be eulogized. In any case, come

up with ten ideas based on the occasional and elegy prototypes (or combine elements of both). Work out those ideas in your journals by asking yourself basic questions about research, theme, epiphany and ending for all types of occasion poems (along with "principle of life" for elegies).

ADDITIONAL EXERCISE FOR ALL LEVELS: "THE IDEA FILE"

You have finished the first and, perhaps, most important section of this book — conceiving ideas for poems and writing about them in your journal. Now it is time to review your journal entries and ideas for the various kinds of verse. On a separate piece of paper for each poem, or in separate files in your computer, make final notations and improve each idea until you are satisfied with it. When you are, put the ideas for each work in a folder or file to be used for Notebook exercises in the final two sections of this text: "Tools of the Trade" and "Formats and Forms."

PART TWO

Tools of the Trade

In this section you will learn the basics of craft, from voice to rhyme. At the end of each chapter you will select ideas from your "Idea File" and write drafts of poems. At this time you need another folder titled "Work in Progress." When you compose a poem based on an idea, mark it "first draft" and put it in the file. Each time you rewrite the poem, mark it "second draft," "third draft" and so on, and paper clip all drafts of the same poem. This way you can chart your progress and determine which element of craft works for you or needs improving.

Chapter Eight

Voice

In literary circles, you'll hear a lot of talk about famous poets finding their voices after years of struggle and apprenticeship. You'll read *juvenalia* — the early work of Sylvia Plath, for example — and discredit it because, as someone is bound to say: "She had not yet discovered her voice." You'll hear the same arguments about the early work of such poets as Theodore Roethke and James Wright who, like Plath, wrote formal poetry before turning to free verse later in their careers. Generally speaking, it is more difficult to compose in a natural voice if you are employing rhyme and meter, which, if poorly executed, can sound artificial or ornamental. But that wasn't the case with Plath, Roethke and Wright. When they matured as poets, they began to write about people and topics that thoroughly consumed them and, to convey their complex truths, relied on the vehicle of voice.

Once they had discovered their subject matter, voice followed.

On the other hand, some poets — the late poet and writer Raymond Carver comes to mind — based their early work on epiphanies and experience: highs, lows and turning points. They began with a subject matter and didn't lose sleep waiting to find their voices.

I like Carver's poems because they demystify the issue of "voice." Consider his lyric "Margo":

His name was Tug. Hers, Margo.
Until people, seeing what was happening,
began calling her Cargo.
Tug and Cargo. He had drive,
they said. Lots of hair on his face
and arms. A big guy. Commanding
voice. She was more laid-back. A blond.
Dreamy. (Sweet and dreamy.) She broke
loose, finally. Sailed away
under her own power. Went to places
pictured in books, and some

not in any book, or even on the map.
Places she, being a girl, and cargo,
never dreamed of getting to.
Not on her own, anyway.

That easy-going, conversational voice is Carver's trademark, and it explains, in part, why he's still widely read as a writer. In a word, he *relates*.

I wish I had read his poetry earlier in my own career.

Like many young poets, I had developed a Shakespeare complex, assuming when I wrote verse that I, too, was speaking to the ages. This is romantic nonsense. Poetry speaks to people, and people decide whether it is good enough to share with future generations. But nobody had explained this to me. So instead of writing poems in the voice of a sassy, savvy, streetwise teenager, I used a formal, objective, Anglo tone when, in actuality, I was informal, subjective and all-Mediterranean.

The result was artificial writing. The issue, then, was not finding my voice—I always had one!—but *losing* it.

For years I composed awkward-sounding poems that nobody wanted to read. Then I met Bruce Weigl, whose war poems appear in chapter five. At the time, Weigl was promoting his first collection in Oklahoma where I worked as a journalist and studied English. He was a guest in my poetry class, and my work was up for critique.

I have since lost the draft of a poem that Weigl analyzed that night. But I recall that I had cast it in blank verse—the meter of Hamlet's soliloquy—intending to reflect upon a sensitive topic: infidelity. (The piece was about my mother suspecting that her husband was having an affair.)

As you might expect, Weigl began his critique by focusing on the voice in the poem. He said it sounded artificial. "Come on," Weigl taunted me. "Tell us what it was like—in your own words."

I looked down at my poem. Didn't it contain *my own words*?

"Put the poem away," Weigl said. "Look at me and explain why you want to write about your mother."

"I often think about this," I began. "I know it happened—"

"Stop," he said, putting my words on the board. "You just wrote your first line."

I was amazed. Poetry was supposed to be difficult.

"And lose the blank verse," Weigl added, as if reading my mind. "For the time being, just make your lines as long as they need to be to express an idea."

At first I was put off by Weigl's critique. He was assaulting my notion of what a poem should be and that was a big hurdle for me to overcome. But I decided to trust him rather than cling stubbornly to my beliefs — a turning point in my career — and revised the piece according to his instructions.

In a few days, I had a final draft:

THE ONLY MORNING MY MOTHER DIDN'T WORSHIP HER HUSBAND

I often think about this. I know
it happened: My mother comes to me,
crosstown before breakfast,
the look of "someone's dead"
in the Maltese black eyes. She cries
Mickey — my nickname — an E-vowel perfect
for Mediterranean sorrow.
She won't tell me what's wrong.
She repeats my name, getting softer
while I get the brandy. I pour myself
a drink, too, and we sip
like it's Sunday dinner
minus Father.
I ask what I suspect
is too hard for her. "Is Papa dead?"
She focuses on me with eyes
drier now, breathes deep for the words.
"Papa. Another woman."
I cradle her against the cotton
of my pajama top. She leaves
two wide stains, much larger than eyes.

Later that year I entered the poem in a university-wide competition, and it won first place. The judge praised my "voice." Being a savvy lad, I knew that I had not found my voice . . . but had reclaimed it.

Let's see how you can reclaim yours.

EMPLOYING A PROPER VOICE

Consider how Bruce Weigl confronted me in the classroom. He was able to speak to me so directly because he was wearing the mask of teacher and I the mask of student. If he had confronted me in the street or the restroom, the topic of our conversation and his tone of voice would have been inappropriate for the setting. Thus the mask, or role a person plays, influences the type of voice that he or she uses to address somebody in a particular place.

On any given day, a person wears several masks:

- *6:30 A.M.* You need to wake your spouse for work — we'll call him

"Tug" — and he is grumpy in the morning. You nudge him gently on the shoulder and wear the mask of wife, whispering to your other half in a voice that sounds loving, prodding and firm: "Come on, now, darling. Time to get up." You are playing the role of dutiful spouse and employing an appropriate tone at dawn in the typical bedroom.

• *8:15 A.M.* You arrive at work and your manager summons you to his office, wanting to know the status of a report you promised to complete yesterday. "I ran into some snags with the budget," you say, "and worked them out last night at home. With any luck, I'll have it done by five." He replies, "I need it by noon." In this scenario, the manager wears the mask of boss and you, the mask of employee, using a tone that is confident, energetic and responsible: "I'll get right on it." Such a response is appropriate during hours in the office. But if you and your manager spoke to each other like this after hours, the boss would come off as arrogant and you as ingratiating.

• *Noon.* You met your deadline, and now you are having lunch in the cafeteria with a colleague. You are wearing the mask of friend and the colleague, confidant. Your colleague asks what is wrong, so you glance at nearby tables — you don't want other employees to overhear — and use a hushed, frustrated, serious voice to explain: "I'm putting in more than sixty hours a week, and my boss is a jerk." Such a statement may be appropriate with a friend in the cafeteria, but *not* with an upstart rival in the parking lot.

• *5:15 P.M.* You are driving home when you see the flashing lights of a state patrol car. You have been caught speeding, realize it and pull over. The peace officer who approaches you is wearing the mask of trooper and you, law-abiding citizen when you ask: "Is there anything wrong, officer?" The trooper ignores you: "License and registration, please." You don't need another ticket so you use a respectful, ingratiating, *innocent* voice: "I know I exceeded the speed limit, officer. But I had to pass that truck — it was *tailgating* me — and I wanted to concentrate on the road." The trooper hands back your license, says your registration is expired, and writes up *another* ticket. You take your citations, roll up your window, and wait until the trooper is out of earshot. "Damn," you say, "they all must have some sort of quota!"

Your mask, as it were, has been dropped.

Wearing masks is not deceitful in real life or in poetry. We relate to each other by accepting or resisting certain roles. Instinctively you know what tone of voice is appropriate with each person and in each situation. Once you realize that you wear masks routinely during the day, you will be able to call upon that ability to compose poems in an appropriate or natural voice.

A FOUR-STEP PROCESS TO DEVELOP VOICE

Before you write your next poem, ask yourself:

1. *With whom am I speaking?* Perhaps you are addressing someone specific in the poem. If so, use a voice to suit the occasion as you normally would during heightened moments (when feeling happy, angry, betrayed or some other emotion). Or you may want to address a person who never even makes an appearance in your poem. If so, this person is "implied." For example, in "The Only Morning My Mother Didn't Worship Her Husband," I'm not addressing my mother but a friend in a private talk. The friend doesn't make an appearance, of course; however, by imagining him across from me, I was able to employ a compassionate tone of voice to suit the occasion.

Finally, you may want to address yourself in a poem as actors sometimes do in soliloquies. Of all the people you will talk to in life, you will talk most often — and openly — to yourself. Every day we congratulate, berate or encourage ourselves in response, usually, to other people or circumstances. Simply align the tone of voice with the latter as you would internally in real life.

2. *Where is this conversation taking place?* Again, you can include a specific setting in a poem and shape your voice accordingly. Or you may want to imagine a place that is never mentioned in the poem. If so, the setting is "implied." In "The Only Morning My Mother Didn't Worship Her Husband," I evoked the setting of a bar and pictured myself confiding in my friend in dim light across a table. The imaginary surroundings played no role, of course, in the poem; but they helped to shape my voice.

3. *What is the nature of the epiphany that you want to share?* As you learned in chapter one, each poem should include a moment of truth. In "The Only Morning My Mother Didn't Worship Her Husband," I saw my mother as a woman for the first time. By contemplating your epiphany, you will be able to conceive a tone that conveys your truth with the most clout.

4. *What voice is appropriate for Questions 1, 2 and 3, above?* After you have selected or imagined the setting and the person whom you are addressing in a poem, and contemplated your epiphany, you should be able to jot down some adjectives describing the voice you want readers to "hear" on the page.

In "The Only Morning My Mother Didn't Worship Her Husband," I wanted to convey a "compassionate, tense, descriptive" voice, which, I thought, would convey my epiphany.

To convey yours, put your poems through this four-step process . . . and you will also reclaim your voice.

TUNING YOUR EAR

One way to sharpen your voice is to listen to the voices of other poets. In a typical poem, you will hear distinctive tones, just like string instruments in a quartet. Here are excerpts from famous poems and, in parentheses, adjectives to describe the tones I hear on the page:

THE CANONIZATION
By John Donne

For God's sake hold your tongue, and let me love,
    Or chide my palsy, or my gout,
My five gray hairs, or ruined fortune flout; . . .

(*Voice*: impatient, testy, self-effacing)

JENNY KISSED ME
By Leigh Hunt

Jenny kissed me when we met,
    Jumping from the chair she sat in;
Time, you thief, who love to get
    Sweets into your list, put that in!

(*Voice*: breathy, excited, bold)

THE COLLAR
By George Herbert

I struck the board, and cried, 'No more!
                            I will abroad.
    What? shall I ever sigh and pine?
My lines and life are free; free as the road,
    Loose as the wind, as large as store. . . .

(*Voice*: direct, complaining, aloof)

NO COWARD SOUL IS MINE
By Emily Brontë

No coward soul is mine,
No trembler in the world's storm-troubled sphere!
I see Heaven's glories shine,
And Faith shines equal, arming me from Fear.

(*Voice*: confident, intelligent, philosophical)

THE QUEEN OF HEARTS
By Christina Rossetti

How comes it, Flora, that, whenever we
Play cards together, you invariably,

However the pack parts,
Still hold the Queen of Hearts?

(*Voice*: suspicious, sly, questioning)

BEAT! BEAT! DRUMS!
By Walt Whitman

Beat! beat! drums! blow! bugles! blow!
Through the windows — through doors — burst like a ruthless force,
Into the solemn church, and scatter the congregation,
Into the school where the scholar is studying; . . .

(*Voice*: loud, oracular, commanding)

THE VOICE
By Thomas Hardy

Woman much missed, how you call to me, call to me,
Saying that now you are not as you were
When you had changed from the one who was all to me,
But as at first, when our day was fair.

(*Voice*: plaintive, repetitive, sad)

It's perfectly all right to disagree with my adjectives and to substitute your own when analyzing these selections. All you need to hear
are distinct sounds. Contemplate those sounds and see how they harmonize with the subject matter. Then consider the various aspects of
voice that you will bring out in your poems — *before* you even begin to
write them.

This way you can envision your poem and hear how it will sound
on the page. You will have an easier time writing verse and can concentrate on other basic elements — line, stanza, title — discussed in upcoming chapters.

For now, you want to collect words as some people collect coins.
Many poets jot down new sounds in their journals when they hear
them. The Canadian poet George Whipple, author of two collections,
advises, "Keep paper and pencil with you at all times. They are your
best friends when the poem starts to whisper in your ear while you are
riding the bus or ready to fall asleep at night, or getting up in the
morning."

Whipple notes that poems, lest we forget, are made of words. He
recommends keeping lists of words in your journal. "New and strange
ones you meet on the street (the names of cars — Bronco, Mustang,
Protégé) or in advertisements (Velcro, spiffy, munch) or in conversations (sleaze, blooper, skateboard)." He adds that such words "help
to ground the music of your poem in the everyday."

To appreciate the power and music of words:

1. Listen to how you relate to your family, friends and strangers in particular settings.

2. Isolate intriguing or unusual words you hear in everyday conversations.

3. Read the quotations of people featured in newspaper stories and popular magazines and circle words or phrases that you find intriguing enough to use one day in a poem.

4. Read back issues of a poetry magazine and jot down adjectives to describe the various tones of each verse. This will give you an idea of the range of voices in a typical publication.

5. Buy a book of poetry. Study the voice of each poem, circle words that interest you, and jot down adjectives to describe the various tones. This will give you an idea of the range of voices used by one author in a typical collection.

6. Read the dictionary. (Every poet ought to do this at least once in his or her career.) If you find this too tedious, skip several pages at a time. Jot down at least five new words for each letter of the alphabet and list them in your journal.

To get you started, let's preview poems in the mini anthology:

• "A Hymn to God the Father" by George Whipple. Whipple's work and voice are distinct because of the words that pepper his poems. In the poem reprinted here, he employs a formal, jazzy and scientific tone — quite a combination!

• "Tell Her" by Judith Kitchen, author of the 1985 award-winning collection *Perennials* (Anhinga Press, 1986), whose essays and criticism appear regularly in such journals as *The Georgia Review*. In the poem reprinted here, she employs a direct, descriptive and insistent tone to explain pictures of starvation to a child.

• "Daily Horoscope" by Dana Gioia, whose journal and poetry we sampled in the first section. One day, he explains, he scanned the newspaper and focused on the horoscope column. Says Gioia, "I was interested in the way that horoscopes adopt an intimate, second-person voice when predicting your future."

As you can see, words and tones surround us. Tune into them, and you will have earned your voice.

Mini Anthology of Voice Poems

A HYMN TO GOD THE FATHER

O God invisible as music, let me know
Thee in the least reflection of Thy much,

in termite, tick and earwig, in the glow-
worm striking matches on the dark, the house-
fly scratching his humungous-huge orbed head;
in all the creepy, crawly, earthbound things,
the bandy ant in black fatigues, the slow
gelatinous, fat snail.

           And when I climb
to Thee in prayers that fall as if unsaid,
O Alpha and Omega, Logos, great I AM,
I know Thee in the nit, mosquito, flea;
in pollywog, boll weevil, gnat and louse
— and with the praying mantis, worship Thee.
                        — George Whipple

TELL HER
(Explaining Pictures of Starvation to a Child)

Tell her they are real. That
hunger has lived in them so long
they've come to resemble it.
That each night they lie down
on the line between living and dying.

Tell her there are many ways
to die, and each is lonely.

And there are many hungers —
that somewhere at this moment
a man is praying to a telephone pole.
When he is brought in,
he will claim to be his own
vision of God.

Or that now an old friend has gone silent
in the wake of a stroke
that spilled out his words
like the unmatched pieces of a jigsaw puzzle.

Talk about what it is to want.
To want to live, knowing, as you do,
that all our lives our real work
is to move, moment by moment,
closer to their tiny wasted faces.
                        — Judith Kitchen

DAILY HOROSCOPE
(an excerpt*)

Today will be like any other day.
You will wake to the familiar sounds
of the same hour in the same room,
sounds which no alarm is needed to announce.
And lying in the warm half-darkness, wish
for any of the dreams you left, convinced
that any change would be an argosy —
an hour's sleep, an unexpected visit.

But they are lost to you — the dreams, the sleep,
the faceless lovers you desire. Lost
as if your eyes were shut against the light,
and only these dull colors have remained,
the vision never coming into focus,
blurred or obscured this morning and forever.

Beyond your window, something like a wind
is filling in the emptiness of air.
Vast, hungry, and invisible it sweeps
the morning clean of memories, then disappears.
The weather changes randomly. Rain
is falling from another planet
but cannot wash the daylight off
into familiar shapes. These walls, these streets,
this day can never be your home, and yet
there is no other world where you could live,
and so you will accept it.

                              Just as others,
waking to sunlight and the sound of leaves,
accept the morning as their own, and walk
without surprise, through orchards crossed by streams,
where swift, cold water is running over stone.
                              — Dana Gioia

Notebook

LEVEL ONE

By now you have organized your "Idea File" so it contains as many
as one hundred ideas for poems. Choose three that feature a specific

---

*This excerpt originally was part one of a six-part sequence.

setting. For instance, ideas based on your list of highs, lows and turning points from chapter one might feature an exotic vacation (high),
the scene of an accident (low) or a place of employment (turning point).
Now do the four-step process (page 114) for each idea. Once you have
established the right tone of voice for each poem, do first drafts. (Note:
Don't worry about the form of your poems — rhymed, metered, free
verse. Just write your drafts in a style that pleases you. The focus now
is on *voice*.)

LEVEL TWO

1. By now you should have done several of the exercises recommended earlier in this chapter (listening to everyday conversations,
analyzing poems for voice in magazines and books, keeping lists of
words, etc.). If not, do them now.

2. Choose three ideas from your "Idea File" that feature *weak* or
vague settings. For instance, in your updated list of highs, lows and
turning points, you might have described "coming to terms with childhood" (high), "feeling like a failure" (low) or "deciding to become
more independent" (turning point). Enhance each idea by conceiving
a specific setting, apply the four-step process (page 114) and do first
drafts.

LEVEL THREE

1. Choose three ideas from your "Idea File" that feature something
or someone you would be most apt to find in specific settings. For
instance, a mayor at City Hall, a parrot in the rainforest or an apparition in a graveyard. Apply the four-step process and do first drafts.

2. Now switch settings for the three poems, coming up with the
most unusual or intriguing combinations, say: the parrot at church,
the mayor in the rainforest and the apparition at City Hall. Compose
these poems and compare them to your earlier drafts, analyzing
changes in voice.

Chapter Nine

The Line

P oetry is the highest and most complex form of human speech. It includes terms as difficult to pronounce as medical ones: amphibrach, dactyl, onomatopoeia — to name a few. Suffice it to say that encyclopedias of poetry often number one thousand pages or more, chock full of words like these, with examples and definitions. And yet poetry has one characteristic on which all its other elements must rely: the line. Eliminate *rhyme*, and you still have *free verse*. Eliminate *simile*, and you still have *symbol*. Eliminate *line*, and you have *prose*.

The line is the jugular vein of poetry. What you will learn about it in this chapter applies to free and formal verse, making free verse less free . . . and formal verse more difficult. Moreover, if you truly master the line, something magical will occur within you: You will discover that poetry is as close to music as it is to writing.

For the time being, let's look at these building blocks to see how you can structure your verse via the line:

Building Block #1: *The first line should be a zinger.* Too often poets back into their work, composing throwaway first lines to get going and then neglecting to revise them later. Read the front page of your daily newspaper, especially the wire reports, and you'll see how reporters pack as much information as possible into the first sentence of their stories, to keep the reader's interest.

Shouldn't a poet do the same?

Consider some of these opening lines:

- *Dear Chloe, how blubbered is that pretty face!*
from "Answer to Chloe Jealous" by Matthew Prior.
- *An old, mad, blind, despised, and dying king —*
from "England in 1819" by Percy Bysshe Shelley.
- *My pictures blacken in their frames*
from "Death of the Day" by Walter Savage Landor.
- *She walks in beauty, like the night*
from "She Walks in Beauty" by Lord Byron.

- *When the dead in their cold graves are lying*
  from "Memory" by Charlotte Brontë.
- *Well hast thou spoken, and yet, not taught*
  from "My Comforter" by Emily Brontë.
- *The Soul selects her own Society*
  from "303" by Emily Dickinson.
- *Bald heads forgetful of their sins,*
  from "The Scholars" by W.B. Yeats.
- *Something there is that doesn't love a wall*
  from "Mending Wall" by Robert Frost.

Reading these examples, you can see why people often quote first lines of poems at parties to impress each other. The opening lines of immortal works are strong and we tend to remember them as often as we remember their titles. To show how a good first line can improve a poem, consider the first and second drafts of a verse titled "Realism":

(First draft)

I posed for a portrait.
"Make me look like that," I said,
And you stepped back, *hmmm*-ed.

(Second draft)

We began to lose our love because I wanted yours
Before it changed as a portrait often does
Too long on the easel. . . .

In the first draft, the second and third lines are interesting; but the opener is a dud. It simply describes the topic of the poem, and that could have been done with a good title. In the second version, however, the new first line is improved, setting the mood and generating stronger lines than in the original.

Every first line ought to encourage the audience to read on. If readers become bored by the second or third line, chances are they will abandon the poem. The opening lines, if strong enough, imply that the poem will build in intensity as it continues.

Building Block #2: *A line should work as a unit of speech.* It also should contain an idea or image that melds with the idea or image in the next line. Often it will convey one meaning when read across and another when read down, in tandem with the next line. Ideally, it should begin and end with strong words — vivid nouns or verbs, for example — or unanticipated ones — unusual adjectives or adverbs, for example. Avoid too many pronouns (*I, we*) or definite and indefinite articles (*the, a*) at the ends of lines because they seem to dangle and call attention to themselves.

Let's study excerpts from poems to illustrate these points:

Whenas in silks my Julia goes,
Then, then, methinks, how sweetly flows
That liquefaction of her clothes!
—from "Upon Julia's Clothes"
by Robert Herrick

Note how each line conveys one image or idea and how meanings of each line blend. The second line, for instance, not only depicts the woman's silks but also implies the sweetly flowing thoughts of the poet. Then, in the third line, Julia's clothes become fluid. Now that's poetry in motion!

When the dead in their cold graves are lying
    Asleep, to wake never again;
When past are their smiles and their sighing,
    Oh! why should their memories remain?
—from "Memory" by Charlotte Brontë

Consider the double meaning generated by the ending word: *lying*. Are the dead telling untruths . . . or merely reclining in the ground? The answer to that question is both: the first line means one thing when read across and something else when read with the next line: "Asleep, . . ." Remaining lines work as units using strong words: "again," "sighing," "Oh!" and "remain."

It is a beauteous evening, calm and free,
The holy time is quiet as a Nun
Breathless with adoration; the broad sun
Is sinking down in its tranquility; . . .
—from "It Is a Beauteous Evening"
by Wordsworth

Note how the first and fourth lines of the excerpt convey a clear image or an idea and how, again, the meanings of the second and third lines harmonize. Also, each line ends with a strong word, and the third line begins with one.

He hears with gladdened heart the thunder
    Peal, and loves the falling dew;
He knows the earth above and under—
    Sits and is content to view.
—from "He Hears with Gladdened
Heart the Thunder" by Robert Louis
Stevenson

Once more the first and second lines play off each other, conveying multiple meanings: the thunder of a heart and of the sky. Each line acts as a unit to convey an image or idea and all end or begin with strong words.

Building Block #3: *The length of a line can help you express feelings or evoke moods.* In general, the shorter the line, the greater the drama. The longer the line, the greater the emotion. (Medium-length lines of about seven or eight words suit poems in which drama or emotion is not a factor.)

Let's illustrate drama by using a William Carlos Williams poem to prove that even kitchen memos can convey tension in taut, slim, suggestive lines:

THIS IS JUST TO SAY

I have eaten
the plums
that were in
the icebox

and which
you were probably
saving
for breakfast

Forgive me
they were delicious
so sweet
and so cold

The final lines, "so sweet/and so cold," imply a certain spite. Marital friction. Watch how the lines defuse, however, if rewritten into long lengths:

I have eaten the plums that were in the icebox and which
    you were probably saving for breakfast.
Forgive me. They were delicious, so sweet and so cold.

Reads like a kitchen memo again, doesn't it? The voice suddenly sounds like a family doctor late for a house call. Worse, the darker meaning is lost so the last line seems like a consolation.

The poem self-destructs.

Long lengths are for outbursts like the opening lines, say, of Allen Ginsberg's "Howl":

I saw the best minds of my generation destroyed by madness,
                                                        starving

hysterical naked,
dragging themselves through the negro streets at dawn looking
                                                              for an
angry fix, . . .

That's a howl heard across the fifties. The long line allows Ginsberg
to vent his fury and feelings for generations to come. Watch what
happens when we chop it into inappropriate short lines meant to dramatize a situation:

I saw the best
minds
of my
generation
destroyed
by madness
starving
hysterical naked
dragging
themselves
through
the negro
streets
at dawn
looking for
an angry fix. . . .

This sounds like a beatnik lobotomized, not a prophet proclaiming
his loss in the voice of Solomon's "Song of Songs." As you can see,
short lines ruin Ginsberg's "Howl," altering voice and undermining
meaning and design, just as the Williams "plum" poem was ruined
by long lines.

I routinely check my line lengths while polishing my verse. Here
are three poems from my files, using short, medium and long lines
and all dealing with the same subject — the loss of a baby:

INVOCATION

Till the sun falls
Below that tree line
And light stops
Coloring stained glass,
I want to talk
With the Virgin Mother
Who the saints say
Always listens. I won't

Worry about my wife
Who waits outside
The mountain chapel.
She has a pastel sky
For company, though
She must share it
With tourists at the peak

Season. She refuses
To share her grief
With you and the stone
Jesus, cold at your breast.
Our child was colder,
Even in the red
Sunset that was a gift
In the birthing room:

Sculpted forever
To your baby, you can turn
Light to life. Do it
Again. Do it for the mother
Who holds her infant
Only once and in that
Moment is as holy.

NO STRINGS

We keep finding on our doorstep
Rattles too big for the post box.
They arrive with offers from a company
No parent can refuse, clean diapers
Being next to God. The Ivory Snow mother

Thinks so in baby magazines on trial
Subscription. And if we don't want
The bedtime books, we still get to keep
The Disney mobile. It hangs above the crib
Littered with coupons for free formula,

Gerber, Johnson's "no more tears" shampoo.
We send for everything. They don't know that
After the stillborn, somebody forgot
To pull our name from the mailing lists.
We'll write, if at anytime we're unhappy.

SNOWHEAD, AFTER THE ACCIDENT

That year, that awful year I'll remember in the next century
When somebody's striking daughter rings up $19.81
For whatever I'll be drinking then, I want you to remind me
The snow was whiter than we'd ever seen it in Oklahoma
And that for one chill day toward sunset, we stopped
Crying as a baby would stop, suddenly, to play
In it and roll in the back yard one huge belly-
Ache of a snowball, layer on layer until stripes
Of dead grass showed below the bedroom window;
How hour by hour the form we never planned took shape,
From bulbous head to lump-bottom, arm to outstretched arm
Welcoming us as if just arrived, as if to say: *I am still
With you*: beckoning the moon that night to cast those arms
And head on our pale bedspread that seemed a continuum of snow
Covering our bodies, not touching, until you reached
Over me for the curtain, missed it, and by accident, found me.

Read each poem aloud. The short lines of "Invocation" were meant
to provide dramatic tension; the medium lines of "No Strings," to
focus on an idea without muddling it with drama or emotion; and the
long lines of "Snowhead, After the Accident," to convey emotional
release.

Now take a scratch pad and cast "Snowhead, After the Accident"
in short lines; "Invocation," in long lines; and "No Strings," in short
and long lines.

Read them again and you'll see each flounder.

Building Block #4: *The last line should be as powerful as the first
line.* But it shouldn't simply restate the same idea, image or thing.
Ideally, it should leave the audience feeling satisfied or startled, resolving a problem or situation or tantalizing readers with an ending image
or outburst.

To illustrate, I'll repeat some of the powerful opening lines mentioned earlier in this chapter . . . and juxtapose them with ending lines
of the same poems:

- Whenas in silks my Julia goes. . . .
  — O how that glittering taketh me!
- She walks in beauty, like the night. . . .
  A heart whose love is innocent!
- An old, mad, blind, despised, and dying king— . . .
  Burst, to illuminate our tempestuous day.
- Well hast thou spoken, and yet, not taught. . . .
  Evince my gratitude!

- When the dead in their cold graves are lying. . . .
  The soul lives in glory and light.
- The Soul selects her own Society. . . .
  Like stone.
- He hears with gladdened heart the thunder. . . .
  Expectant of the certain end.
- Something there is that doesn't love a wall. . . .
  He says again, "Good fences make good neighbours."

After I complete a poem, I make sure to juxtapose my first and last lines to see if I can improve either of them. If the first line is much stronger than the last, I'll revise. I'll do the same if the last line is better than the first. Then I evaluate each line of the poem to see if it works as a unit to convey an idea or image or suggests other meanings. Finally, I determine whether the length of the line is appropriate for the subject matter.

To assess the importance of the line in contemporary poetry, try these exercises:

1. Determine the length of lines (mostly short, medium or long) in each poem appearing in at least three literary magazines. Now assess whether the line length blends with the subject matter, helping to produce a dramatic-, focus- or emotional-based work. This will give you an idea of the myriad ways lines are used by poets publishing in different magazines.

2. Analyze the line according to the above methods as it is used in at least three new collections of poetry. This will give you an idea of the myriad ways that individual authors call upon the line to enhance poems.

3. Analyze the line again in poems appearing in *The Norton Anthology of Poetry*. This will give you an idea of how important the line is in works by various authors from different backgrounds and eras.

To emphasize these lessons, let's preview poems in the mini anthology by past masters of the line, focusing on their uses and/or innovations that are still being practiced today:

- "Lines From a Dream" by Walter Savage Landor. A two-line work, this shows how the first and last lines should startle the reader. Also note that the first contains two levels of meaning and that the second one begins and ends with vivid words.
- "Unfolded Out of the Folds" by Whitman. This, of course, illustrates the long line as emotional outburst. Despite the length, however, each line is crisp as a unit; moreover, the first and last lines brilliantly counterbalance each other.
- "Portrait of a Lady" by Williams. The short line adds tension

and controls how we read the work, so that images piece together slowly, as they do when an artist paints on canvas. Only this is a portrait in verse, illustrating the power of the line.

If you master the line as these poets did, your work will stand out from that of others because of craft. You'll also strike a chord within readers who will hear — and remember — the music of your verse.

Mini Anthology of Line Poems

LINES FROM A DREAM

O Friendship! Friendship! the shell of Aphrodite
Lies always at the bottom of thy warm and limpid waters.
—Walter Savage Landor

UNFOLDED OUT OF THE FOLDS

Unfolded out of the folds of the woman man comes unfolded, and is
                                       always to come unfolded,
Unfolded only out of the superbest woman of the earth is to come the
                                       superbest man of the earth,
Unfolded out of the friendliest woman is to come the friendliest man,
Unfolded only out of the perfect body of a woman can a man be form'd of
                                       perfect body,
Unfolded only out of the inimitable poems of woman can come the poems
                                       of man, (only thence have my poems come;)
Unfolded out of the strong and arrogant woman I love, only thence can
                                       appear the strong and arrogant man I love,
Unfolded by brawny embraces from the well-muscled woman I love, only
                                       thence come the brawny embraces of the man,
Unfolded out of the folds of the woman's brain come all the folds of the
                                       man's brain, duly obedient,
Unfolded out of the justice of the woman all justice is unfolded,
Unfolded out of the sympathy of the woman is all sympathy;
A man is a great thing upon the earth and through eternity, but every jot
                                       of the greatness of man is unfolded out of woman;
First the man is shaped in the woman, he can then be shaped in himself.
—Walt Whitman

PORTRAIT OF A LADY

Your thighs are appletrees
whose blossoms touch the sky.
Which sky? The sky
where Watteau hung a lady's
slipper. Your knees

are a southern breeze — or
a gust of snow. Agh! what
sort of man was Fragonard?
— as if that answered
anything. Ah, yes — below
the knees, since the tune
drops that way, it is
one of those white summer days,
the tall grass of your ankles
flickers upon the shore —
Which shore? —
the sand clings to my lips —
Which shore?
Agh, petals maybe. How
should I know?
Which shore? Which shore?
I said petals from an appletree.

— William Carlos Williams

Notebook

LEVEL ONE

1. Take out the three drafts of poems from your "Work in Progress" file that you did in the last notebook exercise on voice. Revise them according to the four building blocks discussed in this chapter.

2. Select three ideas from your "Idea File" — one suited to short-line lengths (drama), one to medium-line lengths (clarity), and one to long-line lengths (emotional release). Now compose first drafts, heeding all that you have learned thus far about voice and line.

LEVEL TWO

1. By now you should have done the exercises recommended earlier in this chapter (analyzing the use of the line in magazines, books and anthologies). If not, do them now.

2. Revise the three drafts from the previous Level Two notebook exercise according to the four building blocks in this chapter.

3. Choose an idea from your file that lacks a strong element of drama or emotion — in other words, an idea based on an intellectual concept (contemplation of love, nature, goodness, violence, death, etc.). Compose a draft of that poem using medium-line lengths. Now return to your original idea and revise it to make it more dramatic or emotional; for instance, you might want to insert action (along with a tense voice) to achieve drama or comment (along with a passionate

voice) to achieve emotion. Compose a draft of the dramatic-revised idea using short-line lengths and a draft of the emotional-revised idea using long-line lengths. Compare all versions of the same idea and discuss which draft you like best/least in your journal.

LEVEL THREE

1. Revise the six drafts from the previous Level Three notebook exercise according to the four building blocks in this chapter.

2. Read your journal entry based on the Level Two, Assignment Three. Identify which version you liked least — the drama/short-line length, the concept/medium-line length, or the emotion/long-line length. Now choose three ideas from your "Idea File" best suited to the version and line-length that you liked *least*.

Compose drafts in the same style.

Chapter Ten

The Stanza

A fter the line, the most basic unit of poetry is the stanza. It's a powerful tool. So powerful, in fact, that even its absence in a poem is an element of craft, a deliberate move by the artist in the creation of a work.
Among other things, a stanza:

• Pivots the poem like a chapter in a book.
• Mimics the mind in remembering events.
• Mimics nature in depicting events.
• Helps set the mood and the pace of a poem.
• Creates a pattern to guide the poet.
• Empowers the patterns of formal verse.
• Pleases the senses with new shapes.

A little white space goes a long way if you know *how* and *when* to use it. Unfortunately, because a stanza seems so basic, so second nature, too many poets treat it casually or not at all during composition, missing opportunities to enhance their work.

The stanza helps poets express their ideas or express them in complex ways. In fact, a lot of funky things can happen *off* the page in the white space of a stanza. The narrator or character of a poem can have an epiphany there. Or the poet can change the subject or setting and even flash forward or backward as needed.

As an exercise once, I wrote the following poem to show the power of the stanza. I'll number the spaces between stanzas because I'll refer to them later:

WHAT THE WAITRESS SEES
Her life is like ours. One day
Something went *snap!*, and she found herself
In the service of businessmen. More bread,
They call to her, and she responds
     (1)
As if known by that name. More Bread.

We want burgundy, lots of it, and then
We would like her to leave. She sees
Couples all the time: married, pretending
    (2)
To be, not to be, about to be. Yet
We are different. A man of dangerous
Middle Age: suited, tied. And you are younger
Of course: casual, cute. That says plenty,
    (3)
But how we carry on! How we huddle
Over paper! You yell, redden, are ready
To wash my face with wine. I cannot argue
With you anymore. I reach for a napkin,
    (4)
A pen. "Don't give me a line," I write,
"Give me a stanza." You are quiet again
So I add, "It will work. Trust me."
In an hour, you tell me *We can't go on*
    (5)
Like this, I want to be whole for you.
She cannot hear us. But she sees you
Crying now, and no one has raised
A voice. A glass. Or a fist. Later
    (6)
She finds the napkin with a tip. Stanza?
A type of dance maybe, a Latin one like tango.
Last stanza in Paris. How we belong there!
But this is Oklahoma where something goes
    (7)
Snap!. Dancers. She wants us to be dancers
Who stanza in a honky-tonk. She looks
At the clock. She will meet someone tonight.
It will work this time. It will be good.

Let's see what happens in the white spaces as numbered:

1. *Scene shift*. The waitress responds, moving from the table of businessmen to the couple.

2. *Focus shift*. The point of view switches from the waitress alone to the couple and the waitress.

3. *Mood, scene and focus shift*. The couple seems to be fighting, the waitress observing from a distance and the man reaching for a napkin (as if to dry his face or tears).

4. *Mood, focus and time shift*. No, he is going to write. Then the

scene flashes forward to the woman's italicized outburst, cut off, as if she's struggling to get out her words.

5. *Focus shift.* The waitress tries to figure out what is happening at that table.

6. *Time and scene shift.* The customers have left. The waitress tries to decipher the note at the couple's table and has an epiphany about romance.

7. *Mood, time, scene and focus shift.* Like a dancer's fingers going *Snap!*, the mood of the poem suddenly becomes magical, the scene shifts to a honky-tonk, and time pushes forward again as the waitress makes her wish.

If you want to measure what, exactly, the stanza is doing in "What the Waitress Sees," type the poem out in a single column without any breaks. It probably will confuse you. You'll wonder from whose viewpoint this story is being told and question why scenes and time elements change without warning.

In this case, the stanza makes the poem.

END-STOPPED AND RUN-ON STANZAS

Let's define them: When a punctuation mark, usually a period, appears at the end of a line, the line is *end-stopped.* In other words, the reader is forced to take a pause before continuing to the next line. That pause is even greater when the last line of a stanza is end-stopped, because the reader must take *two* pauses — one for the end-stopped line and another for the white space that follows. When no punctuation mark appears at the end of a line, the line is called *enjambed* or *run-on.* Now the reader freely continues from one line to the next, without much of a pause. When the last line of a stanza is run-on, however, the reader hesitates momentarily to span the white space between stanzas.

An end-stopped stanza is especially effective if the poet wants to suggest memories punctuated, as it were, by long pauses or shifts in time. To illustrate, let's consider an early Bruce Weigl poem from his book *A Romance* (University of Pittsburgh Press, 1979):

THE HARP

When he was my age and I was already a boy
my father made a machine in the garage.
A wired piece of steel
with many small and beautiful welds
ground so smooth they resembled rows of pearls.

He went broke with whatever it was.
He held it so carefully in his arms.

He carried it foundry to foundry.
I think it was his harp,
I think it was what he longed to make
with his hands for the world.

He moved it finally from the locked closet
to the bedroom
to the garage again
where he hung it on the wall
until I climbed and pulled it down
and rubbed it clean
and tried to make it work.

As you can see, Weigl end-stops stanzas with each memory, giving his voice a plaintive, almost halting quality. Time lapses in the white space of any stanza, but when stanzas are end-stopped as above, they seem to move more slowly — almost deliberately. Weigl uses this to good effect, probing his epiphanies about his father as if he sits across from us and relates the story of "the harp."

Weigl doesn't use formal stanzas, uniform patterns of lines as in "What the Waitress Sees." I use such stanzas in my free verse because they help me discover the poem (the same way meter and rhyme do in formal work). But Weigl's lyric is the better for lack of such structure. It would undercut the epiphany of the memories and make them seem preconceived.

Here's Judith Kitchen's poem from her book *Perennials* (Anhinga Press, 1986) that uses run-on uniform stanzas:

WALKING ON ICE
We walk out testing the
surface, the currents
beneath. You push   off

and slide, your body young
and gentle. This could easily
be another time — the wind

reaching for my scarf,
other fingers on my waist,
skates glinting in the late

afternoon. But here,
at the intersection, the ice
sighs. Under our feet, under

our children's feet, the shiver,

star-shaped, spreads
the length of the canal.

Kitchen's stanzas slip easily into each other to recreate the tension
of "walking on ice," her title. (She even indicates the slippery ice
visually in the third line of her poem, leaving white space between
the words "push" and "off.") You usually don't find run-on stanzas
used in formal ways. But in this poem, the run-ons suggest ice and
the tercets, or three-line stanzas, the elegance of skating. They rub
against each other, and shards fly as if from skates of the poet's youth.

MANY AND NO BREAKS

The more stanzas you use, the greater their pull on lines, as if white
space is a force of poetic gravity. Some poems require that force to hold
the structure together. Other poems seem weightless, fragile, unable to
withstand any breaks. Let's consider the two types and their effects.

This is the ending of "An Abandoned Farm in the West," a poem
in unrhymed couplets from *Lower-Class Heresy* (University of Illinois,
1987) by T.R. Hummer, who has edited *The Kenyon Review* and *New
England Review*:

She mumbles *Heresy, heresy* and does not hear.
Anyone might have been born here, might have named

The light-jagged mountains thrown down in June sun,
Anyone among us might have scattered these small stones

In the oblivious story of our play while the woman sings
Her mother-song from the bedroom window

And the man drags his crippled foot in sheets
Of what he would have sworn would soon be snow:

Anyone might have loved anyone, anyone might have married
The first body come whistling down the slow-dusked road,

Anyone might be your brother, lifting the blue flowers
Of your dress in the corncrib's innocent dark:

And you love him as long as you can, hold on to the hard
Life he makes while he shivers in the heat

This shadow means, not knowing it is you, torn
To the shape of a man in the field of your own failed season.

The second sentence of this excerpt is more than 140 words, a
passionate outburst. But it succeeds solely on the merits of Hummer's
stanza-making. He knows that a many-stanzaed work parcels images

and ideas of a long poetic phrase into units. The units, or couplets here, make the poem understandable. Otherwise, it would be hopelessly complex.

Let's consider the opposite now, a poem by Louise Glück from her book *The House on Marshland* (Ecco, 1976):

FLOWERING PLUM

In spring from the black branches of the flowering plum tree
the woodthrush issues its routine
message of survival. Where does such happiness come from
as the neighbors' daughter reads into that singing,
and matches? All afternoon she sits
in the partial shade of the plum tree, as the mild wind
floods her immaculate lap with blossoms, greenish white
and white, leaving no mark, unlike
the fruit that will inscribe
unraveling dark stains in heavier winds, in summer.

This poem's structure is fragile, blossoms afloat in the wind and flooding a girl's lap. To break the lyric into couplets would intrude on its magic — the last moments of innocence — so fleeting that the lines must flow mostly run-on, to conclusion. Cast the lyric into unrhymed couplets, as in the Hummer poem, and watch the poem's beauty deflate.

In this case, the absence of breaks is evidence of craft as much as the plethora of breaks was in Hummer's poem. While he needs many stanzas to hold the structure of his poem together, Glück requires the weightlessness of no breaks to depict the girl's essence.

Again, the stanza is at work behind the scenes.

MID-LINE BREAKS

No one says that a stanza has to follow the end of a uniform line. You can break into the white space of a stanza at any point in a line if that will aid in the reading of a poem. Originally this was the norm in verse plays on stage during the Elizabethan era. One actor would say half a poetic line, and another actor would finish it. Poets adapted this playwriting technique to the page, usually in narrative verse that features more than one speaker. Later this metamorphosed into a bona fide stanza break in poems that lacked playlike dialogue. A good example is Wordsworth's "Tintern Abbey," written in blank verse (as were the earlier plays) but broken at strategic points in a passage without quotations:

Once again I see
These hedge-rows, hardly hedge-rows, little lines

Of sportive wood run wild: these pastoral farms,
Green to the very door; and wreaths of smoke
Sent up, in silence, from among the trees!
With some uncertain notice, as might seem
Of vagrant dwellers in the houseless woods,
Or of some Hermit's cave, where by his fire
The Hermit sits alone.

These beauteous forms,
Through a long absence, have not been to me
As is a landscape to a blind man's eye: . . .

In this excerpt, Wordsworth end-stops the midline stanza break to augment the solitude of the hermit. The white space that follows implies that the narrator is pondering some deep truth. Then the poem continues, articulating that truth — again, via the stanza.

DESIGNING STANZA PATTERNS
Stanza patterns are just that — lines with indentations and white space that constitute visually appealing units. These function like regular stanzas, controlling how we read a poem and enhancing content; however, they also serve as an element of design on the page.

The goal is to please the ear *and* the eye.

Such patterns have been composed since Shakespeare's day. He used them in his songs so they resemble measures of music:

Blow, blow, thou winter wind,
Thou art not so unkind
	As man's ingratitude;
Thy tooth is not so keen,
Because thou art not seen,
	Although thy breath be rude.
Heigh-ho! sing, heigh-ho! unto the green holly:
Most friendship is feigning, most loving mere folly:
	Then, heigh-ho, the holly!
	This life is most jolly.

Since the Elizabethan era, these patterns have been adapted to free verse with more ornate structures and indentations. Here's an example from my files:

WHITE NOISE
To make sound, I need peace
	so the disturbance may pass
		through a medium. To make love,
I need sound so peace ensues

as bodies become equal
again. Love is greater
Than sound and subsumes it
as light subsumes the same
properties at higher frequency.

I am on the same property,
common ground, hearing our talk
at the log fence, Queen Anne's lace
Like so many silicon
microphone heads at the hip,
recording the disturbance.
We are magnetic now as love
happens without sound,
silent movie in black & white,

White noise as it is known
in circles of science
encompassing all frequencies
Within the ring cycle of wood,
logging our longing so when
you leave and I pass this place,
I can hear the timbre
rewind or fastforward at will,
pause and play back the sound

Love makes when peace has no medium,
no body to balance the wave.

Analyze the shape of the above excerpt, and you will see that it consists of three units of three indented lines. (More about the last two lines later.) The units are not typical stanzas because no white space separates them. Space is inserted, however, between each three-unit shape (or stanza pattern). You can design any shape, of course, but you should repeat it—at least until it is recognized as a pattern. In my poem, the last two lines violate the pattern intentionally. Read them again for theme—"peace has no medium/no body to balance the wave"—and you can see the pattern break down visually on the page as it does thematically in the poem.

To familiarize yourself with the myriad uses of the stanza, try these exercises:

1. Analyze the stanza in works appearing in *The Norton Anthology of Poetry*. This will give you an idea of how poets have used the stanza in past and recent eras.

2. Analyze the stanzas in works appearing in at least three literary

magazines. This will give you an idea of how contemporary poets use the stanza in different publications.

3. Analyze poems in three new collections of poetry. This will give you an idea of how individual poets call on the power of the stanza to enhance their verse.

To get you started, let's preview the poems in the mini anthology:

• In "Stanzas" by Byron, note the indented formal end-stopped stanzas that punctuate his pithy observations on war.

• In "This Living Hand" by Keats, note the run-on lines in one fragile stanza.

• Laurence Lieberman, poetry editor at the University of Illinois Press and author of several collections, is a master of the modern-day stanza pattern. When you read his "Tartine, for All Her Bulk," you'll encounter a pattern that not only contains units and indented lines but three individual stanzas (mostly run-on) of five, eight and six lines. Instead of white space to signify the start of a new pattern, he starts each by flushing left on the page *and* using white space. Each nineteen-line pattern is repeated four times in his ninety-five-line mosaic.

After you read this and other poems reprinted here, you should appreciate the power of the stanza, an important tool in the making of verse. The more tools you have at your disposal, the easier it will be to compose, revise and express yourself as a poet.

Mini Anthology of Stanza Poems

STANZAS

When a man hath no freedom to fight for at home,
    Let him combat for that of his neighbors;
Let him think of the glories of Greece and of Rome,
    And get knocked on his head for his labors.

To do good to mankind is the chivalrous plan,
    And is always as nobly requited;
Then battle for freedom wherever you can,
    And, if not shot or hanged, you'll get knighted.
                                        —Lord Byron

THIS LIVING HAND

This living hand, now warm and capable
Of earnest grasping, would, if it were cold
And in the icy silence of the tomb,
So haunt thy days and chill thy dreaming nights
That thou wouldst wish thine own heart dry of blood

So in my veins red life might stream again,
And thou be conscience-calmed — see here it is —
I hold it towards you.
                                    — John Keats

TARTINE, FOR ALL HER BULK

Tartine, for all
her bulk outsweep — pumpkin hips
        and rump — pivots and revolves with burly grace
        across the several acres
        of yard, dashing from one garden corner to the next

                amid the gush
                of wit and loquacious repartee with Thom and myself.
        Two donkeys and one calf,
                on separate ropes, get tangled
                        in the pair of hoses, strategically set, placed
                to hit most key targets
        of her sprawled vegetable and fruit gardens,
                evenly: the calf keeps trying to munch the colorful

        leafage from young papaya and christophene
                plants, her prize crops,
                        while a burro starts zigzagging, his rope
                        crisscrossing the hoses,
                        so we can hardly tell where any rope, hose or thick
                        vine starts or stops. But she unravels

the loose flux
of knots, saves the tender shoots
        and battens down all free-floating livestock
        like so many sails or tarps
        in a gale at sea, with no loss of her verbal pizzazz.

                Steepest grades
                of garden, here and there, must be traversed if she's
        to keep one jump ahead
                of the hemp and rubber entanglements,
                        those hooved prancers grooved to outwit her, to do
                her one better — they lose!
        She wields her fulsome girth, brawny and agile
                to spare, over those abrupt dips and ascents, perhaps two

        house stories' elevation at the loftiest
                plateau, where one hose —
                        propped on a forked limb — splits its geyser

into three or four streams
aimed toward lowest fringes of her many crops. My eye
cannot discern the measure of her amplest

haunch or loin,
what with ballooning skirts,
    pleated ruffles billowing in and out —
    those immensities veiled
as she whirls about her garden. She waves her lavish

                    satin guilt hems
            with a gypsy dancer's flourish, parading her costume
flash with as much deviltry
        as the carriage she half conceals, half
            divulges: *oversize clothes*, she croons (picking up
        my gasps and dazzlement
at the very sashaying of her skirt flounces),
            have frequently been a sideline and avocation of hers . . .

    In Britain, she'd travelled for some years
        as saleslady clothier
        and agent, modelling — from door to door —
            those prodigious garments
        she offered at slashed warehouse prices to corpulent
    sad-faced buyers. Tartine made a *Royal Killing*

of her walkup/
walkaway business, soonest won
    top honors for best sales on her twenty-square-
    miles route, three years running.
    She kept the most capacious outsize smocks and slacks,

                    pleated cape
            jackets and horsy riding britches, in *High Fashion*
    by adorning their inflated
        hulks with her rotund-but agile-charms.
        Chunky allure, she terms it. Wherever she sojourned,
        on holiday, she could garner
    quick pin money by peddling a ready-to-wear
stack of eye-fetching ruffly blouses, or expansive gowns.
        Oddshaped folks, in City or Province,
            often too submissive
                and shy about their disproportioned limbs
                to shop in the marketplace,
                    thus paying dear prices to local seamstress or tailor
        for radical alterations of drab fabrics,

jumped at the chance
to embrace puffy shapes and offbeat
   sizes on their very doorstoop, while Tartine
   endowed many an article
   she wore with raw earthly glamours into the bargain,

        her sales pitch
        the Latin dance trot she varied to make each outfit
shine forth with proper flare.
   None haggled over price, so cheered
      they were to be lifted from a hopeless morass: hunts
   to clothes marts that catered,
only, to midrange norms . . . Today, since her return
      to Montserrat in nineteen eighty, she can hardly find

true fit duds for herself, much less a sales
   career which pays
      half so well — hard pressed for Overseas Mail
      Order garb from America
      or Britain: *I can't be sewin' up tentsized parachutes*
   for me own glum bloody stay-at-home backside!
         —Laurence Lieberman

Notebook

LEVEL ONE

1. Revise the drafts of poems in your "Work in Progress" file and improve your stanzas according to precepts learned in this chapter:

- *Formal stanzas*: For poems using the same number of lines in each stanza, to give a structured appearance.
- *Freestyle stanzas*: For poems in which content calls for stanzas at irregular intervals.
- *Many stanzas*: For poems using long sentences; conveying many facts, ideas or images; or utilizing scene or time shifts.
- *No stanzas*: For poems whose content seems too intense or fragile.
- *End-stopped stanzas*: For poems whose content is enhanced by pauses or hesitations.
- *Run-on stanzas*: For poems whose content is enhanced by white space but not by long pauses or hesitations.
- *Midline stanzas*: For poems whose content contains or implies conversation and/or whose truths are enhanced or clarified by breaks.
- *Stanza patterns*: For poems in which the author desires greater

control over how the audience reads a work and who wants to make the work appeal visually on the page.

2. Choose three ideas from your "Idea File" — one directly related to memory, one to emotional release, and another to a fragile moment. Before you write, determine the voice and line length for each idea according to lessons learned in previous chapters. Now compose a draft of (a) the memory idea using only a few irregular and end-stopped stanzas, (b) the emotional release idea using at least ten uniform run-on *and* end-stopped stanzas, and (c) the fragile moment idea using only run-on lines with no stanza break.

LEVEL TWO

1. If you haven't done the reading exercises mentioned earlier in this chapter (analyzing the stanza in the Norton anthology and in at least three magazines and new collections), do them now.

2. Review the final drafts of poems in your inventory and determine whether you are relying on only a few of the stanza's uses in your work. Now review the drafts of poems in your "Work in Progress" file and compose new versions using those stanza techniques that you have been avoiding.

3. Select three ideas from your "Idea File" that concern aspects of beauty — an element of nature, say, or a concept of love. Compose a draft using a stanza pattern whose design enhances the topic, theme or truth of your poem.

LEVEL THREE

Review the drafts of poems in your "Work in Progress" file and select three. Compose new drafts of each poem using no stanzas, many stanzas, formal and freestyle ones, end-stopped and run-on ones, midline breaks and stanza patterns. Add or delete lines as needed to make the new versions as polished as possible . . . and then compare. Make notations in your journal, describing what you have discovered about the stanza on your own and how you will apply those discoveries in future poems.

Chapter Eleven

The Title

O nce I was a guest poet visiting a creative writing workshop and critiquing a woman's untitled poem. I thought she had missed an opportunity by not titling her work and told her so. She replied that she disliked titles. "Why?" I asked. "Well," she said, pausing a moment to ponder her feelings, "it's too much of a commitment."

I couldn't have phrased it better myself. A title is just that — a commitment — promising a payoff if the audience will invest a little time to read your work. In essence, you are asking people to stop their lives and dwell awhile in yours. Why should they?

The title addresses that question. It promises that the poem will transform the ordinary — "Snowflakes," say, by Longfellow — into the extraordinary. Or it suggests that the work will make us wise — "Hymn to Intellectual Beauty," say, by Shelley — or will intrigue and entertain us: "The Rape of the Lock" by Pope.

The poet had better meet those expectations, or else readers will feel shortchanged. For instance, if you title your poem "Snow," the reader will anticipate learning about the mystery or beauty of that common noun and natural phenomenon. If you simply depict pretty flakes that melt when the weather becomes warmer in spring, the reader will shrug and complain: "So what?" Likewise, if you title your poem "Hymn to Intellectual Hunger," the reader will anticipate learning about ennobling truths and again will feel let down if you depict a person with an appetite for knowledge the way most people have an appetite for food. The reader will shrug and complain, "Hasn't that been done before?"

Typically, beginning poets do not appreciate the power of a good title.

Let's illustrate:

Picture a poem about an ex-radio announcer wasting away in a hospital for the criminally insane, taunted by "feeble-minded felons in pajamas" as he repents his sins and accepts his plight. Close your

eyes for a few seconds and visualize this poor soul in a deck chair.
Ready?

Now title the poem "Ezra Pound," as Robert Lowell did after visiting the canto-writer at St. Elizabeth's Hospital in Washington where Pound was detained because of his anti-American broadcasts during World War II.

As the anecdote illustrates, a title can transform an entire work. It's the first thing a reader sees . . . and the last thing that he or she remembers about a poem.

The real question for the poet, though, is what comes first—the title of the poem or the content?

CHICKEN/EGG QUESTION

The answer is simple: whatever works for you. Some poets need a title to help clarify or enhance content. Others think a working title—one they plan to revise—eases stress and eliminates writer's block. And some prefer to compose the poem without a title, worrying about that requirement later. A few do all three, depending on the content or difficulty of the poem. These poets realize that sometimes the title will come naturally, sometimes not; when it doesn't, they use a working title or none at all in the early stages.

Allow yourself that freedom. What has worked once—or even often for you—may not work all the time. If you force yourself to adhere to rigid rules, title-writing can overinfluence or even block your poems.

Say, for instance, that you always need to know the title before you can write a poem. If so, you don't have to spend hours thinking up various versions of titles in search of a final one. To get going, simply compose a working title, a few words or a phrase that you plan to revise later. Base it on your epiphany.

Consider this scenario: One night, before writing a poem, I wandered outdoors and felt betrayed by a full moon that was supposed to inspire romance but seemed instead to be passing me by. Later I based a working title on the experience: "Swearing Never to Write About the Moon." As soon as I wrote that, I knew that it sounded clunky, as many working titles do. But it did the job, jump-starting my muse.

I began:

Worse, Oklahoma moon. Big, luminous,
Pure enough to read poetry by
Shakespeare, the balcony scene,
Our hero ababble with love, high

On star and simile, run out
Of metaphor, light—it would seem—
Of language: false dawn. . . .

The rest of the poem came easily, describing how a man walks alone in a city and pays a late-night visit to an ex-lover, silhouetted with another man in the window. The poem ends: "You'll say your *wherefores* soon/Enough. And I shall sing no more of love,/Whose mask is still the moon."

Now it was time to return to the title. I was using a Romeo and Juliet allusion to power my poem and wanted the final title to reflect that. By the time I had finished the lyric, I knew the content so well that the final version was a snap to write: "Moon, Love: Whereof I Swear Never Again to Write."

I would have blocked the poem if I had spent hours trying to come up with a title like the one above. And then, if I did, I would have run the risk of letting such a title overinfluence content. The solution, then, was to employ a working title and concentrate on content, worrying about the final title after the poem was completed.

If you use working titles to help you concentrate on content, don't be awed by the power of your lines and then put off writing a final title. I suspect that my poem would never have been printed if I hadn't reworked the "working" title.

But suppose you have an easy time with titles, knowing what the final one will be from the start. If so, by all means compose the title first. Just don't let it overinfluence content or else your poem may sound forced or artificial.

On occasion this has happened to me.

Once I visited the Oklahoma City zoo and saw the dolphins there leap for a fish in return for a little attention. Their plight reminded me of desolate lovers. By the time I drove home and settled in to write, I knew that my poem would be called "Dolphins." The opening lines came easily enough:

All day as we wander again
Miles apart, I take in show after show
At the aquarium. The dolphins
Begin to notice me, deadpan
By the holding tank, their lingo
Primal as love. . . .

But the poem bogged down as I tried to describe dolphins using biological terms. My voice changed from sounding plaintive or yearning in the opening lines (appropriate for a love poem) to one that sounded dull and scientific. In other words, I was forcing my lines to conform to the title and limiting the scope of what I usually discover during the writing process, how one word sparks another, how one image melds with another and so forth.

A final title is important, but not if it blocks the poem (as was the case here). So I scrapped my title and composed without one, concentrating as much on lovers as on the dolphins: "They have two names/As we have two names. 'Dolphin'/Is pretty enough, but 'porpoise'/Sounds too much like another word,/Purpose. What is the purpose/of a dolphin who leaps 18 feet for a fish?"

Again, the rest of the poem came easily; so easily, in fact, that I was able to use my original title after all.

Here's a third scenario: You're in such a hurry to compose a poem that you skip the title. Maybe the muse has paid you an unexpected visit, and you can feel your lines forming already inside your head. Quickly you reach for a pen or a keyboard. All you want is to get your words down so you won't forget them.

In this case, content comes first.

Again this has happened to me. Once, after a winter storm, I wanted to write a mood piece featuring a man who has stayed awake all night watching snow and worrying about a relationship.

The lines came relatively easy, but the title didn't:

All night, as I lay in the spare room
Thinking of us, the snow has been falling
On the car, on the evergreen and hedge. It grows
Sudden and cold as our love. We should revel tonight
In sub-zero, cover the tracks: our souls are together,
Twined as any limb. I can't even wake you.
In the blue-grey light the window allows, you'd see me
Stroking a lock of hair from the delicate cheekbone
I might kiss, and ask me *What are you doing? Why*
Are you awake? You would brush my hand like snow.
I want to whisper, we are alive. We feel the same
Love for the other. But you sleep and I watch
The flurry outside conceal what remains
Of metal and wood. By morning, the snow
May drift like a dream and embed us
Or may melt like beauty and be gone.

To come up with a title, I had to go through each line and word of the poem, circling words for inspiration: "sudden," "cold," "love," "snow," "drift," "melt," "beauty," etc. In essence, I was compiling an "objective correlative," a term coined by T.S. Eliot that means, in plain talk, a string of words or images that in itself tells a story.

Every poem has a correlative upon which you can base a title. Typically, your list of words will also indicate a deeper level of meaning. In my poem, the deeper meaning was obvious: *Love can be as cold or as fleeting as snow.*

After several dozen attempts, I came up with: "The Brevity and Permanence of Snow."

If your poems usually come first, without regard to titles, you have to be disciplined. The tendency will be to give up the search too soon, going with what actually is a working or half-baked title. But if you circle words as I did in the above example and ponder your correlative, you should be able to come up with a title that enhances your work.

Now that you know the three methods to compose a title, let's review the three basic types.

DESCRIPTIVE, SUSPENSE AND LABEL TITLES

A descriptive title depicts content, a suspense one sparks interest, and the label variety is just that — a word or two as on a can of vegetables: "Beans" or "Creamed Corn."

Let's use a poem by Judson Jerome — "Oil of the Pecos Valley" — to illustrate how each functions.

Study the above title for a moment. Now imagine it in a trade publication, accompanying an article on drilling in the Southwest. A magazine editor would call this a *descriptive* title because it informs the audience what the content is going to be.

Jerome's first line reads: "In that kind of country even the yellowest blossoms. . . ."

Now imagine "Even the Yellowest Blossoms" as a title in the trade publication, illustrating the same article. A magazine editor would call this a *suspense* title because, on reading it, the audience would have no inkling that the story is about oil in the Pecos Valley. But they might be intrigued by the image of yellow blossoms.

Finally, imagine "Oil" or "Pecos Valley" as possible titles in this trade publication. Either one would be a *label* title, a generic tag describing news about petroleum or its availability in the valley.

Imagining a descriptive, suspense and label title in a trade publication is a good exercise because we often encounter these types of titles in magazines. You also can familiarize yourself with such titles by paging through an anthology in the library. You'll find many examples of descriptive and label titles and only a few suspense ones. That's because the best titles for poems ground the reader in time or place or set the mood so the audience knows what to anticipate. An occasional suspense title adds a little contrast, a bit of spice.

Nonetheless, there are problems associated with all titles. Descriptive ones can be boring, safe. Label ones, cryptic. Suspense titles, confusing.

Here's how you can lessen the risks.

SOLVING COMMON PROBLEMS

A good descriptive or label title is deceptively simple. It seems at first to define content or set the scene so the poet can continue. True, it does that. But if that is all your title accomplishes, then it has fallen short of its mark. A descriptive or label title also has to convey another level of meaning — usually associated with an epiphany or a peak experience.

Let's use another excerpt from the poem by Judson Jerome to illustrate this concept.

In the middle stanzas of "Oil of the Pecos Valley," he writes:

The first million years were likely the most absurd,

until, in its gully, indifferent, reluctantly fertile,
it ran more like plasma than blood, like lymph in the land,
colder than night in the night, colder in sunlight,
slick under bluffs, greener than thorn trees, and while

rabbits drink elsewhere, cedars absorb it, and cottonwoods,
continuously quivering, turn it to pulp and pale green.

When we finish the poem, we realize that oil pulses through the land as plasma pulses through the body, a "lifeblood" analogy endowing "Oil of the Pecos Valley" with a second level of meaning. This helps to convey Jerome's epiphany. Thus, his title succeeds.

Label titles especially need to encompass more than one meaning. Consider this made-up poem "Corn":

It sells for four bits
per can or a nickel
per ounce or 0.02
pennies per kernel.
You can afford it.

Boring stuff. The title has one meaning: "corn." Worse, the content doesn't convey much either: "corn's cheap." The title remains static. Now consider this made-up poem "Beans":

Somebody buy me
a can, quick.
You can afford it.
I weigh my life
in beans, bites.

The second poem is better than the first because the title harmonizes with content and thus increases meaning. We read the poem and contemplate "Beans," which now suggests poverty as in "I don't have beans" and frustration: "Beans!"

In the hands of a good poet, a label is elusive, changing how we view the world, as Longfellow illustrates in his famous lyric "Snowflakes":

Out of the bosom of the Air,
　Out of the cloud-folds of her garments shaken,
Over the woodlands brown and bare,
　Over the harvest-fields forsaken,
　　Silent, and soft, and slow
　　Descends the snow.

Even as our cloudy fancies take
　Suddenly shape in some divine expression,
Even as the troubled heart doth make
　In the white countenance confession,
　　The troubled sky reveals
　　The grief it feels.

This is the poem of the air,
　Slowly in silent syllables recorded;
This is the secret of despair,
　Long in its cloudy bosom hoarded,
　　Now whispered and revealed
　　To wood and field.

As you can see, each time Longfellow describes "snowflakes," we realize that he is comparing them to words—"silent syllables"—to explain how nature mourns. Since reading his poem, I often think about snowflakes as "divine expression." Longfellow has transformed the ordinary into the extraordinary by endowing his poem with a deeper level of meaning. Such is the beauty of a good label.

Nonetheless, you will want to use a suspense title occasionally because a good one can entice a reader and is a welcome change of pace. First a word of caution: Suspense titles sound more sophisticated, artsy; but, in reality, they are the adjectives of titles. Use them sparingly as you would use adjectives in your prose.

Think of a suspense title as a slogan or an advertisement that promises a big payoff to pique the audience's interest. Many ads do not live up to expectations, but at least we usually know what product is being peddled. This is not always the case with poems employing suspense titles. Often the reader, attracted by the title, will scan the opening lines, still not know what the poem is about, and lose interest.

If you decide to use a suspense title, be sure to define the topic or set the scene as soon as possible. This way readers will be grounded in the poem from the start, able to understand content without feeling confused. To illustrate, consider how Hilda Raz grounds the following poem in the first four lines:

WHAT HAPPENS

In Alma, Nebraska, at midnight
into a spring storm the young doctor
goes out. He says he is going
to deliver the widow's baby.
I am sitting in the parlor
with my new friend, our landlady,
who is painting my nails
what she calls *a good color*.
She paints her own and tells
the story of the widow.
Outside the window the rosy snow
comes down on the crocus.

After explaining the situation in the opening lines, Raz sets the poem in the parlor with a friend and uses images to highlight the irony of painting her nails "a good color" (as the narrator longs to paint the world a rosier hue). What happens, then, is an epiphany.

As a general rule, you should link the title to the epiphany in a poem. This approach not only will help you conceive the best title for your work, but also will forebode key elements therein.

Now let's consider other elements of craft involving titles.

VARYING AND AVOIDING CERTAIN TITLES

Here are two variations of basic titles:

1. *The Statement.* Instead of a word or phrase, compose a complete sentence. The sentence can function as a suspense, descriptive or label title, as in:

- "When I Feel Your Soul, I Reach for You With These Arms" (suspense)
- "Caution: This Poem Is Armed and Dangerous" (descriptive)
- "Jump!" (label)

2. *The Question.* Again, cast your title as a complete sentence in question form, as in:

- "Who in the Green Hate Would Have Known?" (suspense)
- "In Whom Now Shall I Place My Trust?" (descriptive)
- "Huh?" (label)

Here's a short list of titles that look gimmicky or outdated and turn off readers:

Bleeding Titles. These are ones that contain a word or phrase in the title that connects linguistically to the first line of the poem, as in the made-up poem "Sleepwalkers" connecting to the line: "Already were bedded."

Option: If you like such titles, try to compose them so the first line can stand alone:

FOR ALL I KNEW

Sleepwalkers already were bedded. . . .

Generic Titles. These are ones that call attention to form, rather than content, as in "Sonnet," "Pantoum" or "Villanelle." (We'll learn about these form poems in later chapters.) Some poets, proud that they can execute a form as difficult as the pantoum, and not wanting readers to overlook that fact, cannot resist using a generic title.

Option: If you want to call attention to the form of your poem in the title, add a phrase as in, "Pantoum for My Side of the Family."

Untitled. Poems that use "Untitled" violate a basic pact with readers who look to the title to anticipate the contents of a poem. Use of "Untitled" became vogue after poems by famous people — I'm talking ladies and lords of royal courts — were found untitled and published posthumously. If you use "Untitled" for your poems, readers might wonder why you passed up an opportunity to grace your poem with a real title.

Option: None.

First-Line Titles. These types employ the same phrases, statements or questions as titles *and* as first lines. This too has to do with tradition. Some poems were taken from longer works, as in Shakespeare's "Soliloquy" from *Hamlet* or William Blake's "And Did Those Feet" from *Milton*. Other poems bore numbers instead of titles, as in Shakespeare's "Shall I Compare Thee to a Summer's Day" or Dickinson's "Because I Could Not Stop for Death." These were marked #18 and #712, respectively, in original manuscripts. So instead of saying, read me Shakespeare's 18th or Dickinson's 712th, people repeated the first line. Eventually, poets began mimicking the practice in an attempt to sound as immortal as Shakespeare, Blake and Dickinson.

Options: If you still feel that you should repeat the title, do so only if it is:

- So odd that repetition may enhance content. (See poem by Henry David Thoreau in the mini anthology.)
- An element of voice expanded upon in the first line. (See poem by John Clare in the mini anthology.)

You should use even these optional titles sparingly. Otherwise some readers will suspect that you're trying to elevate yourself to master poet status. Again, others may wonder why you are avoiding real titles.

Last-Line Titles. These poems use the same phrase, statement or question as the title *and* the last line of the poem. If you repeat the title as the ending of your poem, you're missing yet another opportunity to enhance the clarity or meaning of your work. Again, either rewrite the title or the ending so it echoes an aspect of your epiphany or peak experience. For instance, once I wrote a poem originally titled "The Boy Who Made the Wicked Witch Cry," for the actress Margaret Hamilton, whom I met in the late fifties at a flower shop. The poem ended naturally with the same line as the title, so I changed the original title to "After Oz."

Option: If your poem would be harmed by changing the title or the last line, keep the work as is. (The longer the work, the better your chances of getting away with a last-line title.)

To sharpen your understanding of the title as an element of craft, try these exercises:

1. Go through all the poems in a year's issues of a literary magazine like *Poetry* and identify the type of title: label, descriptive, suspense. This will give you an idea of how contemporary poets employ the various titles to enhance the meaning of their work.

2. Go through the collections of the last three Pulitzer Prize winners for poetry and identify the type of title in each poem: label, descriptive, suspense. This will give you an idea of how individual poets employ the various titles in a single long work.

3. Go through all the poems in *The Norton Anthology of Poetry* and identify the type of title: label, descriptive, suspense. This will give you a historical perspective about the use of the title as an element of craft.

To illustrate the basic types of titles, I have selected poems in the mini anthology that vary the same phrase in different works:

- "I Am" by John Clare as label *and* statement.
- "I Am a Parcel of Vain Strivings Tied" by Thoreau as suspense *and* statement.
- "Who Am I?" by Carl Sandburg as a descriptive *and* question.

After reading these and other poems in magazines, books and anthologies, you'll see how title writing can deepen the meaning and augment the message of your verse.

Mini Anthology of Title Poems

I AM

I am—yet what I am, none cares or knows;
   My friends forsake me like a memory lost:

I am the self-consumer of my woes —
    They rise and vanish in oblivion's host
Like shadows in love-frenzied stifled throes
    And yet I am, and live — like vapours tost

Into the nothingness of scorn and noise,
    Into the living sea of waking dreams,
Where there is neither sense of life or joys,
    But the vast shipwreck of my life's esteems;
Even the dearest that I love the best,
    Are strange — nay, rather, stranger than the rest.

I long for scenes where man hath never trod
    A place where woman never smiled or wept
There to abide with my Creator, God,
    And sleep as I in childhood sweetly slept,
Untroubling and untroubled where I lie
    The grass below — above, the vaulted sky.
                                        — John Clare

I AM A PARCEL OF VAIN STRIVINGS TIED

I am a parcel of vain strivings tied
        By a chance bond together,
    Dangling this way and that, their links
        Were made so loose and wide,
                Methinks,
        For milder weather.

A bunch of violets without their roots,
        And sorrel intermixed,
    Encircled by a wisp of straw
        Once coiled about their shoots,
                The law
        By which I'm fixed.

A nosegay which Time clutched from out
        Those fair Elysian fields,
    With weeds and broken stems, in haste,
        Doth make the rabble rout
                That waste
        The day he yields.

And here I bloom for a short hour unseen,
        Drinking· my juices up,
    With no root in the land
        To keep my branches green,

But stand
In a bare cup.
— Henry David Thoreau

WHO AM I?

My head knocks against the stars.
My feet are on the hilltops.
My finger-tips are in the valleys and shores of universal life.
Down in the sounding foam of primal things I reach my hands and play
with pebbles of destiny.

I have been to hell and back many times.
I know all about heaven, for I have talked with God.
I dabble in the blood and guts of the terrible.
I know the passionate seizure of beauty
And the marvelous rebellion of man at all signs reading "Keep Off."

My name is Truth and I am the most elusive captive in the universe.
— Carl Sandburg

Notebook

LEVEL ONE

1. Select your best draft of each poem in your "Work in Progress" file and circle the words or lines that contain your epiphany. On a separate sheet of paper, type the title of your draft, the first line, the line(s) containing your epiphany, and the last line. Example:

Title: The Brevity and Permanence of Snow
First Line: All night, as I lay in the spare room
Epiphanies: I want to whisper, we are alive. We feel the same
Love for the other. . . .
Last line: Or melt like beauty and be gone

The first, last and epiphany line(s) are the key elements of any poem. Meaning should somehow be reflected or enhanced by the title. In the outline above, the first words of the first line — "All night" — play off the title, and the rest of the line grounds the reader as it should with a suspense title. The lines conveying the epiphanies enhance the poem with a love theme whose message, again, is *love can be as cold or as fleeting as snow.* The final line echoes that truth. In sum, the title succeeds.

Of course, the epiphany and truth of each poem will differ. But analyze these key elements and apply lessons learned in this chapter until you are satisfied with your descriptive, suspense or label title.

2. Select three ideas from your "Idea File" and do a first draft for each according to these methods:

• Write the final title first and then the draft.
• Create a working title first and then the draft.
• Compose the draft first and then the title.

In your journal, discuss which method was the most/least effective for you.

LEVEL TWO

1. Analyze the titles of the best drafts in your "Work in Progress" file and determine whether you are satisfied with them. If not, revise according to methods explained in this chapter.

2. If you haven't done the reading exercises (analyzing the use of titles in magazines, prizewinning collections and the Norton anthology), do them now.

3. Read the passage in your journal from the Level One, Exercise Two. Identify the method of title writing that was *least* effective for you. Now select three ideas from your "Idea File" and employ that method again. Once more, write about the experience in your journal, discussing why you may be having trouble or how you overcame the trouble composing via this method.

LEVEL THREE

1. Analyze the titles of the best drafts in your "Work in Progress" file and determine whether you are satisfied with them. If not, revise according to methods explained in this chapter.

2. Read the passage in your journal concerning the Level Two, Exercise Three. If you are still experiencing problems composing titles by this method, again select three ideas from your "Idea File" and compose titles according to the troublesome method. If you have overcome problems with that method, return to the journal passage concerning the Level One, Exercise Two. You should have described the method that was most/least effective for you. Eliminate these methods. You should have one remaining method. Take three more ideas from your "Idea File" and compose drafts according to that method.

Chapter Twelve

Meter

I fell in love with poetry because of meter. When I was a boy, my mother read lyrics by the great English poets to lull me to sleep at night. She had been given an anthology of "immortal" poems by her eighth grade teacher and cherished the book. By the time I was in the eighth grade, I had read every poem in the collection. Included was "The Bells" by Edgar Allan Poe, a stanza of which is quoted below. I would read the poem—*chant* is a better word—with my nine-year-old sister Lori, and soon this became a rainy-day game with us. We would huddle in her bedroom on the floor with the book and read the poem slowly at first, building up speed with each line until our voices rose finally into one amazingly rapid *rap*:

> Keeping time, time, time
> In a sort of Runic rhyme,
> To the throbbing of the bells —
> Of the bells, bells, bells —
> To the sobbing of the bells: —
> Keeping time, time, time
> As he knells, knells, knells,
> In a happy Runic rhyme,
> To the rolling of the bells —
> Of the bells, bells, bells: —
> To the tolling of the bells —
> Of the bells, bells, bells, bells,
> Bells, bells, bells —
> To the moaning and the groaning of the bells.

When my sister and I finished the poem, we would burst out laughing, exhilarated and exhausted by Poe's chiming bells. We were as proud as any siblings double jump-roping in the city streets. (By the way, you also can jump rope to "The Bells.") You can rap to it, too, thanks to *meter*—the rhythm or cadence that you hear in a poem.

Learning meter should be easy. The hardest part, it seems, is overcoming fear of the strange words—anapest, iamb, etc.—that describe certain sounds or rhythms. The good news is that English has a natural rhythm. So if you use a natural voice in your poems, as described in chapter eight, chances are your lines will convey a pleasing cadence. In fact, English sentences often fall into an "iambic pentameter" beat. Don't let those words scare or impress you. An *iamb* is simply a two-syllable word (or two one-syllable words) with the inflection on the last syllable, as in "toDAY" or "a DAY." If you designate those words with the symbols for a light or *unaccented* stress (ˇ) and for a hard or *accented* stress (´), those words would be marked "tŏdáy" and "ă dáy." Each iamb, or pair of light and hard syllables, equals a "foot." *Pentameter* means five pairs of such sounds, or five "feet."

If you marked off each foot with this symbol (|), an iambic pentameter line would look like this: " | Ĭ thóught | yŏu sáid | yŏu tóok | ă bús | tŏdáy. | "

English, though mainly iambic in tone, is a rich language. It borrows words from other tongues, so variations in inflection are bound to occur. That's why you want to familiarize yourself with all the possible sounds and rhythms you can employ in poems.

When we speak of meter in poetry, usually we mean two things:

- A *regular* rhythm—a sound that you can tap your feet to—like music.
- An *accentual-syllabic* rhythm—a sound that takes into account the number of accents (or hard stresses) along with the number of syllables in each line.

Let's look at the history behind the term *accentual-syllabic*.

We inherit accentual meter from our old German and English influences. Centuries ago, poets simply counted the number of accents and usually employed alliteration—words beginning with the same letter—to mark off time, as in:

The Roman retreated on the road,
Vanquished by the victorious Vandal,
Banished in battle, broken,
Shields in shards, severed,
Longing to lie in his land.

Likewise we inherit syllabic sounds from Romance languages that influenced English in the past. (Asian poetry also is heavily syllabic.) Let's cast the above stanza into lines using the same number of syllables, to illustrate this type of meter:

The Ro-man re-treat-ed on the road,
Van-quished by vic-tor-i-ous Van-dals,
Ban-ished now in bat-tle, and bro-ken,

His shield in so man-y shards, sever-ed,
As he longed to lie down in his land.

As your ear becomes more attuned to slight variations in sound, you'll begin to see the problems with accentual and syllabic meter. Accentual meter is too unnatural-sounding in modern English. (Who deliberately speaks with words that begin with the same letter?) Syllabic meter, on the other hand, is extraordinarily subtle. (Who can claim that all four of the syllables in a word like *victorious* are equal in duration or importance?)

Accentual-syllabic meter, perfected in the Elizabethan era, is inherited from ancient Greek poetry. Unlike Anglo accentual or Romantic syllabic meters, classical meter conforms better to modern speech inflections and tightens the standard line for more impact on the ear. To illustrate, let's rewrite that same stanza about the beaten Roman, using traditional meter (along with standard symbols for light and hard stresses and traditional feet):

Whĕn thĕe Ró-	măn ă-bán-	dŏned hĭs róads
Aňd sŭrrén-	dĕred, thĕe Ván-	dăls pŭrsúed;
Thĕe ĭmpér-	ĭăl afm-	ŏr ĭn shárds
Aňd thĕe árt-	ĕrĭes śev-	eřed, hĕe loňged
Tŏ lĭe dówn	ĭn thĕe pás-	tŭres ŏf hóme.

As you can see, the above stanza eliminates much of the alliteration and subtlety of the earlier versions. Yet it has a distinct beat like accentual meter and equal number of syllables per line like syllabic meter. The beat is derived from the hard stress of words as they normally would be pronounced in English, and the syllable count occurs automatically because a certain tone is repeated. As such, classic meter works almost like a measure in music. (The word *meter*, by the way, comes from the Greek word for "measure.")

To help simplify the basics of accentual-syllabic meter, I've composed an outline below. Study it if you have never learned formal meter, or review it if you know formal meter but want to brush up on the basics.

METER PRIMER

Prosody, or the study of meter, is more complex than outlined here. But these are the basics that poets need to compose formal verse, to smooth lines of free and formal verse, or to enhance meaning with meter.

How to Scan

The word *scan* means "analyze a poem to determine its meter." If you have never scanned before, follow this method:

1. Read the lines of a poem aloud a number of times until you can feel or sense a rhythm.
2. Mark the unaccented (˘) and accented (´) stresses of each word in the poem.
3. Identify the sound(s) employed most often in the poem.
4. Mark off each sound with the symbol (|) to designate feet per line. (Consult the section below to identify the various types.)
5. Combine the name of the sound with the name that represents the number of feet per line . . . and you will have determined the meter.

Types of Sounds

These are the primary combinations of light and hard stresses that make up accentual-syllabic meter:

Iamb (pronounced *ī-am*): One word or two monosyllabic words with a light/hard stress as in "tŏdáy" or "ă dáy." (This sound is conversational, a workhorse of the English language.)

Trochee (*trō-kē*): One word or two monosyllabic words with a hard/light stress as in "tímĭng" or "tíme mĕ." (This sound adds emphasis, typically varying the iambic beat at the start of a line, or after a comma or other punctuation mark *within* a line. When used repeatedly in a line, it has an incantation tone.)

Anapest (*an' -a-pest*): One word or a combination of words yielding two light stresses followed by a hard stress as in "vĭllănélle" or "ĭn ă fórm." (The anapest has a tripping sound and usually quickens the pace of a poem.)

Dactyl (*dak' -til*): One word or a combination of words yielding one hard stress followed by two light stresses as in "cálĕndăr" or "príŏr tŏ." (The dactyl varies the anapest in the same manner that the trochee varies the iamb. When used repeatedly in a line, the dactyl has a more grotesque incantation effect.)

Types of Variants

Meter analysis, or *scansion*, is an inexact science. For instance, one-syllable words may be light or hard, according to the preferred meter. One person may hear or pronounce a word differently from another person, as in "hăráss" or "hárăss" or "háráss."

To adjust for pronunciation, poets employ two basic variants:

Pyrrhic (*pir' -ik*): Two light syllables usually (but not always) occurring at the end of a line: " | wĕ héar | thĕ soúnds | ŏf | vói- | cĕs éch- | ŏĭng" with the final *oing* as the pyrrhic. (Note: When a pyrrhic ends a line, as above, the poet may count it as a complete foot or disregard it, depending on the desired meter.)

Spondee (*spon' -dē*): Two hard syllables usually (but not always)

following a pyrrhic: " | th̃e sóunds | ŏf vói- | cĕs sígh- | iñg fŏr- | évér | "
with the *ever* as the spondee. (Note: When a spondee follows a pyrrhic
and ends a line, as above, the poet *must* count the pyrrhic and the spondee as two feet.)

   Other Variants: Less common alternate sounds are the *amphimacer (am-fim' -e-ser)* — hard/light/hard stress, as in the word *várĭánt)* —
and *amphibrach (am' -fe-brak)* — light/hard/light stress, as in the word
ĕnjámbmĕnt. Although the practice is discouraged, some poets claim
the last hard stress of an amphimacer or the last light one of an amphibrach is *hypermetric* (beyond the measure) or *truncated* (below the
measure), as needed, at the end of a line. Hypermetric syllable(s) are
not counted but truncated ones are.

   Here are some examples:

- *Hypermetric*:
  | th̃is fóur | bĕat líne | ĕxclúdes | várĭ- | ~~ants~~
  | th̃is fŏur| bĕat líne | ĕxclúdes | ĕnjámb- | ~~ment~~
- *Truncated*:
  | th̃is fíve | bĕat líne | ĭnclúdes | várĭ- | ánts |
  | th̃is fíve | bĕat líne | ĭnclúdes | ĕnjámb- | mĕnt |

Types of Feet

   One iamb, trochee, anapest, dactyl, pyrrhic or spondee equals *one
foot*. If you use one foot per line, you are writing *monometer* as in
" | ẃe wrĭte | / | tíñy | / | p̃oĕms | / | bút ŭe | / | névĕr/ | / | públĭsh | / |
áný | / | óf thĕm. | " Here are other meters (note the use of trochee):

   Dimeter: two feet per line as in " | ẃe wrĭte | tíñy | / | p̃oĕms | bút
ŭe | / | névĕr | públĭsh | / | áný | óf thĕm. | "

   Trimeter: three feet per line as in " | wé wrĭte | tíñy | p̃oĕms | / |
ánd ŭe | séldŏm | públĭsh| / | áný | óf thĕm | qúicklý. | "

   Tetrameter: four feet per line as in " | wé wrĭte | stándărd | p̃oĕms
| ánd ŭe | / | óftĕn | públĭsh | ṁaňy | óf thĕm. | "

   Pentameter: five feet per line as in " | wé wrĭte | stándaŕd | p̃oĕms
| aṅd ŭe | óftĕn | / | públĭsh | ṁaňy | óf thĕm | aṅd wĭn | cóntešts. | "

   Hexameter: six feet per line as in " | ẃe wrĭte | loñğer | p̃oĕms |
aṅd ŭe | séldŏm | públĭsh | / | ṁaňy | óf thĕm | ánd wĭn | ṁonĕy | ín
ă | cóntĕst. | "

   Heptameter: seven feet per line as in " | ẃe wrĭte | réal lŏng |
p̃oĕms | aṅd ŭe | rárĕly | públĭsh | áný | / | óf thĕm | iṅ ă | lítĕr- | árý
| mágă- | ziñe oř | jóurnăl. | "

   Octameter: eight feet per line as in " | ẃe wrĭte | p̃oĕms | ẃith
sŭch | lóng lĭnes | th̃at ŭe | ñevĕr | públĭsh | áný | / | iṅ ă | wéll-knŏwn
| líttlĕ | mágă- | zíne ŏr | ácă- | deṁĭc | jóurnăl. | "

Types of Meter

To determine the meter for your poem, do a scansion (according to the methods explained at the beginning of "Meter Primer"). In other words, read each line of your poem and mark each iamb, trochee, anapest, dactyl, pyrrhic or spondee. Count them and then designate the feet per line. Combine the predominant sound with the feet per line, and you will have identified the meter.

To practice, scan this excerpt of an Emerson poem:

> By the rude bridge that arched the flood,
> Their flag to April's breeze unfurled,
> Here once the embattled farmers stood
> And fired the shot heard round the world.

(Note: Answer provided in the Level One notebook exercise at the end of this chapter.)

METER AND MEANING

When should you use regular meter in a poem? If you decide that you only want to compose formal verse (see part three), then most of your work should be metered. If you decide that you only want to compose free verse (see chapter seventeen), you should understand meter nonetheless because you may want to employ a certain type of sound in your poem. As we learned earlier in the chapter on voice, sound enhances meaning.

Let's see how meter does.

To illustrate, I've composed a poem featuring two people talking on the telephone, going through all the phases of a typical argument:

THE CONVERSION

I. *Iamb: Rising Meter, for Conversation*

"Hello?"
"I want to talk."
"Will wonders ever cease?
"I won't apologize, you know."
"I don't have anything to say to you."

II. *Trochee: Falling Meter, for Emphasis*
"Later."
"*Don't* hang up yet."
"Like I said I won't a-" —
"If you don't then I will leave you."
"-pologize until I'm good and ready."

III. *Anapest: Tripping Meter, for Excitement*
"Eat a rock."
"Do you think we can talk?"
"Don't you *dare* condescend anymore!"
"Do you think we can talk without fighting awhile?"
"Not unless you apologize, buddy. Take back what you said."

IV. *Dactyl: Awkward Meter, for Grotesqueness*
"Sorry then."
"*What* are you sorry for?"
"Calling you. Hating you. Loving you."
"Never accuse me again of dishonesty."
"How could you blame me when my lines were lifted verbatim?"

V. *Spondee: Hard Meter, for Stress*
"STU-PID!"
"PO-ET-AST-ER!"
"A-POL-O-GIZE RIGHT NOW!"
"I CAN'T BE-LIEVE YOU STOLE MY LINES!"
"I CAN'T BE-LIEVE I MAR-RIED YOU, YOU CREEP!"

VI. *Pyrrhic: Soft Meter, to Soothe*
"sorry."
"why do we fight?"
"oh we fight when we write."
"why don't you hang up and come home?"
"i plan to soon as i write this poem."

Now let's see how these precepts hold up when applied to actual poems.

Below are excerpts from two poems—the first by Emily Brontë and the second by Anne Brontë. I'll scan each work and then make some observations about meter and meaning:

TO IMAGINATION

Whĕn wéa-	r̆y wíth	thĕe lóng	dăy's cáre,
Ănd eárth-	lў chánge	frŏm paín	tŏ páin,
Ănd lóst	ănd réa-	dў tó	dĕspáir,
Thў kińd	vŏice cálls	mĕ báck	ăgáin:
Ŏ, mу́	trŭe fríend!	Ĭ ám	ñot lóne,
Whĭle thóu	cañst spéak	wĭth súch	ă tóne!

Sŏ hópe-	lĕss ís	thĕe wórld	wĭthoút;
Thĕe wórld	wĭthín	Ĭ doúb-	lў príze;
Thў wofld,	whĕre guíle,	ănd háte,	ănd doúbt,
Ănd cóld	sŭspíc-	iŏn név-	ĕr ríse;

| Whĕre thóu, | aňd I, | aňd Líb- | ĕrtý, |
| Hăve ún- | dĭspút- | ĕd sóv- | erĕigntý. |

(Meter: iambic tetrameter)

LINE COMPOSED IN A WOOD ON A WINDY DAY

M̆y sóul	ĭs ăwák-	ĕned, m̆y spír-	ĭt ĭs sóar-	iňg,
Aňd cár-	riĕd ălóft	ŏn tȟe wiňgs	ŏf tȟe bréeze;
Fŏr, ăbóve,	aňd ăroúnd	m̆e, tȟe wíld	wĭnd ĭs róar-	iňg
Ăróus-	iňg tŏ ráp-	tŭre tȟe éarth	aňd tȟe séas.

Tȟe lóng	wĭthĕred ģrass	ĭn tȟe sún-	shȟine ĭs glánc-	ĭng,
Tȟe báre	tȟrees aȟre tóss-	iňg tȟeir bȟranch-	ĕs ŏn hĭgh;
Tȟhe déad	leăves bĕnéath	tȟem ăre mér-	rĭly̆ dánc-	iňg,
Tȟe w̆hite	clŏuds ăre sćud-	dĭng ăcróss	tȟe blŭe sky̆.

(Meter: anapestic tetrameter)

Discussion: Although both excerpts are in tetrameter, the sound is different in each. Emily Brontë employs the iamb because her poem is a meditation. She focuses clearly on an idea: Imagination (or her inner world) helps her cope with the realities of the outer world. Conversely, Anne Brontë employs the tripping sound of the anapest to augment the topic: wind. Her lyric has no great truth to explore; instead, she captures our imagination with sound. (Even her hypermetric endings — those falling tones on the first and third lines of each stanza — combine with iambs at the beginning of the second and fourth lines of each stanza, effectively making more anapests.)

As you can see, the meaning of each poem is enhanced by sound.

Watch what happens when I recompose their verses, switching the meter so that Emily Brontë's poem employs anapests and Anne Brontë's poem, iambs:

> When I weary of everyday trouble and care,
>   And I swing from a feeling of joy to deep pain,
> And grow lost, and am ready too quick to despair
>   Then thy kind lulling voice calls me back once again:
> O my true faithful friend! I am not so alone,
> While thou canst speak to me using such a full tone!

> When the hopeless realities of the harsh earth
>   Oft intrude on the one that I thoroughly prize;
> When the hate and the doubt overshadow my worth,
>   And the cold of suspicion in me doth arise;
> I withdraw, and within I find Liberty rare,
> And imagine a realm of enlightenment there.

My soul awakes, my spirit soars
  Aloft on wings of morning breeze;
Above, around, the wild wind roars,
  Arouses rapture of the seas.

The withered grass in sun may glance,
  The trees may toss their branches high;
The leaves beneath them also dance,
  When clouds are scudding cross the sky.

Each excerpt is weaker because the sound of the meter does not harmonize with the subject matter, as musical instruments must harmonize with singers. The anapests of the rewritten Emily Brontë poem cheapen the meditation because the tripping sound distracts us from focusing on her idea. (Imagine a polka band accompanying an opera star singing a requiem, and you'll understand what I mean!) On the other hand, the serious tone of the iamb changes the meaning of the rewritten Anne Brontë poem about wind. It makes her lines sound almost dirgelike, as if something ominous will happen in the woods. (Now imagine a philharmonic accompanying a pop star chanting a rap!) In each case, the sound of the meter undermined the meaning.

To see how other master poets use meter:

• Research issues of magazines published between 1900 and 1950 (*Poetry*, founded in 1912, is available at most libraries) and scan the poems, evaluating how meter and sound harmonize with subject matter.

• Purchase or check out collections of formal poetry from the library and do a scansion on each poem, again evaluating the effects of meter and sound on subject matter in long individual works by at least three different authors.

• Page through the Norton anthology, scanning at least one poem from each author listed in the table of contents.

For the mini anthology, I've selected poems whose sound and meter are aligned with subject matter:

• "A Cradle Song" by W.B. Yeats. Consider how the dimeter, combined with the alternating light/hard stresses and tripping sounds of iambs and anapests, might approximate a cradle's rocking to lull a child to sleep.

• "Now" by Robert Browning. See how the grotesqueness of his dactyls and trochees in the beginning lines burst into anapests and spondees in this passionate sonnet variation. (Note: The four-beat meter deviates from the usual pentameter of the form, condensing the

sense of time and implying an inability to achieve song.)
  • "Mowing" by Robert Frost. Note how the iambic pentameter
mimics the movement of the hand-held blade, swinging with a regular
rhythm (iambs) in some lines and moving more easily (anapests) or
more slowly (dactyls, trochees) over other patches.

  In this and other poems included here, meter is the driving force
behind the scythe of the poet.

Mini Anthology of Meter Poems

A CRADLE SONG

The angels are stooping
Above your bed;
They weary of trooping
With the whimpering dead.

God's laughing in heaven
To see you so good;
The Shining Seven
Are gay with His mood.

I kiss you and kiss you,
My pigeon, my own;
Ah, how I shall miss you
When you have grown.

                              — W.B. Yeats

NOW

Out of your whole life give but a moment!
All of your life that has gone before,
All to come after it, — so you ignore,
So you make perfect the present, — condense,
In a rapture of rage, for perfection's endowment,
Thought and feeling and soul and sense —
Merged in a moment which gives me at last
You around me for once, you beneath me, above me —
Me — sure that despite of time future, time past, —
This tick of our life-time's one moment you love me!
How long such suspension may linger? Ah, Sweet —
The moment eternal — just that and no more —
When ecstasy's utmost we clutch at the core
While cheeks burn, arms open, eyes shut and lips meet!
                              — Robert Browning

MOWING

There was never a sound beside the wood but one,
And that was my long scythe whispering to the ground.
What was it it whispered? I knew not well myself;
Perhaps it was something about the heat of the sun,
Something, perhaps, about the lack of sound —
And that was why it whispered and did not speak.
It was no dream of the gift of idle hours,
Or easy gold at the hand of fay or elf:
Anything more than the truth would have seemed too weak
To the earnest love that laid the swale in rows,
Not without feeble-pointed spikes of flowers
(Pale orchises), and scared a bright green snake.
The fact is the sweetest dream that labor knows.
My long scythe whispered and left the hay to make.
                                        — Robert Frost

Notebook

LEVEL ONE

1. Here's the answer to the scansion of Emerson's poem:

Bў thĕ	rúde brídge	thăt arćhed	thĕ flóod,
Thĕir flág	tŏ Aṕ-	rĭl's bréeze	ŭnfúrled,
Hére onće	thĕ ĕmbát-	tlĕd fárm-	eřs stóod
Aňd fíred	thĕ sĥot	hĕard róund	thĕ woŕld.

The above excerpt of "Concord Hymn" has thirteen iambs, one pyrrhic, one spondee and one anapest. Emerson uses four feet per line. If you combine the sound with the feet, you should have identified his meter as *iambic tetrameter*.

2. Select the best drafts of three poems from your "Work in Progress" file. If you have composed free verse, recast your poems in a regular meter (without worrying about rhyme). If you have rhymed and metered your work already, chose another meter and compose another version. Compare versions and discuss results in your journal.

3. Consult your "Idea File" for at least three ideas for poems involving some sort of movement — the arc of a swing in autumn, say, or the kick of a fired pistol — and compose first drafts, choosing the appropriate sound and meter to enhance the subject matter. (If you do not have three such ideas, conceive three now and compose first drafts according to methods explained above.)

LEVEL TWO

1. If you haven't done the scanning exercises (using issues of older magazines, books of formal verse and the Norton anthology), do them now.

2. Select at least three ideas from your "Idea File" and compose drafts of each idea in monometer, dimeter, trimeter, tetrameter and pentameter. Compare versions and choose the best draft of each idea, discussing the process in your journal.

LEVEL THREE

1. Review your journal entries from exercises in Level One and Two. Discuss what you have come to believe about meter. For instance, how have you used it to enhance content? To accompany voice? Epiphany? How can you improve these aspects of your work? Come up with specific suggestions that address your strong and weak points concerning meter.

2. Choose three ideas from your "Idea File" that would best suit your *weak* points concerning meter. For instance, if you have trouble using meter to accompany voice, select ideas — concerning extranatural themes, say — whose success depends largely on voice. Then choose the sound and meter to harmonize with each specific idea and attempt to turn your individual weakness concerning meter into a strength.

Chapter Thirteen

Rhyme

I f you bought this book because you love poetry and want to compose it, chances are you already know about rhyme — at least from a typical reader's perspective. Doesn't everyone? As children, we are enthralled by words that sound the same and laugh at all those *Horton Hears a Who* or *The Cat in the Hat* rhymes by Dr. Seuss. Or we memorize Mother Goose rhymes and sing along. Then, in elementary school, we try our own hand at rhyming poems, usually finishing the ditty "Roses Are Red, Violets Are Blue" with something sweet or clever: "I love my mother/And she loves me too!" or "Flamingoes are pink/And live in the zoo!" Soon we encounter our first serious poems in middle school, and they almost always rhyme, from Edgar Allan Poe's "The Raven" to Robert Frost's "Stopping by Woods on a Snowy Evening." Finally, in high school, we meet and memorize Shakespeare and attempt to pen our first sonnet — rhyming fourteen lines according to a predetermined scheme. Thereafter some of us decide to keep reading and writing poetry . . . and others vow *never* to touch the stuff again!

But, no matter how we feel about poetry, we all associate rhyme with it.

There is more to rhyme, though, than choosing words with exact or approximate sounds and tacking them on the ends of lines. Used in such manner, all rhyme does is help the poet end a line so he or she can hurry to the next one, without caring much about the effect the rhyme is having on the poem proper.

Rhyme is capable of accomplishing much more. Not only can it help shape a work, it also can:

- Enhance the sound of a poem.
- Combine with meter to add melody to a beat.
- Augment the meaning of a poem.
- Set the mood for the content.

To illustrate the power of rhyme, here is a sentence in prose, free verse, meter, meter and slant rhyme (approximate-sounding but unrhyming last syllables), meter and rhyme, and meter and double rhyme (two or more ending syllables that rhyme):

(Prose)

Since the dawn of time, people tap fingers and toes to music. It seems we are pentadactylic for a reason.

(Free Verse)

We are pentadactylic. We tap toes and fingers for a reason.

(Meter)

Mortals mark time on their fingers and toes,
Humming the mantras of Adam and Eve.

(Slant Rhyme and Meter)

We are pentadactylic, as everyone knows,
Marking off meter according to laws.

(Rhyme and Meter)

We are pentadactylic, as everyone knows,
Marking off meter with fingers and toes.

(Double Rhyme and Meter)

Adam and Eve were made pentadactylic.
Only a snake would find *that* idyllic.

As you can see, each time the rhyme combines with meter or changes mode, the sound of the couplet also changes, even though the meaning of the words basically remains the same: an observation about the human having five fingers on each hand and five toes on each foot. In each version, we can sense how sound — especially rhyme — affects or shades that meaning. The slant rhyme and meter version, for instance, has a slight tension to it, whereas the double rhyme and meter version has a comic element. The power of rhyme is even greater than illustrated above, depending on the sound, placement and emphasis given to words whose vowels and consonants blend to produce certain effects in poems.

Let's study them.

RHYMER PRIMER
As in the previous chapter on meter, I have devised an outline to cover the principles of rhyme:

How to Designate Rhyme

Rhyme schemes are cast in italicized codes, like this one for a Shakespearean fourteen-line sonnet: *abab cdcd efef gg*. To decipher that code, you need to know these basics:

• To indicate rhyme, designate the last word of each line with a letter of the alphabet. Lines whose last words share the same rhyme also share the same letter. For instance, this quick poem would be shown as *aa:*

Let the words at the end of a *line*
Take letters that you should *assign*

• To add a new rhyme, use the *next* letter of the alphabet. This poem's pattern would be shown as *ababcc:* —

Let the word at the end of a *line*
No matter how short or how *long*
Take letters that you should *assign*
In the pattern in which they *belong*
And then you will know how to *chart*
The requisite craft to make *art*.

• To designate a stanza, insert a space between the letters, as in this version, indicated as *ab ab cc*:

Let the word at the end of a *line*
No matter how short or how *long*

Take letters that you should *assign*
In the pattern in which they *belong*

And then you will know how to *chart*
The requisite craft to make *art*.

Types of Sounds

Here are the primary tones of rhyme and their effects on the content of a poem:

• *Full* or *True Rhyme*: The juxtaposition of exact-sounding vowels and consonants in two or more words located at the ends of different lines in a poem. This type of rhyme is the workhorse of formal poetry and lends a clarity or conciseness to lines.

Sure thou didst flourish once! and many *springs*,
Many bright mornings, much dew, many *showers*
Passed o'er thy head; many light hearts and *wings*,
Which now are dead, lodged in thy living *bowers*.
                                    — Henry Vaughan

• *Slant* or *Near Rhyme*: The juxtaposition of two or more words with approximate-sounding vowels or consonants at the ends of different lines in a poem. This type of rhyme causes a feeling of uneasiness or tension in a poem, especially when it appears in a short line.

The Bustle in a House
The Morning after *Death*
Is solemnest of industries
Enacted upon *Earth*. . . .
— Emily Dickinson

• *Double* or *Multiple Rhyme*: The juxtaposition of two or more approximate- or exact-sounding vowels or consonants in two or more words, usually found at the ends of lines in a poem. This type of rhyme startles the reader with an unanticipated sound, almost always humorous.

(Double Approximate Rhyme)

A strange Erratum in all the Editions
Of Sir Joshua Reynolds' *Lectures*
Should be corrected by the Young Gentlemen
And the Royal Academy's *Directors*
— William Blake

(Multiple Exact Rhyme)

About binomial theorem I'm teeming with *a lot o' news* —
With many cheerful facts about the square of the *hypotenuse.*
— W.S. Gilbert

• *Rising* or *Masculine Rhyme*: A full-rhyming word that ends on a hard stress or whose exact-sounding last syllable does. This type of rhyme produces a strong beat and emphasizes the sound of a word.

As from the darkening gloom a silver *dove*
Upsoars, and darts into the Eastern *light,*
On pinions that naught moves but pure de*light;*
So fled thy soul into the realms *above*; . . .
— John Keats

• *Falling* or *Feminine Rhyme*: A full-rhyming word that ends on a light stress or whose exact-sounding last syllable does. This type of rhyme adds a soothing, echoing or humorous tone, depending on the poem in question.

And after April, when May *follows,*
And the whitethroat builds, and all the *swallows!*
Hark, where my blossomed pear-tree in the hedge

Leans to the field and scatters on the *clover*
Blossoms and dewdrops — at the bent spray's edge —
That's the wise thrush; he sings each song twice *over*, ...
				— Robert Browning

Types of Placement

Rhymes can occur anywhere in a line. Here are basic placements and their effects in a poem:

• *End-Stopped Rhyme*: A rhyme word followed with a punctuation mark, usually a comma or a period. This type of placement helps shape the line as a unit, giving it a crisp feel. It also calls attention to the rhyme word, emphasizing its meaning and its music.

Look back with longing eyes and know that I will follow,
Lift me up in your love as a light wind lifts a swallow,
Let our flight be far in sun or blowing rain —
But what if I heard my first love calling me again?
				— Sara Teasdale

• *Enjambment* or *Run-On Rhymes*: A rhyme word not followed by a punctuation mark. This type of placement de-emphasizes the line as a unit and the sound of the rhyme so the content may continue without interruption, producing a tripping, breathless or rambling tone.

And I wish that the baby would tack across here to me
Like a wind-shadow running on a pond, so she could stand
With two little bare white feet upon my knee
And I could feel her feet in either hand

Cool as syringa buds . . .
				— D.H. Lawrence

• *Internal Rhyme*: Two or more words whose vowels and/or conso- nants make approximate or exact sounds or rhymes on the same line. (Note: When a certain vowel is repeated at the beginning or within unrhyming words in a line, *assonance* is produced, as in "a *su*dden *hu*mming *u*nder stars." When a certain consonant is repeated at the beginning or within unrhyming words in a line, *consonance* occurs: "a *s*udden *s*ummer of *s*unflowers.")

Here are lines illustrating internal rhyme and slant rhyme, respec- tively, from Wordsworth's "Stanzas." This type of placement produces more music, making an entire line melodious instead of the ending word, and as such adds yet another layer of sound, especially when combined with meter.

As pleased as if the same had *been* a Maiden-*queen*

For never *sun* on living creatures *shone*

Now that we have covered the basics of several types of rhyme, let's proceed to how you can invent them for your poems.

How to Use a Rhyming Dictionary

Many contemporary poets will tell you never to use a rhyming dictionary because it becomes a crutch. You end up needing it after the first two lines, and then, it seems, the dictionary *dictates* one absurd line after the other:

THE DYNAMO

At Yellowstone I saw a geyser
spew its water in the air,
this was but an appetizer;

the park attendant, debonair,
saw me wearing polyester,
knew at once that I was lost;

how'd he guess my name was Esther?
Then I saw the name embossed
On the tag the park required

When I drove here. (I'm retired.)
He explained what rangers know:
Geysers steam before they blow!

As you can see, if used in this manner, the rhyming dictionary composes mostly nonsense. You begin a work wanting to capture the essence of a natural wonder and end up as Esther wearing polyester. To counter that effect, poets often are discouraged from using such dictionaries and told to think up rhymes in their heads, using the alphabet and imagination.

I've composed dozens of formal poems this way, and it works — after a while. In the beginning, however, a novice poet just cannot conceive enough rhyme words to complete a poem; worse, he or she is spending energy concentrating on the invention of rhyme instead of on the invention of a poem. That's like trying to remember how to spell every word in the first draft of an essay, instead of focusing on the *ideas* you want to convey.

In a word, using a rhyming dictionary unwisely, or trying to remember rhymes while you are writing poems, damages the creative process. Chances are your rhymes will maul meter and devour ideas. The solution, however, is not to shun rhyme or rhyming dictionaries, but to use both appropriately.

I use a rhyming dictionary to help me compose formal work, but I remain in control of the creative process. Before I write, I have a good idea what I want to express because—like you—I keep an idea file and outline a poem (as described in chapter one). Here's a sample from my files:

11/5/85
I want to write a love poem with rhyming stanzas.
Rhyme and meter will become part of a game that
the narrator plays to forget about unrequited love.
I should call it "The Art of Amnesia"!

In my first draft, I decided to use a type of poem called terza rima, which features stanzas with interlocking rhymes according to this scheme—*aba bcb cdc ded*—and so on, for as long as a poet needs to convey an idea. For starters, I concentrated on coming up with strong opening lines:

Maybe if I write this out, give it up
To gears of meter, caesura, and rhyme. . . .

I stopped there. I felt that I had two strong rhyme words and opened my dictionary to look up entries under *up* and *rhyme*. Here is an abbreviated list of what I found:

Up: cup, pup, sup, hiccup, makeup, setup, teacup, etc.
Rhyme: chime, clime, crime, dime, I'm, prime, time, etc.

I circled *cup*, *sup* and *setup* to rhyme with *up* and *chime*, *I'm* and *time* to rhyme with *rhyme*. Then I contemplated my potential rhyme words and evaluated how each related to content: romantic amnesia. I liked the sound of *cup* and imagined one clanging like the heart— "I will not clang inside like a cup!"—and wrote a few sentences using the word *time*: "I will tap my foot on shards, keeping time" and "I will count the shards, keeping time." As you can see, the lines using the word *time* sounded forced, and I felt myself straining to keep the meaning of my poem clear in my mind. So I abandoned the rhyme word *time* and pondered *I'm*, changing it to *I am* to smooth the meter and slant the rhyme. It worked:

Maybe if I write this out, give it up
To gears of meter, caesura, and rhyme,
I will not clang inside like a cup

Stung by a spoon, cracked by it. I am. . . .

Without consulting the dictionary, I saw the opportunity now to pun *I am* with *iamb*. I kept this word in the back of my mind. The next step was to compose another line without regard to rhyme, to focus again on my subject:

That breakable. My all-important id. . . .

Back to the dictionary again:

Under *-id* I found: *bid, did, grid, hid, kid, lid, mid, slid, squid,* among others. Immediately I was attracted to *lid* to play off *cup* . . . but that was leading me farther away from using *iamb*. So I abandoned *lid* after a few attempts. This is where novice poets usually get stumped, forcing rhyme or allowing the dictionary to take over. Suddenly the poet is either wrenching rhyme to remain true to meaning or wrenching meaning to remain true to rhyme.

When you find yourself in that situation, the solution is to open another reference book: the thesaurus. Using a thesaurus to locate better rhyme words is similar to using one in tandem with a standard dictionary to spell difficult words. For instance, say you want to find the correct spelling of *diverse*, but can't locate it in the dictionary because, alas, you can't spell it. So you think of a synonym: *different*. Under the entry of *different* in the thesaurus, you'll find the correct spelling of *diverse*.

The process is the same with rhyme words a poet cannot locate. In my case, a quick check in the thesaurus under the entry *id* yielded these words: *self, ego, identity, selfhood, personality* and *psyche*. I opened my rhyming dictionary again. Under *self*, I found the word *shelf* and composed a few draft lines, happy that I could use my cup metaphor again by linking it to the concept of meter:

Stung by a spoon, cracked by it. I am
That breakable. Say I time this self-
Consuming prophecy just right with iamb

And measure, lyric and line on a shelf
Beside amphibrachs in a cupboard.

Those lines worked well, but the dilemma now was that the word *self* did not have many rhymes. I needed one more to propel me to the next stanza, and I couldn't find it. In such a situation, you have two options: You can abandon your previous line using the poor rhyming word and start again. (In my case that would mean throwing away my meter/shelf metaphor and using a richer rhyme word, like *identity*.) The other option is to slant rhyme.

Let's take a closer look at the words *self* and *shelf*. The important vowel/consonant sound is *-el*, and under that entry in the rhyming dictionary I found several approximate rhymes, including the one I used: *quell*.

The rest of the poem came easily after that. Using the process described above, I was able to complete my poem with a rhyming dictionary and thesaurus without wrenching sound or changing meaning:

And measure, lyric and line on a shelf
Beside amphibrachs in a cupboard.
Would canon or craft in any way quell

The desire tonight to hold her, hoard
Lover-like the anapest of her heart?
I don't know. So imagine my working toward

Conclusion, the easy denouement, the sort
A reader with a yen for Jung would prove
My kind of broken dish. It is a start,

However dim, for when the triplets move
Leisurely as these, when they weave
Their web among the trinkets of

Formality, at least I forget about love.

Now that you know how to use a rhyming dictionary, let's consider the various patterns you can employ via the stanza and rhyme.

Rhyming Patterns

Of course, you can rhyme lines of a stanza any way you wish. For instance, you can rhyme the first two lines and then alternate the rhymes in the next four lines of a stanza. Such a pattern would be outlined like this: *aabcbc*. Or you can alternate the rhymes of the first four lines and rhyme the last two: *ababcc*. Or design these variations — *abcabc* or *abbcac* or *abccba* — or whatever pleases your fancy (and ear).

Some rhyming patterns have traditional names, such as the interlocking three-line stanzas called *terza rima* mentioned earlier: *aba bcb cdc ded*. Another popular rhyming pattern, usually composed in pentameter, is the seven-line stanza called "rhyme royale": *ababbcc*. Although often mistaken as "form" poems (discussed in chapter nineteen), these are powered by the stanza and, as such, can be as long or short as required to convey a message or idea.

Whether you design your own rhyming pattern, or employ an established one, you should focus on the stanza as a vehicle for sound. To illustrate, let's sample some of the rhyming patterns of Robert Herrick, a seventeenth-century master poet whose melodies can be touchstones for your own:

(Couplet)

The mellow touch of music most doth wound   a
The soule, when it doth rather sigh, then sound.   a

(Triplet)

I do love I know not what;   a
Sometimes this, & sometimes that: a
All conditions I aim at.   a

(Quatrain)

Gather ye rosebuds while ye may   a
   Old Time is still a flying: b
And this same flower that smiles today,   a
   Tomorrow may be dying.   b

(Five-Line Stanza)

Go happy Rose, and interwove   a
With other flowers, bind my love.   a
   Tell her too, she must not be,   b
   Longer flowing, longer free,   b
   That so oft has fetter'd me.   b

(Six-Line Stanza)

Glide gentle streams, and bear   a
Along with you my tear   a
   To that coy girl;   b
   Who smiles, yet slays   c
   Me with delays;   c
And strings my tears as pearls.   b

(Seven-Line Stanza)

   Not all thy flushing suns are set,   a
     Herrick as yet: a
   Nor doth this far-drawn hemisphere   b
   Frown and look sullen, everywhere.   b
Days may conclude in nights; and suns may rest,   c
     As dead, within the West;   c
Yet the next morn, re-guild the fragrant East.   c

(Eight-Line Stanza)

Agyge's Ring they bear about them still,   a
To be, and not be seen when and where they will.   a
They tread on clouds, and though they sometimes fall,   a
They fall like dew, but make no noise at all.   a
So silently they one to th'other come,   b

As colours steal into the pear or plum,   b
And air-like, leave no 'pression to be seen   c
Where e're they met, or parting place has been.   c

These are a few rhyming patterns that Herrick used in his work. You can design dozens of variations of the above stanzas. Keep in mind there is no formula to align a melody with content because both depend on your idea, truth and imagination. As always, the best way to learn about possibilities is to read poems and determine which ones move you most . . . and why.

Toward that end, I have assembled a mini anthology of poems whose use of rhyme is innovative, musical and effective — given the subject matter of each selection:

• "Kismet" by Diane Ackerman. In a sonnet variation about the philosopher Wittgenstein, Ackerman, a poet and an essayist for *The New Yorker*, uses rhyme to enhance her epiphany: *Love speaks in tongues*. Her stanzas are not based on a formal pattern but on a syllogism (a type of logical argument) for an added sense of irony. Note her many ingenious rhymes — "lovers kiss/aurora borealis," "other's mouth/azimuth" — that surprise us, well, like unexpected kisses!

• "Early Brass" by Ronald Wallace. Another sonnet variation, this poem's music resounds with every line. When you read it, focus on the intriguing, unexpected rhymes: "tuxedos/O/bravado's" and "brass/sass/surpass" in the first stanza. Note the enjambment of the first stanza mimicking the sliding sounds of trombones and brass and the second stanza's humorous multiple slant rhymes — "oversized trombone-/altogether un-" and "slapstick recital/Sacbut Ensemble." Also note the end-stopped rhymes in the second stanza, focusing on the slant multiple rhymes as if they were somehow off-key, in keeping with an amateur recital. Finally, study the way the choral last lines of each stanza make the entire poem "a little song" of early brass.

• "The Palace Cafe" by Jim Barnes. We read Barnes's free verse in the chapter on extranatural poetry; in this selection, he uses terza rima to produce an ominous tone. Note how the poet's lines build on each other, working as units; some suggest one meaning when read across and another when read in tandem with the line below. According to Barnes, "Poems that do not employ form are by definition formless." However, Barnes transcends the form of a terza rima, retaining the natural sound of his voice, using slant rhyme for tension, and employing enjambment to forebode the cyclone winds that haunt the town.

• "The Crash" by Frederick Feirstein, a New York City psychoanalyst and Guggenheim fellow for poetry. This poem is part of a dramatic sequence from *Manhattan Carnival* (Countryman, 1981), featuring street scenes from New York and depicting the life of a man who is estranged from his wife. Although this poem can stand alone, consider it an excerpt of a larger work and focus on its rhyme words. For Feirstein, rhyme is a rhythmic device as much as a melodic one. He says, "I find it important to be as original in using rhyme as in using metaphor. Only occasionally will I use one-syllable rhymes, and only when I'm trying for a certain effect." In "The Crash" you'll see how the mostly one-syllable rhymes and end-stopped lines add to the drama and confusion of an accident.

Although each of the above poems is a work of art, I know that rhyme, as a tool of craft, is responsible for it.

Mini Anthology of Rhyme Poems

KISMET

> "What can't be said can't be said,
> and can't be whistled either."
> — Wittgenstein

Wittgenstein was wrong: when lovers kiss
they whistle into each other's mouth
a truth old and sayable as the sun,
for flesh is palace, aurora borealis,
and the world is all subtraction in the end.

The world is all subtraction in the end,
yet, in a small vaulted room at the azimuth
of desire, even our awkward numbers sum.
Love's syllogism only love can test.

But who would quarrel with its sprawling proof?
The daftest logic brings such sweet unrest.
Love speaks in tongues, its natural idiom.
Tingling, your lips drift down the xylophone
of my ribs, and I close my eyes and chime.
                                        — Diane Ackerman

EARLY BRASS

When five balding men in long-tailed tuxedos
rise to the bright occasion, their brass
sacbuts, cornet, and slide trumpet in hand, O
the chansons and canzoni, the madrigals, the sass
they pull out of their bold embouchures! Their bravado's
a coinage of lieder and light so daft
no music could, under sweet heaven, surpass

the New York Cornet & Sacbut Ensemble's.

Yet last night in the lunchroom of Van Hise School,
when my sixth-grade daughter and her oversized trombone—
all silverware, sour milk, and John Philip Sousa—
sashayed on stage at a slapstick recital,
she sounded (by God!) not altogether unlike the New York Cornet & Sacbut Ensemble.
                                        —Ronald Wallace

THE PALACE CAFE

We sit here with our backs to the wall and drink
to all the things we should have done before
Armageddon fell upon this town. We think

we know it well, the mountainous cloud that bore
the very soul away, its winds whipping
roofs away, walls. It took the wives we swore

to God we'd love forever, honor, and sing
the seasons to. And took our sons. And then
our farms. There was total nothing on the wing

but cloud and wind. If we are lucky when
the waitress comes, coffee in hand, she might
say a word that will take our minds up wind

from this stinking town, what's left of it.
But we do not know it well: the changing sky
does not allow forecast. The winds that hit

us in the back that day filled the blank eyes
on the square with debris. The Palace lost
its shade, the window and a rack of pies

gone without a trace. The tornado cost
the Sabre Jet a wing, the park its trees
and tulips that survived the last hard frost.

With all the loss you'd think we'd want to leave
the state. We stay with nothing like we want,
save The Palace where we don't have to serve.
                                        —Jim Barnes

THE CRASH

I hear a crash and turn. A wall of flame
Surrounds a car. I'm hollering your name.

The passersby first freeze, then screaming run.
The burning car is like a loaded gun.
A doorman grabs my belt to hold me back,
"That woman" — Woman! — "must be charcoal black."
I shout, "The cab that hit her . . . over there!"
The doorman pleads, "He doesn't have a prayer!"
I pry the door. He's married to the wheel.
He doesn't look alive. I reach to feel
His pulse. "You nut, get out before it blows!"
The cabbie's life is ebbing from his nose.
"Exhaust pipe's catching fire, hurry up!"
I pull him free and make my palm a cup
To stop his bleeding. Someone hugs his feet.
We lug him way past safety down the street.
  I'm suddenly in Lenox Hill berserk,
Bellowing at an intern, "Hurry, jerk!"
A fire engine's siren tears the air,
Then hundreds more — lunatics at their hair.
The cabbie's face has dribbled into gray.
I squirm from pats and handshakes, storm away.
I won't look back as hoses douse the pyre.
Remember how my greatest fear was fire?
And if I was a hero, would you love me?
At least, Marlene, you'd think much better of me.
— Frederick Feirstein

Notebook

LEVEL ONE

1. Take three drafts of poems from your "Work in Progress" file
and cast them in rhyme according to the precepts in the "Rhymer
Primer" outline and using a rhyming dictionary and thesaurus.
(Note: If your drafts are already rhymed, revise the poems using
new rhymes and you will be composing completely different drafts.)
In each case, compare versions and ask yourself:

- Are the meanings of my poems changing simply to meet the
  rigors of rhyme or am I controlling meaning in my work?
- Am I coming up with new, interesting or unusual rhymes?
- Are the placements of my rhymes enhancing sound and meaning?
- Am I honoring the precepts of line and stanza when I use
  rhyme, or am I simply using rhyme to end a line and the rhyme
  scheme to determine my stanza breaks?

- Is the voice in my poem still aligned with subject matter and epiphany, or am I warping voice by using rhyme?

Discuss these elements of craft in your journal.

2. Review entries under slant rhyme, rising rhyme and falling rhyme in the "Rhymer Primer," studying the effects of each sound. Now select three ideas from your "Idea File" in which each of these rhymes would be appropriate and compose first drafts. (If you lack such ideas, devise them now and compose the drafts.)

LEVEL TWO

1. Do both Level One assignments again with at least three new drafts of poems from your "Work in Progress" file and three ideas for new poems from your "Idea File." Compare this set of poems with your Level One set of rhymed work. Ask yourself:

- Are my rhymed poems improving with each set?
- Am I increasingly in control of my rhymed work?
- Are my rhymes becoming more innovative?
- Has it become easier to honor the precepts of line and stanza when I rhyme?
- Is my voice as natural in rhymed work as in free verse?

Discuss these elements of craft in your journal.

LEVEL THREE

1. Select three ideas from your "Idea File" and compose drafts via rhymed patterns. (Design your own patterns or use terza rima or rhyme royale.)

2. Reread your journal entries for the Level One and Two assignments. Isolate any weaknesses you still have concerning the use of rhyme. Select three more ideas from your "Idea File" and compose drafts focusing on those weaknesses until they become strengths.

PART THREE

Formats and Forms

In this section you will learn about modes and methods of expression, from narrative, lyric and dramatic verse (the traditional formats) to poems in fixed, free and sequence styles (the traditional forms). Chances are, the drafts of poems you composed doing notebook exercises in the previous section fall into one or more of the above categories. Now it's time to study them in depth and improve those drafts, in addition to composing new ones.

Chapter Fourteen

The Narrative Poem

N arrative poems come in all shapes and sizes, but they all have one thing in common: They tell stories. People have been telling stories since the dawn of creation, and the great religious and poetic works reflect this. For instance, a parable is a story. Throughout time, in cultures around the world, the person who tells an enlightened tale has been honored as a priest or visionary with unique powers. Even the word *poet*, used today in conversation, implies that a person has a special gift that distinguishes him or her from other writers.

Children, of course, love stories. Typically, a narrative poem — heard in childhood — ignites the muse within us, so we vow to become poets when we grow up. Such was the case with me upon hearing "Paul Revere's Ride" by Henry Wadsworth Longfellow whose first stanza begins:

Listen, my children, and you shall hear
Of the midnight ride of Paul Revere,
On the eighteenth of April, in Seventy-five;
Hardly a man is now alive
Who remembers that famous day and year.

I can still remember my mother reading that poem to me in our living room, transporting me to the Revolutionary War via Longfellow's tale. Reading it again for this chapter almost thirty-five years later, I am moved more by the memory of narrative verse — and how it inspired me — than by the poem; however, without "Paul Revere's Ride," I might never have been moved to become a poet and share my stories with others.

"Since I was a small child, I have loved to hear a good story," says Jim Peterson whose first book, *The Man Who Grew Silent* (Bench Press, 1989), features several narrative selections. "In fact, I'd rather *hear* a good story than read one. A narrative poem between, say, two and six pages is ideal for oral delivery. It doesn't last so long that the listener loses interest. It is condensed, avoiding the lengthy build-up and detail that novels and even short stories usually require." Peterson observes that a narrative poem usually is stripped to the barest essentials, "the basic actions and transactions of its characters."

Thus, it can pack more punch than fiction.

But many poets (including me) believe that narrative verse has suffered in modern times. Poet Robert Kinsley notes: "It's shameful that we have lost so much in terms of the narratives of our lives. No more real myths in the world, so very few stories that are larger than our immediate selves. I suppose in some ways that's why narrative verse has fallen out of favor in poetry, and with good reason perhaps. Too much of it is so narrow. So little goes beyond the immediacy of the moment."

Two points:

1. When Jim Peterson says that a narrative poem has appeal because it is stripped to its barest essentials, he is talking about structure — the craft involved in making such verse.
2. When Robert Kinsley notes that narrative verse has fallen out of favor because much of it is too narrow, he also is talking about structure — or *lack* of craft involved in making story poems.

True, some people are natural storytellers. They spin their tales and enchant others without stopping to consider how they are able to do this. If they are also poets, they intuit basic elements of a story but, alas, cannot explain why theirs succeed. If you are like most of us, however, sometimes you can tell a good story and sometimes not; thus, by knowing the basic elements of narrative verse, you'll be able to improve your poem or detect why it will succeed or fail — often before you even begin to compose the work.

SIX ELEMENTS OF NARRATIVE VERSE

If you know these elements — topic, theme, voice, viewpoint, moment, ending — and how they affect your story, you'll also be able to envision your narrative and simplify the creative process.

Topic: The subject matter has a beginning, middle and end. (Sometimes the ending comes first, the beginning second and the middle third — or some other combination — but all narratives, however innovative, contain all three.) Moreover, because of such a structure, you'll be able to sense a passage of time: First this happened, then this, and finally this.

To determine whether your topic suits the narrative mode, ask yourself: "What happens?" In every story poem, something has to occur or else you'll end up with a lyric — a work in which the poet fixes or focuses on a moment, feeling or concept. In narrative verse, action is required. But it need not be significant, as this poem by Corrinne Hales illustrates:

HOW IT WORKS

My grandmother picks through
Snapbeans. Her lap full of the best ones,
The ends fall down around her feet.

Holding the basket, I wait
While she empties her apron and sweeps
What's left into a neat pile.

You'll be eating this stuff
Long after I'm gone, she tells me.
It's true. When I was a child

I ate what she and my mother had done
Long before I was born.

Hales's poem employs one significant scene depicting the narrator as a child with her grandmother. Though quite brief, the action has a beginning ("My grandmother picks through/Snapbeans"), a middle (I wait/While she empties her apron," etc.) and an end ("You'll be eating this stuff/Long after I'm gone, she tells me").

General Rule: The simpler the action, the smaller the poem.

Theme: An undercurrent of meaning runs through a narrative poem. All types of poems have themes, but narrative ones usually feature scenes that also *imply* or forebode the theme. In other words, any action in a narrative should also illustrate thematic concerns as well as articulate those concerns via voice.

Ask yourself, "What is the theme of my work and how does it relate to each scene or action in my story?"

Whenever a narrative poet mentions an act or introduces a scene, each must be significant with regard to theme or the reader will not fully understand or appreciate the story. Moreover, those acts or scenes must build so they forebode the climax (or high point) in the story or otherwise resolve or imply the conflict via a closed or an open ending. If, for instance, your poem has a theme of forgiveness, action or scenes should echo or show that feeling or indicate that a change associated with that feeling is imminent.

In Hales's poem above, the grandmother's act of picking through snapbeans is symbolic as is the narrator's waiting and grandmother's final comment. They imply what is broken and passed on in mother-daughter relationships, as indicated in the title — "How It Works" — and in the last two lines: "I ate what she and my mother had done/ Long before I was born."

General Rule: After you have identified the topic and theme, break the story into the beginning, middle and end, and identify how many acts or scenes you will need to convey the theme. Then rank order those acts or scenes so they build to an ending.

Voice: The voice of a narrative poem should be aligned with the subject matter (as you learned to do in chapter eight). In addition, you have to make one more determination: Should you use the first person (I/we) or the third person (he/she/they) to tell your story?

If you chose the first person, you are employing a narrator. If you choose the third person, you are employing a storyteller. Here's the difference:

- *Narrator*: You must use *I* or *we* in the poem; thus, your narrator must make an appearance, either alone (*I*) or with others (*we*). Moreover, tones of voice become aspects of the narrator's personality. If you tell the story with angry, hip and savvy tones, your narrator also is angry, hip and savvy.
- *Storyteller*: You cannot use *I* or *we* in the poem; thus, if people appear in the work, he, she or they are characters (depicted in the third person). Moreover, tones of voice in the poem belong to an unseen character on the page. Now if you tell your story with angry, hip, savvy tones, those traits do not belong to any character but to the storyteller who *never* appears in the piece.

Ask yourself: "Do I have a significant role in this story or am I simply telling it secondhand?" If you have a role, chances are you will use a narrator. If you are telling it secondhand, you may want to use a storyteller—someone who might have heard the tale or known the person(s) involved in the action.

Let's discuss using a narrator first. A common mistake is to use the first person simply to describe what happens in a piece.

Consider this quick poem:

TWISTER

I see the farmer in the fields and hear
the thunder. I watch as the lightning
illuminates his path back toward the house.
I listen to his wife calling him.
Now I witness his children leaving the shelter.
Everyone runs toward the funnel of their lives.

As you can see, the *I* in the poem lacks a significant role. (Substitute *we* for *I* and you'll get the same result.)

As a rule, if you can eliminate the first person in a poem—in effect, eliminating the narrator—and the poem remains basically the same, you don't need to use *I* or *we*:

TWISTER

The farmer in the fields hears
the thunder. The lightning
illuminates his path back toward the house.
His wife is calling him.
Now his children leave the shelter.
Everyone runs toward the funnel of their lives.

In the second version, the farmer, wife and children are characters depicted in the third person; hence, an unseen character, or story-teller, must be relating events without commenting on or filtering them (more on that later).

In this poem by Robert Kinsley, the narrator also is a witness but his passivity plays a role in the action that occurs:

THE UNIVERSE EXPLODING

At the mall in Parkersburg
my son and I wander among
the displays at the Home Show
while my wife shops.
A sign in front of the furnace display,
"most efficient in the world" and I have to
stop. Soon a small crowd
gathers and the salesman starts his pitch—
"this is the one ya want to buy, no doubt about it"
he says looking straight at me, taught I suppose
to pick out one vulnerable looking
soul to make it seem more real, and I'm
caught in the spiel. "How's it work you ask"
he says before the words leave my mouth. "Well,"
he starts looking deadly
serious, "the gas sort of forms little balls and then
explodes, hundreds of times a minute, like . . ."
he's looking for words, "sort of like" he says
"the way scientists say the universe started."
"Yea" he says, looking
skyward, hesitating a moment in his sudden
discovery. "Just think of it" he says, looking
back at me, "everytime you kick that baby on you're
making a new universe, exploding stars, making black
holes, charting new planets," and he laughs a little back

in his throat, like he thinks he knows something you don't.
"Maybe," he says, "you wander down there one cold morning
to watch it happen, and you never come up."

Although Kinsley gives more lines to the salesman than to the narrator, the narrator's presence in the poem is crucial—he's the target of the spiel—and his son's presence also is important—it depicts the narrator's personality—a man who cares for his boy so his wife can shop at the mall. Maybe an easy target. Moreover, his voice is factual ("At the mall in Parkersburg"), descriptive ("Soon a small crowd/gathers") and intelligent ("taught I suppose/to pick out one vulnerable looking/soul").

Those traits also blend with the narrator's personality and are aligned with topic and theme. The factual voice contrasts with the salesman's glib speech, the descriptive voice sets the scene and the intelligent one adds a sense of irony: Alas, the salesman has not picked out a vulnerable person, but one who understands the meaning of the salesman's final words.

Here's one of my poems to illustrate a storytelling voice in the third person:

THE OLD TRICK

It happened once that a woman who couldn't conceive
Paradise without her adopted daughter,
And the natural mother who all her life held out
Hope for a celestial reunion, approached

The wise judge, prepared to yield custody
At the sight of a sword. Beyond Solomon
A girl scaled the pearly gates like an acrobat.
"Hi, mommy!" she called, and both women waved.

That didn't work. So Solomon heard the arguments,
How the natural mother labored while the other
Simply waited, and how the adoptive mother
Forsook career while the other followed her fancy.

Neither gave an inch. Then be it decreed,
Said Solomon, that the natural mother keep
The child for the nine months she carried it,
And the adoptive mother keep it for the time

She lived on earth. Then what? they wanted to know.
This was paradise and supposedly eternal.
Who got the child next? Solomon shrugged.
Depends, he said, and noted how heaven was

That-a-way, through the gates the girl played upon
But hadn't quite entered, if they got his drift.
The women beheld each other in new light.
"You're very beautiful," the natural mother said.

"She has your eyes, you know," said the adoptive mother.
They embraced. Then Solomon sang hallelujah,
And the girl did a triple toe-loop on the highest bar,
And the women strolled toward the gates, arm in arm.

The tones in this poem — official ("It happened once"), conversational ("That didn't work") and humorous ("heaven was/That-a-way") — don't belong to any of the four characters mentioned in the poem: the two mothers, the girl and Solomon. They depict an unseen character, the storyteller, who filters what we see and hear in the poem (unlike in the Kinsley example). Furthermore, although Solomon is the main character, we never hear the voice of the wise judge or hear him sing hallelujah. Again the persona filters these sounds. By doing so, the storyteller adds another level of narration. Not only are we told a story, we hear it from the voice of a storyteller who puts us in the right mood for the epiphany at the end.

A common mistake with storytelling poems is employing an unseen character who never comments on action in a narrative — as was the case in the second "Twister" poem earlier.

To illustrate, analyze a version of my poem "The Old Trick" without any comment from the storyteller:

A woman couldn't conceive paradise without
Her adopted daughter, and the natural mother
Held out hope for a celestial reunion.

They approached the wise judge. Beyond Solomon
A girl scaled the gates like an acrobat.
"Hi, mommy!" she called, and both women waved.

Solomon heard the arguments. The natural mother
Said she labored while the other simply waited,
And the adoptive mother said she gave up her

Career while the other pursued hers.
Then Solomon decreed that the natural mother
Could keep the child for the nine months

She carried it, and the adoptive mother
Could keep it for the time she lived on earth.
They wanted to know what would happen next.

Solomon shrugged and pointed at the gates.
"You're very beautiful," the natural mother said.
"She has your eyes," said the adoptive mother.

They embraced. Solomon sang hallelujah,
And the girl did a triple toe-loop on the highest bar,
And the women strolled toward the gates, arm in arm.

The second version is weaker because the storyteller is no longer filtering events with his comments.

General Rule: After you have aligned the topic with theme and have decided whether to employ a narrator or storyteller, make sure that (a) your narrator has a role and that voice tones reveal his or her personality or (b) your storyteller filters events and that voice tones reveal his unseen personality.

Viewpoint: Each person or character who could convey the drama or conflict in a narrative does so from a different viewpoint. Use the viewpoint that will have the maximum impact. That is not necessarily yours. If it is yours, employ a narrator. If it isn't, employ a storyteller and relate the tale through *another* character's eyes. (The storyteller is *not* that character but remains unseen and simply knows the character well enough to tell his or her tale, coloring it with comments as explained previously.)

Ask yourself: "From whose eyes is the story best depicted?"

To answer that question, consider each of the characters in your poem and imagine how events in your story would affect them.

Clearly, in Kinsley's "The Universe Exploding," the narrator's viewpoint is the correct one. The wife is absent and the son is too young to interpret the spiel. The salesman's viewpoint would result in an entirely different poem, because we wouldn't have the added sense of irony at the end of the salesman's pitch. Such a version might begin:

Another sucker. Look at him with his son:
sensitive. Caring. Let me teach him
a thing or two. "Hey buddy," I call,
"this is the one ya want to buy," etc.

Obviously, Kinsley knew that such a viewpoint would yield a static poem depicting a shallow, cynical sales pitch at the mall, and so he avoided it.

In my poem, "The Old Trick," the right viewpoint is equally as obvious. The girl is too young to be wise, and each of the mothers has a special interest in the outcome before the judge. To promote one mother's viewpoint is to downplay the other's, when both are so powerfully strong that the wisdom of Solomon is needed to decide the case. Thus, we are privy to the various "tests" through which Solomon puts the mothers. In the end, his viewpoint is the one through which this story is best depicted.

General Rule: If you cannot decide which character best depicts the drama or conflict in a narrative, write a poem from each perspective and compare.

Moment: A poet must choose the point in time to relate events in a story. There are three possibilities:

1. Close to when an event happened, so the details and scenes are fresh and unravel as if we are there.
2. Relatively close to when an event happened, so we have some perspective about the meaning of those details and scenes.
3. Removed from when an event happened, so our perspective is more important than the details or scenes of the story.

Keep in mind that the moment of a narrative poem is *not* the time element: the date something happened. Neither is it grammatical, entailing the use of the past, present or future verb tenses. It is that moment the reader is allowed to enter the story — as it happens, near to when it happened, or removed from it.

Ask yourself: "When is the best moment to enter the story: one in which the drama or conflict can speak for itself, one in which some comment is needed to put the drama or conflict into perspective, or one in which comment is most crucial?"

For purposes here, let's label each of the three moments:

1. *Now*, for a moment close to when an event happened (as in the story is happening *now*) so the narrator seems to be reliving the action or the storyteller transfers the reader to the scene where action occurs.
2. *Now and Then*, for a moment relatively close to when an event happened (as in the story happens *now and then*) so the narrator or storyteller relates action in some parts of the poem and comments on it in other parts.
3. *Then*, for a moment removed from when an event occurred (as in the story happened *then*) so the narrator or storyteller comments on or filters events, putting them into perspective.

When you tell a story in the *Now*, you simply relate what happens; you *cannot* comment on the events. When you tell a story in the *Now and Then*, you relate *and* comment on the events. When you tell a story in the *Then*, you simply comment on events without putting the reader at the original scene.

Let's illustrate each concept with poems by R. Nikolas Macioci:

(Now)

THE 1945 POKER GAME TRANSCENDENCE

I am five.
Wrinkled voices of grown-ups unfurrow
like smoke toward the ceiling light.
Someone hands me a Seven-Up
and blows a wheezing beer-kiss against my arm.
My aunt tops a Queen of Hearts
with a King of Diamonds.
Another heaves up an Ace
and smothers the pile with success.
Beside the cocker spaniel,
with clock-life hugging midnight,
I settle beneath the table.
Through eyes opening to stars and music,
I, in a smudged sailor suit,
disappear into sun-white sleep
as soft as rainbows.

(Now and Then)

FORTY YEARS LATER, THE FATHER'S REMAINING DEBT

Bad sleep breaks, and I become alert
again to childhood's ongoing abuse,
remembered images of his overt
violence alive in my mind, diffuse
as pain: He pulls my hands behind me, ties
them to the back of a kitchen chair, bends
over me with fists full of meat, and tries
to force it down my throat. Our struggle ends
like a weary dance, his pulling away
bringing only momentary escape
from bonds of homemade torment on that day.
Now, prods of sleeplessness assume his shape.
In dreams I wait for his apology;
his head bends down but never weeps for me.

(Then)

KNIFE

The point of my father's knife thunked into
the arm of the rocker in which my mother
held me, exposing tiny tendrils of wood
less than an inch from my infant head.

My mother's eyes had tried to freeze
the knife's motion, reverse it to the hand
from which it had flown.

The first time I heard the story
I went immediately to the rocking chair
to find the scar, the steel
claw mark of what could have killed me. I
scrutinized the wood, ran a hand over
the arm. I asked my mother

if she was sure it had ever happened.
She too ran her hand over the worn pine,
discovering nothing but the blood-
sticky residue of furniture polish.
She seemed amazed that something so cruel
could have vanished so completely.
Eventually the rocker disappeared,

but not the habit of feeling chair arms
for the knife cut, for the sudden change
in grain from smooth surface to raw edge,
the smallest rip in the wood
a sliver of surviving proof.

Now let's discuss each poem briefly, with regard to the moment:

In "The 1945 Poker Game Transcendence," the reader is put at the scene of the story and allowed to hear, feel and experience what the narrator did at age five under the table. The *Now* adds tension, especially when coupled with a child's viewpoint. But the poet cannot comment about the adults playing poker above him. We do not know their nature; neither does it seem important, as the word *transcendence* in the title implies.

In "Forty Years Later, the Father's Remaining Debt," the reader is at times kept from the original scene and then placed in it. The *Now and Then* moment adds perspective and tension. On the one hand, we see the results of abuse in the adult narrator and then experience the abuse as a child, building to the epiphany at the end of the poem.

In "Knife," we never get to experience what the infant or mother did at the precise moment when the father thunked the knife into the arm of the chair. What we lose in tension — the witnessing of such horror — we gain in perspective, as the final lines of his poem skillfully articulate.

General Rule: If you use a moment close to the *Now*, be sure the reader will understand all aspects of the drama or conflict in question (without your explanation or comment). If you use the *Now and Then*, be sure your comment is needed. If you use the *Then*, be sure you are still telling a story — secondhand, perhaps — or your poem will be lyrical.

Ending: As we learned in the chapter on occasional verse, there are two basic ways to convey this:

1. *Open Ending:* The conclusion is not spelled out or explained but illustrated with an image or scene that implies it.
2. *Closed Ending:* The conclusion is stated, wrapping up loose ends.

Ask yourself: "What do I want to leave my reader with — a lingering presence, image or feeling, or a sense of satisfaction or resolution?"

An open ending features a final scene that implies an outcome or establishes a milieu. It results in that lingering presence in the reader's mind. Nothing may be resolved, but feelings are evoked. A closed ending, in which the outcome is final, satisfies the reader. Questions are answered. Everything is resolved.

To illustrate the two types, look again at two of R. Nikolas Macioci's poems: "The 1945 Poker Game Transcendence" and "Forty Years Later, the Father's Remaining Debt." In the first poem, he employs an open ending — "I, in a smudged sailor suit,/disappear into sun-white sleep/as soft as rainbows" — evoking a feeling with images and leaving the reader with a milieu. In the second poem, loose ends are tied in the ending — "In dreams I wait for his apology;/his head bends down but never weeps for me" — resolving the matter.

General Rule: If you decide your ending should be open, but are worried it might be too obscure, try a closed ending. If you decide your ending should be closed, but are worried it might sound forced or too pat, try an open one.

Once you know the basic elements of narrative verse, you should align them in a brief outline so you can envision your story and compose it.

SKETCHING THE STORY

An outline is simply that — a guide to help you picture and depict events in a narrative poem. People who argue against such outlines either are born storytellers or are able to imagine key elements without putting them down on paper first. By making a sketch, you can see what elements might falter and what might succeed — *before* you write your poem. You'll save time and energy, recognizing good stories and avoiding problematic ones that stand little chance of success.

To illustrate, let's make outlines for Macioci's poems to see why they succeed:

1. "The 1945 Poker Game Transcendence"

- *Topic*: Childhood memory
- *Theme*: Transcendence
- *Voice*: Pushed, descriptive, sensual
- *Viewpoint*: Narrator
- *Moment*: Now
- *Ending*: Open
- *Result*: Topic and theme harmonize with voice and viewpoint; moreover, the moment adds tension because the child cannot comment anyway, and the ending enhances theme.

2. "Forty Years Later, the Father's Remaining Debt"

- *Topic*: Child abuse
- *Theme*: Forgiveness
- *Voice*: Intelligent, descriptive, resigned
- *Viewpoint*: Narrator
- *Moment*: Now and Then
- *Ending*: Closed
- *Result*: Topic and theme suit each other, as do voice and viewpoint; thus, the narrator can investigate the incident, using the moment for tension and perspective and coming to a conclusion.

3. "Knife"

- *Topic*: Child abuse
- *Theme*: Survival
- *Voice*: Reflective, descriptive, conversational
- *Viewpoint*: Narrator
- *Moment*: Then
- *Ending*: Closed
- *Result*: Again, topic and theme suit each other and voice allows the narrator to piece together evidence of abuse, reflect on it, and come to a conclusion.

As you can see, such an outline is a blueprint of a writer's style. Contrast one of Macioci's poem's with my own, "The Old Trick":

- *Topic*: Adoption
- *Theme*: Compassion
- *Voice*: Official, conversational, humorous
- *Viewpoint*: Solomon's
- *Moment*: Now and Then
- *Ending*: Open

— and then watch what happens when I insert elements from my outline into Macioci's "Forty Years Later, the Father's Remaining Debt":

- *Topic*: Child abuse
- *Theme*: Compassion
- *Voice*: Official, conversational, humorous
- *Viewpoint*: Solomon's
- *Moment*: Now and Then
- *Ending*: Open

Clearly, the above hybird contains flaws. It indicates that although it would be possible to write a poem about child abuse with a theme of compassion, the poem probably would have a better chance of success if the voice, viewpoint and ending were altered. That's the value of aligning elements of your narrative before you write it, envisioning how your story will sound on the page.

Now let's end with a brief introduction (accompanied by an outline) to narrative verse included in the mini anthology:

- In "The Man Who Beat the Game at Johnny's Truck Stop," T.R. Hummer employs the collective plural first person *we* to add another level of meaning in his narrative. Notice, too, how the moment allows the narrator to depict action and comment and how the theme is resolved in a closed ending.
Outline:

- *Topic*: Friendship
- *Theme*: Acceptance
- *Voice*: Conversational, plaintive, anxious
- *Viewpoint*: Narrator
- *Moment*: Now and Then
- *Ending*: Closed

- In "The Man Who Grew Silent," Jim Peterson employs a complex storyteller; thus, Peterson says, "the reader or listener must remain alert to the fact that the story is being filtered through the eyes and heart of one who has an 'attitude.' " Note how the moment allows the storyteller to relate and filter events and how the main character's fate is implied in the ending.
Outline:

- *Topic*: Losing a job
- *Theme*: Surrender
- *Voice*: Dispassionate, descriptive, unreliable
- *Viewpoint*: Man's
- *Moment*: Now and Then
- *Ending*: Open

• In "Faint-light," Robert Kinsley tries to weave social and mythical elements in his narrative. Note how a simple deed — spending the dawn with his son, swinging — becomes a vehicle of enlightenment, thanks to voice. Note, too, how comment and action blend and then meld into an ending that emphasizes the theme.
   Outline:

• *Topic*: Fatherhood
• *Theme*: Awe
• *Voice*: Introspective, descriptive, philosophical
• *Viewpoint*: Narrator
• *Moment*: Now and Then
• *Ending*: Open

Kinsley says about his poem: "I want to believe in a world larger than myself, in which Gods still do exist."
   If you feel the same way, the narrative is custom-made for your muse.

Mini Anthology of Narrative Poems

THE MAN WHO BEAT THE GAME AT JOHNNY'S TRUCK STOP
for Bruce Weigl

When he put his quarter in
The cowgirl's breasts
Lit up, one red, one green,
And something in her belly came
Up zeroes, opened.
A bell was ringing somewhere
And everybody turned
As the ball jumped
From flipper to bumper so fast
You couldn't tell where it was
Until her eyes went dark
And we all knew the score.

The man didn't say a word.
He brought his hands down hard
On the glass top of the machine
And broke through into the shining
Space we all gaze at, longing
To touch it, never knowing
What we want, or how easy it would be
If you only didn't mind getting a little
Blood on your hands.

We wrapped his
In napkins, and he sat a long time
Not talking, not minding the dark
Blot the bound fingers left
On the table, not listening
When we told him again and again
He had a home.

                       —T.R. Hummer

THE MAN WHO GREW SILENT

He had nothing more to say.
He hadn't gone to work in weeks.
His boss had let him go
After the first three days
When he wouldn't answer
Any of their questions.
But he's sure they parted as friends.

His wife took him by both shoulders
And tried to shake some sense into him.
He had not spoken to her since August
And the nights were getting cold and long.
His fingers trailed down her spine
As she turned away and left the house.
The trunk was packed already, the children
On a bus. He waved from the porch as her car
Disappeared. He turned around and smiled
Into the almost empty room, TV
With a blown tube and a blank face
Like his own, but inside, a storm of dreams

And re-runs.
It felt good to sleep until he woke
To silence in the morning, hands behind
His head deep into the pillow. He watched
The bare limbs shake in the wind outside.
He worked all day to keep everything
In its place and followed all his thoughts
And all his secret voices unwinding
From his head until the tape ran out.

He did not ignore necessities. He stood
Among the gleaming aisles of food
Reading the praises of cereal and beans.
He studied that accumulating silence

Of his friends waiting in the line to pay.
He loved his box grown overstuffed
With mail. He loved the faces of the people
He knew so well calling to him from his lawn
Or pounding on his door. One day
A van pulled up and three men
With dark glasses and a key came in.

He'd been expecting them. They led him
To the van. When he arrived someplace
The rooms were bright and large. A woman
Held his hand and looked into his eyes
But did not persist in speaking. The men
Who led him away did not speak at all.
He loved the way everybody was being
So good about it. They left him in a room
With a table, a chair, and a bed.

He lived there for a long time.
They left him alone. Each night
The lights went out, but the silence
Glowed for him even in the dark. One night
He heard the walls humming
And when they stopped to breathe
He took a breath: a long, deep drawing in
Of air that didn't end. He felt ignored
All the way through, cold from the collapse
Of his presence in the room, and found

Himself outside the wall.
The guards saw him in the yard
But couldn't stop him,
The chain link fence dividing him
Into diamonds
Drifting off in all directions
In the cold night air.

                              — Jim Peterson

FAINT-LIGHT
for Tristan

This is the way the day begins,
the soft moaning of wind in the trees,
dew on the grasses
the faint-light
                    lifting

from behind the hills.

In the yard my son is swaying
to his own song, in his swing
on the air
                   rising
between the trunks of the ancient honey locusts,

the last trees to leaf, in spring,
in Ohio.
Whose bark rejoices in the lastness of things
gray with the color of pain,
knotted and curled, the death-mask
as if all my dead had
                   gathered
here to watch,

my son, who from this angle
seems to rise back and
                   disappear
into the honey locusts, only
to reappear moments later
rising now on the other side
like the dead, this
the song of diminish and return.

And still the morning comes on
and now I am
                   swinging
with my son

between the faces of the dead and buried
between the face of my own death, my diminishing

rising here among the grasses,
the sunlight and the honey locusts.
                   — Robert Kinsley

Notebook

LEVEL ONE

1. Evaluate drafts of poems in your "Work in Progress" file that
seem suited to the narrative mode. Revise them according to precepts
learned in this chapter.

2. Select three ideas from your "Idea File" that suit the narrative
mode. Before you write each poem, ask yourself basic questions about

key elements — topic, theme, voice, viewpoint, etc. Review general rules governing each of those elements. Once you have determined your answers, align them by sketching an outline covering topic, theme, voice, viewpoint, moment and ending. With each poem, envision the work first . . . and then compose.

LEVEL TWO

1. Select three drafts from your "Work in Progress" file. If you have used a narrator to relate events in a poem, rewrite that poem using a storyteller (or vice versa). Compare both versions of each poem. Now evaluate drafts of other poems in your "Work in Progress" file and determine whether you usually prefer a narrator or a storyteller. Discuss why in your journal.

2. Select three ideas for narrative verse from your "Idea File," outline them as recommended, and then employ a narrator or a storyteller — whichever one you usually avoid — and compose drafts.

LEVEL THREE

1. Select three ideas for narrative verse from your "Idea File." Outline them as recommended, with this exception: Sketch three versions of each poem using each of the moments (*Now, Now and Then, and Then*). Compare the three versions for each poem. Now evaluate drafts of other narrative poems in your "Work in Progress" file and determine which moment you find *least* effective.

2. Select three more ideas for narrative verse from your "Idea File" and cast them in the moment you *least* prefer, again attempting to turn a weakness into a strength.

Chapter Fifteen

The Lyric Poem

L yric poems come in all shapes and sizes but share one common trait: They're musical. The word *lyric* is derived from
the Greek *lyra* (musical instrument) and *melic* (melody). It
does not tell a story as narrative poetry does, describing
events or action in the external world, but focuses intensely on a subject and tries to awaken or evoke emotions within the listener (as
music does). Instead of using notes, however, the lyric poet relies on
words and poetic devices—metaphor, simile, cadence, meter, rhyme,
voice, etc.—as in this lovely example by Robert Burns:

A RED, RED ROSE
O my luve's like a red, red rose,
    That's newly sprung in June;
O my luve's like the melodie
    That's sweetly played in tune.

As fair art thou, my bonnie lass,
    So deep in luve am I;
And I will luve thee still, my dear,
    Till a' the seas gang dry.

Till a' the seas gang dry, my dear,
    And the rocks melt wi' the sun:
O I will love thee still, my dear,
    While the sands o' life shall run.

And fare thee weel, my only luve,
    And fare thee weel awhile!
And I will come again, my luve,
    Though it were ten thousand mile.

Seemingly simple, this famous song by Burns focuses on a moment
(a rose newly sprung in June); on objects (seas, rocks, sands); on living
things (rose, bonnie lass); on a concept (love); and on an experience

(parting). His lyric encompasses all of the topics typically expressed in this mode. Moreover Burns relies on language — meter, rhyme, simile — to draw out in the listener the same emotion the narrator feels.

The lyric poet's job is twofold: to investigate and/or re-create moments, objects, living things, concepts or experiences and to expound on them musically, using poetic devices to reveal their true essence.

Few poets have done a better job composing such verse than William Blake. He focuses intensely on each of the typical topics associated with the lyric and uses language and poetic devices — the way a blacksmith uses tools — to shape his songs so they resonate in the reader.

Here is a selection:

(Moment)

TO THE EVENING STAR

Thou fair-hair'd angel of the evening,
Now, while the sun rests on the mountains, light
Thy bright torch of love; thy radiant crown
Put on, and smile upon our evening bed!
Smile on our loves; and, while thou drawest the
Blue curtains of the sky, scatter thy silver dew
On every flower that shuts its sweet eyes
In timely sleep. Let thy west wind sleep on
The lake; speak silence with thy glimmering eyes,
And wash the dusk with silver. Soon, full soon,
Dost thou withdraw; then the wolf rages wide,
And the lion glares thro' the dun forest:
The fleeces of our flocks are cover'd with
Thy sacred dew: protect them with thine influence.

(Object)

SOFT SNOW

I walked abroad in a snowy day
I askd the soft snow with me to play
She playd & she melted in all her prime
And the winter calld it a dreadful crime

(Living thing)

THE TYGER

Tyger! Tyger! burning bright
In the forests of the night,
What immortal hand or eye

Could frame thy fearful symmetry?

In what distant deeps or skies
Burnt the fire of thine eyes?
On what wings dare he aspire?
What the hand, dare seize the fire?

And what shoulder, & what art,
Could twist the sinews of thy heart?
And when thy heart began to beat,
What dread hand? & what dread feet?

What the hammer? what the chain?
In what furnace was thy brain?
What the anvil? what dread grasp
Dare its deadly terrors clasp?

When the stars threw down their spears,
And water'd heaven with their tears,
Did he smile his work to see?
Did he who made the Lamb make thee?

Tyger! Tyger! burning bright
In the forests of the night,
What immortal hand or eye
Dare frame thy fearful symmetry?

(Concept)

INFANT SORROW

My mother groand! my father wept.
Into the dangerous world I leapt:
Helpless, naked, piping loud;
Like a fiend hid in a cloud.

Struggling in my fathers hands:
Striving against my swadling bands:
Bound and weary I thought best
To sulk upon my mothers breast.

(Experience)

LONDON

I wander thro' each charter'd street,
Near where the charter'd Thames does flow.
And mark in every face I meet
Marks of weakness, marks of woe.

In every cry of every man,
In every Infants cry of fear,
In every voice in every ban,
The mind-forg'd manacles I hear

How the Chimney-sweepers cry
Every blackning Church appalls;
And the hapless Soldiers sigh
Runs in blood down Palace walls

But most thro' midnight streets I hear
How the youthful Harlots curse
Blasts the new-born Infants tear
And blights with plagues the Marriage hearse

In each of these lyrics, Blake employs elements of craft to make music on the page. Let's consider a few of those elements to get a glimpse of his genius:

- In "To the Evening Star," Blake composes a ballad to honor the moment — "Now, while the sun rests on the mountains" — using metaphors ("bright torch of love"), personification ("thy radiant crown/Put on") and vivid imagery to capture the essence of cosmic light.
- In "Soft Snow," he focuses on an object, noting that as snow melts it is easier to play with, and the more one plays, the more it melts . . . and that's a crime, according to winter. The metaphor works on several levels, applying to the weather, of course, but also to our mortal condition.
- In "The Tyger," he imagines the hand of the creator assembling the essence of that fearful animal, using rhyme and meter to augment the cadence of his many rhetorical questions.
- In "Infant Sorrow," he probes a concept by focusing on and interpreting movements of a struggling infant and by conveying the sorrow in nursery rhyme fashion, endowing the song with a sense of irony and tension.
- In "London," he uses words and phrases that let us see, hear and otherwise feel the experience of walking among the stricken poor of his era.

Lyrics, ballads and songs by Blake set a standard for other poets to follow (including Wordsworth). In sum, Blake investigated and re-created a wide range of topics — even hitherto taboo ones concerning common people like chimney sweeps and impossible-to-comprehend concepts like infant sorrow — to break new poetic ground and help define the boundaries of the lyric. Moreover, Blake as an artist and engraver had a keen respect for craft and the well-made poem. To this day, lyricists tap the tradition that Blake helped establish so long ago.

"Lyric poems are particularly hospitable to investigation and listening," says Tom Andrews, whom we met in the chapter on nature poetry. "On the one hand, a lyric poet often tries to re-create an experience, re-enact it, embody it through language. On the other hand, he or she tries to remain open to what the language is doing and to explore where the language is heading."

Andrews is discussing the lyric process. Composing such verse is a challenge because language can never quite recapture, re-create or re-enact a moment or experience. Yet words, like musical notes, have their own melodies, and lyric poets have to listen to them. Poets who can balance both elements compose lyrics that transcend the topic and the music and reveal truth.

To illustrate, here's a short lyric by Andrews titled "Ars Poetica" (or one's philosophy of art/poetry):

The dead drag a grappling hook for the living.
The hook is enormous. Suddenly it is tiny.
Suddenly one's voice is a small body falling
through silt and weeds, reaching wildly . . .

The sensitive reader realizes the truth behind the quatrain: The "ars poetica" relates to life as well as art. Using symbolic language — "the dead," "grappling hook," "the living" — Andrews depicts how artists (and people) are influenced by our forebears. At first such influence is great, but it diminishes as we discover that our own small voice (poem/wisdom) cannot encompass the essence of life, a humbling exercise.

Says Andrews about his lyric: "My hope for 'Ars Poetica' is that it engages that tension — between my own desire to speak and the language's tendency to displace the speaker — as straightforwardly as possible. I also hope the poem doesn't seem dry or coldly intellectual."

Andrews is acknowledging the difficulty that all lyric poets face trying to investigate or re-create a topic musically while coping with the limits of language. The more one struggles with concept — working out the central idea of a lyric and expressing it clearly — the more one risks sounding cold and dry on the page.

Ruth Daigon, whose verse and views on love poetry appear in chapter two, is a noted lyricist and former concert soprano. Like Andrews, she's aware of the risks associated with lyric verse and has advice to overcome them: "I associate lyric poetry with strong feeling, some kind of passion, whether it be love, loss, loneliness, the too-quick passage of time. The task of the poem is to translate these feelings or passions into language that will resonate in the mind of the reader so that he or she will not only appreciate this special experience or vision, but also draw upon his or her similar encounters. . . . One of the ways to translate feelings and passions into language is to use the rhythmic disciplines of music. Each word, phrase, sentence must be considered for its sound, cadence, tone, timbre, inflection and how these contribute to making the poem *mean* something—not only cognitively, but emotionally."

FIVE BASIC KINDS OF LYRIC POEMS

Not only can lyric poetry be broken into typical topics—moment, object, living thing, concept or experience—but also into five typical modes of expression. Master lyricists are able to combine these modes or vary them (as an improviser might vary a melody), but the following methods will simplify the process so you can execute well-crafted lyrics:

Investigate the meaning of a concept. Such a poem often focuses on a word or phrase and deconstructs it—takes it apart, bone and sinew as it were—to reveal a meaning greater than any previously stated one. Here is such a lyric from my files:

EVANGELISTS, ENVIRONMENTALISTS

Evangelists like to flash backward
Playing records and tapes,
Listening for Lucifer in the low syllables.

Environmentalists like to flash forward
Taperecording temperatures,
Looking for holes in the high altitudes.

Eva*ngeli*sts have halos; env*iron*mentalists,
Ores. Halogens. *Lists* of souls, species
Near extinction. Both believe in floods,

The mythology of lifeboats and whales.
One wants to save Jonah,
The other the orca whose song is a psalm.

Both damn man, prophesying doom
At the door. Donations are deductible.
One can't wait to get to heaven,

The other can't bear to leave earth.
One thinks that God will reward him.
The other thinks not.

Method of composition: Pick a word or phrase that has particular meaning to you, one that causes you great joy or sorrow — in sum, a concept that speaks to you personally. Then research all shades of meaning in that word or phrase, using standard reference books. Once you have contemplated those meanings, look for a new one — some grain of truth or epiphany to convey how you feel. Then use your mechanical tools (voice, line, stanza, etc.) to link the various meanings and unify them in your ending.

Investigate the essence of an image or object. Such a poem evaluates all aspects, parts, meanings or components of a thing, endowing the image or object with new meaning.

In this lyric, Ruth Daigon probes the essence of a bullet:

LIKE AN IDEAL TENANT

Like an ideal tenant, the bullet fits
precisely in the wound, closer
than a friend, a relative, a lover.
Removing it, what can we give the body
in exchange to accommodate it half so well?

Always the unexpected caller,
it only sleeps with strangers,
never fails to find the perfect host
and it in turn becomes the perfect guest
bringing no gift but itself,
demanding nothing.

Lying cradled in the flesh,
never struggling to emerge,
cushioned in that hollow
as if it knew each curve,
it wraps itself in silence.

Method of composition: Choose an object or image that carries some baggage (connotations) with it, one that by its very nature, a reader might find alluring (crop circles), controversial (cocaine), mythic (cave), powerful (cyclone) or deadly (bullet). Now study your object or image or even look it up in the encyclopedia, if appropriate, to become familiar with all its features and functions. Then find a suitable metaphor or simile for it, as Daigon did by comparing a bullet with a tenant. Draw as many analogies as you can, building from weakest to strongest, to reveal a greater truth than anyone would have realized about the object or image.

Re-create and alter a personal or public experience to understand it. Such a poem satisfies the reader's need to go back in time and addresses the age-old comment, "If only I had a second chance." Content usually focuses on a significant event or experience and reconstructs it—scene by scene—in an attempt to alter, accept or come to terms with the outcome.

Another poem by Ruth Daigon illustrates:

THE DROWNING

We keep pulling him up from the bottom
of the Red River in stop-action or
slow-motion and replay the splash
blooming around his hips.

We correct his dive,
restore the promise
of his form, each movement
clear in the instant of falling.

The moment reversed, we reel him up
to where he's still sitting on the bank.
Mother covers her bare scalp
with hair torn by its roots.

Screams sucked back into her mouth
become soft syllables again.
Her shredded clothes rewoven.
The table set for his return.

Method of composition: Pick appropriate subject matter either from your list of highs, lows and turning points, or from accounts of events you have heard or read about. Re-create scenes from the event and analyze them. Then change the outcome or look for the underlying cause of the outcome or somehow manipulate the outcome to express a greater truth via voice and epiphany.

Re-create a talent or investigate an encounter so others may partake in it. Usually such a lyric focuses on a skill or an experience the poet possesses or knows of and conveys it so the listener knows how it feels.

Here is an example by Mary Martin, a poet, teacher and professional dancer:

THE DANCE TEACHER

The community has seen you thrown
around a man's shoulders, then slung
to his feet smiling, your back
arched, feet pointed, sometimes a shadow
of graceful passion behind
the scrim, other times performed

center stage, his fingers
noticeably pressed into your waist,
your thighs in the light.
Each concert it works
for jazz, ballet,
or modern — the pas de deux
the man, always a new student
who can't move well yet, but
sturdy as a tree trunk,
lifts you, whirls you,
circles the stage with you
above him, your fingers
fanned in bravura, legs
starched in a kick back,
your neck muscles propping up
your grin, just as the fog rolls in
from the wings and the girls
waltz on, laced with garlands
of plastic flowers, surrounding
you like an altar.
This is what you're known for,
to be light enough to be tossed
around on stage, a few moments
of being handled and the audience
squirms and ahhhs! and little girls
with sticky fingers suddenly
want to dance watching you up there,
pretending to be a swan,
a mermaid, a fountainhead, a spout,
a chronic fixture.

Method of composition: Decide what you do best. Or worst. That is a skill (or lack thereof). If this occurs in context with another person, or in front of other people, it is an encounter. In your journal, describe emotions related to this skill or encounter. Focus on how you felt when you performed the skill well, poorly, or uniquely or when you put the encounter into perspective. This represents your peak experience or epiphany. Do not recount mere events leading to your peak experience or epiphany or you will end up with a narrative poem. Instead discuss all aspects of the experience, how each aspect made you feel, and then rank those aspects and emotions from least significant to most, building to an ending.

Re-create an experience that did not, cannot or has yet to happen. Usually such a lyric fulfills the "what if?" impulse that each of us feels on occasion. Ruth Daigon says of such poetry: "It can anticipate what might be the reader's experience in the future and increases the reader's insight about what lies ahead."

An example from my files, set in the future, warns what might lie ahead if we lose our humanity and compassion:

GENERA UBI SUNT

Where are the Mahicans whose name means "wolf"
In the wolf-less mountains of the Catskill?
The Tasmanians whose rocks are relics
In the marsupial uplands of evolution?
The Congoids who met Columbus, the Celts
Who met the Norse in their holocaust sloops?

We, too, are explorers but cannot find them
In our modems and books. We know all about
Eur-asians and -arabs, the yearlings of war.
Show us the lost tribes of Israel and Germania
So we may follow the roads to Rome, annul
The laws of endangerment, and love each other
When love goes the way of the last Aleut.

Method of composition: Answer the "what if?" impulse by imagining scenarios that did not occur (what if JFK had lived?), that cannot occur (what if I were an insect?) or have yet to occur (what if we became extinct?). Pick a topic or scenario that intrigues you or triggers your fantasies. Ask yourself why the topic or scenario excites you, and you should also discover your epiphany. Now imagine the various outcomes or consequences of your "what if?" topic. Rank those outcomes or consequences from least intriguing to most, and build slowly to your epiphany.

Nobody can guarantee that these methods of composition will work for you, but when coupled with all you have learned about craft thus far in this book, they should help you focus on a topic and balance the elements of sense and sound found in good lyrics. Ruth Daigon says that such verse results in an "Aha!" response in the listener, "the sense of discovery, of new understanding."

I experienced the "Aha!" response when I first read these lyrics included in the mini anthology:

- "Tides," by William Stafford. In this poem, Stafford reveals the true essence of the moon's pull on mortals.
- "Not Only the Eskimos," by Lisel Mueller. In this brilliant lyric, the poet reveals the true essence of snow.
- "Most of Us," by Jack Myers. In his poem, Myers investigates

what cannot occur and reveals his own true essence in the process.

• "Eloquent Lingo," by Nuala Archer. In this elusive poem, Archer defines the essence of lyric verse.

Mini Anthology of Lyric Poems

TIDES

The first wave of a new tide hardly
announces itself; but brothers and sisters
confirm that a mighty wave is coming,
and far from shore, bulging in mountain
ranges of ponderous water, the full
universe of the tide leans toward land.

Or winter beginning to move comes
that way, the sun withholding its full
afternoon blessing, a night when frost
creeps out; bones of the glacier
shift and get ready for the powerful surge
when what waits in the sky or mountain descends.

Even inside a cliff, inside that blind
forehead that fronts the ocean, a tide,
or winter, pulses in the gray body
of an earth too slow to respond but thrilled
into being and held in its crystal self,
a jewel of dull intensity inside the stone.

—William Stafford

NOT ONLY THE ESKIMOS

We have only one noun
but as many different kinds:

the grainy snow of the Puritans
and snow of soft, fat flakes,

guerrilla snow, which comes in the night
and changes the world by morning,

rabbinical snow, a permanent skullcap
on the highest mountains,

snow that blows in like the Lone Ranger,
riding hard from out of the West,

surreal snow in the Dakotas,
when you can't find your house, your street,

though you are not in a dream
or a science fiction movie,

snow that tastes good to the sun
when it licks black tree limbs,
leaving us only one white stripe,
a replica of a skunk,

unbelievable snows:
the blizzard that strikes on the 10th of April,
the false snow before Indian summer,
the Big Snow on Mozart's birthday,
when Chicago became the Elysian Fields
and strangers spoke to each other,

paper snow, cut and taped
to the inside of grade school windows,

in an old tale, the snow
that covers a nest of strawberries,
small hearts, ripe and sweet,

the special snow that goes with Christmas,
whether it falls or not,

the Russian snow we remember
along with the warmth and smell of our furs,
though we have never traveled
to Russia or worn furs,

Villon's snows of yesteryear,
lost with ladies gone out like matches,
the snow in Joyce's "The Dead,"
the silent, secret snow
in a story by Conrad Aiken,
which is the snow of first love,

the snowfall between the child
and the spacewoman on T.V.,

snow as idea of whiteness,
as in *snowdrop, snow goose, snowball bush,*

the snow that puts stars in your hair,
and your hair, which has turned to snow,

the snow Elinor Wylie walked in
in velvet shoes,

the snow before her footprints
and the snow after,

the snow in the back of our heads,
whiter than white, which has to do
with childhood again each year.

       —Lisel Mueller

MOST OF US

In another age I would've married a sorry woman
from my small village, had too many children,
broken my back with my hands, and come home drunk.

I would've died early from diseases, having suffered
humiliation after humiliation, my heart twisting at the sight
of a coin, while our hated king lived far off on a hill.

I would've believed in anything that was given,
been on my knees to anything with a singular face.
I would not have been as I am, one who believes in himself

and nothing else, to whom everything else is in service,
and live up here in a bewilderment of choices,
doing what I choose, The King of Everything.

       —Jack Myers

ELOQUENT LINGO

There are many like these
left by who knows who?

In their span of hundreds of
rings or more how many jillions

of leaves dance away, winded?
Simply living, growing, changing

color—or budding, blooming
& bursting—these have been

known & loved as
an eloquent lingo, a fluid

landscape tattoo haunting
as Tarquinia, translated

in our slow tongue as trees.

       —Nuala Archer

Notebook

LEVEL ONE

1. Evaluate drafts of poems in your "Work in Progress" file that seem suited to the lyric mode. Revise them according to precepts learned in this chapter.

2. Review the basic lyric forms discussed in this chapter and select suitable ideas from your "Idea File." Then follow the appropriate methods of composition and compose first drafts. After each draft, describe in your journal how the method of composition helped or did not help you come up with a lyric.

LEVEL TWO

Read your Level One, Exercise Two journal entry in which you discussed how proposed methods of composition worked or did not work for you. Identify those methods that were *least* effective. Then select three suitable ideas from your "Idea File" and compose drafts based on those methods. After each composition, evaluate methods in question again and determine why they now work (or still do not work) for you. If you are still having problems with any, determine whether you can personalize the particular method so it is more in line with your muse. (For instance, you may be dissatisfied when composing "what if" lyrics by ranking outcomes or consequences from least to most important; in that case, you might want to rank them from most to least important.) In any case, discuss all this in your journal.

LEVEL THREE

1. Read your journal entries associated with the Level One and Two exercises in which you discuss the effectiveness of methods of composing lyrics. Evaluate the method(s) that you still find least effective; then choose three suitable ideas from your "Idea File." (Conceive suitable ideas if you cannot locate any.) Compose first drafts.

2. Analyze your drafts again. In your journal, discuss why you might have overcome problems. If you are still experiencing some, however, personalize methods of composition one more time and do second drafts of poems that you composed in the Level Three, Exercise One.

Chapter Sixteen

The Dramatic Poem

I f narrative poems tell stories and lyric ones sound like music, then dramatic poems *characterize*. But again, the mode is more complex than that. Like narrative and lyric poems, dramatic ones come in all sizes, styles and voices. Moreover, a dramatic poem can be essentially narrative or lyric. Skilled poets often cross the borders of these three major verse categories, as they should; nonetheless, every poet should be able to distinguish a predominantly narrative poem from a lyric one (and vice versa) and identify a dramatic poem that borrows from either the narrative or the lyric. If you are able to identify these elementary types, you can go about the business of composing them and, later, more sophisticated fare.

In simple terms, characterization — developing personality, motive and viewpoint — is at the core of dramatic work. Although all poems feature narrators or storytellers who don masks when speaking, characters in a dramatic poem are invented (fictive), historical (real — past or present) or composite (part invented, part real). These characters, like actors, have roles in three varieties of dramatic verse:

The dramatic episode. As its name implies, a dramatic episode features an encounter of at least two characters (one of whom may be silent). This type of poem often contains elements of narrative verse in that (a) a story or incident is related or suggested, (b) appropriate moments of narration are featured (*Now, Now and Then* and *Then*) and (c) readers can sense the passage of time.

The character study. As its name also implies, a character study is just that: an analysis of an invented, a historical or a composite entity. Often it is categorized as a voice poem because the entity speaks without interacting with other characters. Thus, such a dramatic poem is related to the lyric (especially one that focuses on a living thing — in this case, a person).

The dramatic sequence. A series of dramatic episodes or character studies (or combination of the two), this type of poem often combines the best of all modes — narrative, because a tale is told or implied; lyric, because the focus is heightened and intense; and dramatic, because characters are featured. Although a dramatic sequence differs from a poetic play, say, by Shakespeare, in that its form is based on a series of individual poems instead of on acts and scenes, it shares similar traits with its stage cousin. In *Hamlet*, for instance, characters interact with each other in a performed narrative (or series of episodes on stage), character studies are featured via soliloquies (as in Hamlet's "To Be or Not to Be" speech), and actors obviously are fictive, historical or composite entities.

Unfortunately, because of its length and other complexities, the dramatic sequence is beyond the scope of this chapter. However, if tenets of this chapter are combined with those in chapter twenty, about the poetic sequence, you should be able to craft such a poem. (To whet your appetite, I have included opening poems of dramatic sequences in the mini anthology from two contemporary works: "The Psychiatrist at the Cocktail Party" in *City Life* by Frederick Feirstein and "The Homunculus" in *Castle Tzingal* by Fred Chappell.)

To illustrate how dramatic verse characterizes, let's consider one of the best such poems ever made.

THE PROTOTYPICAL DRAMATIC POEM
In all categories of verse, there are poems so excellent that we call them "touchstones"—work that sets standards for generations to come. While we can debate touchstones for narrative and lyric verse, few would object to the following poem by Robert Browning as the touchstone in the dramatic group.

MY LAST DUCHESS

That's my last Duchess painted on the wall,
Looking as if she were alive. I call
That piece a wonder, now: Frà Pandolf's hands
Worked busily a day, and there she stands.
Will 't please you sit and look at her? I said
'Frà Pandolf' by design, for never read
Strangers like you that pictured countenance,
The depth and passion of its earnest glance,
But to myself they turned (since none puts by
The curtain I have drawn for you, but I)
And seemed as they would ask me, if they durst,
How such a glance came there; so, not the first
Are you to turn and ask thus. Sir, 't was not
Her husband's presence only, called that spot
Of joy into the Duchess' cheek: perhaps
Frà Pandolf chanced to say 'Her mantle laps

Over my lady's wrist too much,' or 'Paint
Must never hope to reproduce the faint
Half-flush that dies along her throat:' such stuff
Was courtesy, she thought, and cause enough
For calling up that spot of joy. She had
A heart — how shall I say? — too soon made glad,
Too easily impressed; she liked whate'er
She looked on, and her looks went everywhere.
Sir, 't was all one! My favour at her breast,
The dropping of the daylight in the West,
The bough of cherries some officious fool
Broke in the orchard for her, the white mule
She rode with round the terrace — all and each
Would draw from her alike the approving speech,
Or blush, at least. She thanked men, — good! but thanked
Somehow — I know not how — as if she ranked
My gift of a nine-hundred-years-old name
With anybody's gift. Who'd stoop to blame
This sort of trifling? Even had you skill
In speech — (which I have not) — to make your will
Quite clear to such an one, and say, 'Just this
Or that in you disgusts me; here you miss,
Or there exceed the mark' — and if she let
Herself be lessoned so, nor plainly set
Her wits to yours, forsooth, and made excuse,
— E'en then would be some stooping; and I choose
Never to stoop. Oh sir, she smiled, no doubt,
Whene'er I passed her; but who passed without
Much the same smile? This grew; I gave commands;
Then all smiles stopped together. There she stands
As if alive. Will 't please you rise? We'll meet
The company below, then. I repeat,
The Count your master's known munificence
Is ample warrant that no just pretence
Of mine for dowry will be disallowed;
Though his fair daughter's self, as I avowed
At starting, is my object. Nay, we'll go
Together down, sir. Notice Neptune, though,
Taming a sea-horse, thought a rarity,
Which Claus of Innsbruck cast in bronze for me!

Critics have had field days analyzing this work, but its basic elements are particularly apropos to lessons in this chapter. First, they
cross borders. For one, "My Last Duchess" contains a mini-dramatic

episode — a specific occasion during which the Count's emissary inter-acts with the speaker (though that interaction is implied via voice). In the opening, the emissary makes an inquiry about the duchess upon seeing her portrait. In the ending, the Duke asks the emissary about arrangements to snare another unlucky companion — the Count's daughter. The poem also can be depicted on stage with props (painting with curtain, statue of Neptune, etc.), setting (a room with staircase leading down), and, not the least, two actors: the Duke and the dumb-founded emissary. As such, it also has elements of a poetic play. More importantly, though, is its significance as a character study. This is achieved on two levels: an analysis of the gentle Duchess and of the possessive Duke (who collects women like artwork but cannot see their beauty).

That, of course, is the irony of the poem.

Frederick Feirstein, whose verse we read in the chapter on rhyme, says, "The character study often turns on dramatic irony, a contrast between what the character sees about himself and what the writer and reader see." Feirstein adds that any description in a dramatic work (such as the Duke's commentary about his last duchess) must serve to develop character. Likewise, whatever objects appear in a dramatic episode — e.g., the sculpture of Neptune breaking a seahorse at the end of Browning's poem — must serve a character, a theme or the action, as a prop does in a play.

Here are elements to help you distinguish dramatic poetry from other categories of verse:

- *The title.* This should inform the audience that the poem is in the dramatic mode and also set the stage for the content of the drama to follow. (For example, Browning is no Duke, even though he uses the word *my* in the title "My Last Duchess" — his topic.)
- *The viewpoint.* The poet creates an entity through which events in an episode or topics in a character study are filtered (as comments in Browning's poem are filtered through the Duke).
- *The voice.* Even though the poet may employ the first person, tones of voice are not the poet's but the entity's. (In Browning's poem, the sly, snobby and presumptuous tones are aligned with the Duke's personality.)

You can see how dramatic poems can be confused with narrative poems whose action involves other people and with lyrics whose topics also can be people. Moreover, tributes and epigrams (short pithy poems) often are confused with character studies because they focus intensely on personality traits of an invented, historial or composite entity.

Here's a tribute to an Elizabethan actor by Ben Jonson:

TO EDWARD ALLEYN

If Rome so great, and in her wisest age,
Feared not to boast the glories of her stage,
As skillful Roscious, and grave Aesop, men,
Yet crowned with honours, as with riches, then;
Who had no less a trumpet of their name,
Than Cicero, whose every breath was fame:
How can so great example die in me,
That, Alleyn, I should pause to publish thee?
Who both their graces in thyself hast more
Outstripped, than they did all that went before:
And present worth in all dost so contract,
As others speak, but only thou dost act.
Wear this renown. 'Tis just, that who did give
So many poets life, by one should live.

The poem discusses a historical entity's talent as an orator on stage but the title clearly implies that the views are Jonson's (not the entity's). This, of course, disqualifies it as dramatic work.

Here's a Jonson epigram about a glutton:

ON GUT

Gut eats all day and lechers all the night;
So all his meat he tasteth over twice;
And, striving so to double his delight,
He makes himself a thoroughfare of vice.
Thus in his belly can he change a sin:
Lust it comes out, that gluttony went in.

Again, the title clearly implies that these are the poet's views about a glutton by the name of Gut. Although Gut is a fictive or at best composite entity, voice and viewpoint are not filtered through that entity but belong to the poet. Again, the work is lyric and not dramatic.

Finally, here's a poem by Edgar Lee Masters in which title, viewpoint and voice combine to form a character study:

EDITOR WHEDON

To be able to see every side of every question;
To be on every side, to be everything, to be nothing long;
To pervert truth, to ride it for a purpose,
To use great feelings and passions of the human family
For base designs, for cunning ends,
To wear a mask like the Greek actors —
Your eight-page paper — behind which you huddle,

Bawling through the megaphone of big type:
"This is I, the giant."
Thereby also living the life of a sneak-thief,
Poisoned with the anonymous words
Of your clandestine soul.
To scratch dirt over scandal for money,
And exhume it to the winds for revenge,
Or to sell papers,
Crushing reputations, or bodies, if need be,
To win at any cost, save your own life.
To glory in demoniac power, ditching civilization,
As a paranoiac boy puts a log on the track
And derails the express train.
To be an editor, as I was.
Then to lie here close by the river over the place
Where the sewage flows from the village,
And the empty cans and garbage are dumped,
And abortions are hidden.

The pivotal line — "To be an editor, as I was" — and the other lines that follow, make the piece a character study (as opposed to an epigram on editors or a tribute to one named Whedon). In fact, if you end the poem after this line — "And derails the express train" — and title it "Editors," you would have an epigram. However, after that pivotal line above, the reader realizes that these are the pronouncements of an editor on himself, from the grave.

Now that we have an idea about what constitutes dramatic work — a revealing title plus an entity's viewpoint and voice — let's analyze techniques to help you create a dramatic episode and a character study.

HOW TO COMPOSE A DRAMATIC EPISODE

First, review the process of composing a narrative work as discussed in chapter fourteen. Instead of aligning aspects of voice as personality traits of the poet or of an unseen storyteller, align them with a specific character. Once you do, you will have transformed a narrative poem into a dramatic episode.

Let's illustrate this with two of my poems, the first a narrative and the second a dramatic episode:

BUYING A BETTA FROM THE VIETNAMESE
CLERK AT K MART

I ask how many can live
In a 10-gallon,

And she doesn't bat an eye:
Four, she says.
I like the idea of her lying.
Then the manager passes by
And she sighs: "put more
Than one in a tank, sir,
And they rip each other
To noodles." She goes on
Break, and I follow her
With a betta in a baggie
To the cafeteria.
I have something to hide.
"Sit down," she says and talks
About tropical fish. In Saigon
Men would fight bettas the way
You fight cocks in the back
Alleys, she says, batting an eye.
I reach for her hand
But she leaves
Her address on a napkin.
Later I bring the bourbon
And my betta in a bowl,
Put it between us
On the table in her kitchen.
Maybe something is in store.
She used to breed fighting fish
For her lovers and could do
The same for me, she says.
This time she doesn't bat
An eye but takes me
By the trigger finger
And forgives me.

If you sketch an outline for the above poem, as you learned to do in the chapter on narrative verse, it would resemble this:

- *Topic*: Buying a betta at K mart
- *Theme*: Forgiveness
- *Voice*: Matter-of-fact, savvy, tense (first person)
- *Viewpoint*: Narrator
- *Moment*: Now and Then
- *Ending*: Closed

Watch how the outline changes for a dramatic episode:

- *Topic*: Buying a betta at K mart

- *Theme*: Forgiveness
- *Voice*: Descriptive, conversational, candid (first person)
- *Viewpoint*: Vietnamese Clerk
- *Moment*: Now and Then
- *Ending*: Closed

Voice and viewpoint are affected. Although we are using the first person to narrate the episode, tones of voice are aligned *not* with personality traits of the poet (or implied author of the piece), but with the fictive entity of the Vietnamese clerk.

Consider how that brushstroke, plus an appropriate title, transforms the entire work:

WHAT THE VIETNAMESE CLERK AT K MART SAID BEFORE SHE SOLD THE VETERAN A BETTA

You can find them anywhere, any pet shop,
Even the K mart at Muskogee: fighting fish
That flare so bright you think of dragons,
That come one to a bowl with a story I keep

For the special customer. Long ago a girl
With hair like mine, so black the sun
Sparked in the paddies, dipped her hands
Below some bubbles and scooped a betta

With a little color. The men she knew
Fought such fish as Americans today fight
Cocks in the barns and back alleys.
The betta she held was not purple like yours,

But brown with a promise of purple, and the fins
Sad as a girl whose hair is shorn for punishment.
Still, it was the finest fighter anyone then had seen.
If she brought the fish to her husband

Then and there, I would not be selling you
A betta today at K mart. She put it in a bowl
And vowed to breed this fish until she found
The dragon in its blood, and given a dragon

Her husband, she thought, would love her forever.
Only a girl so gentle could make such magic,
And being gentle this mistake: she bred the best
And did not kill the others, as I might have done.

She put them in the paddies. Soon her neighbors
Brought home bettas more striking than ones she took

To her husband, to keep her secret. He lost
Fight after fight and had nothing left to wager

But the girl. When he told her to serve
A new master, then and there she could have
Given him a dragon — purple with black mask,
Fins like fire. He would have reclaimed her.

Instead, she went quietly to the other man
And vowed to breed the blood of dragons
In their children. One by one she freed
Her fighters that lord to this day in the paddies,

That I sell here at K mart, and when a man
Like you comes along, someone I might have bred
My bettas for in Saigon, I tell this little story
And make us feel okay about what happened.

In the narrative example, the *I* in the poem — along with the actions,
comments, views and tones of voice — can be assigned to the poet, me.
(At least that is what it suggests.) Even the presence of the clerk is
filtered through the narrator. But in the dramatic version — which also
employs the first person — actions, views, comments and tones of voice
obviously are assigned to the clerk. Everything is filtered through her,
and she couldn't possibly be me because I am not Vietnamese or a
woman. The clerk may be invented, historical or a composite — that's
my prerogative as poet — but she is above all a *created* entity.

Now that the dramatic episode has been distinguished from the
narrative, here's how you can compose one:

1. In a page of your journal, make a character sketch of the persons
in your episode. Simply describe them in a few sentences as you would
describe another person to a friend. Discuss aspects of each character's personality and why he or she might have developed certain traits.
For example:

> The clerk, a Vietnamese woman with long black hair, is attracted
> to certain men she thinks are veterans. She likes to tell them a
> story about bettas because that symbolizes the fighting spirit of the
> Vietnamese. She does this to help herself and them forgive what
> happened in her country.

2. Conceive a scene with these characters that has some action
(however simple, such as buying a betta at a pet shop). Write down a
sentence or two in your journal about that scene to remember it vividly
in your mind. For example:

> The selling of the betta occurs at K mart — an American symbol.

I want the clerk to address the customer as she sells him a fighting fish, sharing her folktale about bettas.

3. Decide which character has the most clout. If you can't, funnel a few lines through each character and compare. This should result in your choosing an entity through which voice and viewpoint can be funneled. For example, the the veteran's viewpoint:

> She tells me I can find them anywhere,
> Even the K mart in Muskogee. I listen
> As she says, etc.

Here the narrator is too passive. Try again, this time using the clerk's viewpoint:

> You can find them anywhere, any pet shop,
> Even the K mart at Muskogee: fighting fish
> That flare, etc.

Much better. Now the narrator is engaging.

4. Because the title is so important in a dramatic work, pick one now that introduces your main character. The title should also ground the reader, conveying that the person who speaks is not the poet and setting the stage for the episode to follow (as in the title "What the Vietnamese Clerk at K mart Said Before She Sold the Veteran a Betta").

5. Imagine your episode in three moments of narration ("Now," "Now and Then" and "Then," as decribed in the chapter on narrative verse). Compose a few lines in each moment so you can sense the right one.

(Now)

> A girl went to the paddies. She saw
> Bubbles rise to the surface and
> Dipped her palm, scooping a betta.

Result: No perspective to characterize speaker.

(Now and Then)

> Long ago a girl with hair like mine,
> So black the sun sparked in the paddies,
> Dipped her hands below some bubbles
> And scooped a betta.

Result: Action and perspective via voice.

(Then)

In Vietnam you can still find bettas
In the paddies, under bubbles.
If you scoop your hands quick enough,
You can catch them.

Result: All comment, no tension.

6. Imagine your characters in the scene as if you were viewing them on stage. As you do this, make a list of objects (props) that might depict your actors or help propel the episode. In the "Betta" poem, the list would include such words as *bowl, paddies, hair, dragon, K mart, customer, mask*, etc. This list will help you visualize your piece later.

7. Imagine the ending to your scene (open or closed). Compose an open ending and a closed one and then compare. For example:

(Open)

One by one she freed her fighters
That lord to this day in the paddies.

Result: Too vague, no resolution.

(Closed)

I tell this little story and make us
feel okay about what happened.

Result: Echoes theme of forgiveness.

8. Review all elements thus far: personality sketch, scene, moment, pertinent objects, ending. Now align tones of voice with the viewpoint of your main character. In the "Betta" poem, the tones need to be descriptive, conversational and candid so the clerk can make her point with the veteran.

9. Do a mini-outline as you learned in the chapter on narrative poetry, detailing topic, theme, voice, viewpoint, moment and ending. If you are having trouble distinguishing your dramatic episode from a narrative work, you might want to compose an outline for a narrative poem and then another one for a dramatic episode (as I did earlier in this section).

10. Envision your poem and compose.

HOW TO COMPOSE A CHARACTER STUDY

Review the chapter on lyric verse, paying special attention to lyrics about basic topics (moments, objects, living things, concepts and experiences). If the living thing is a person and you focus on him or her

intensely—funneling tones of voice and viewpoint through that person—you also are composing a character study.

But the transition from the lyric to the dramatic mode can be much
richer than that. All you have to do is:

1. Imagine *the person* who would be intensely interested in a specific moment, object, living thing, concept or experience.
2. Create an appropriate entity.
3. Funnel voice and viewpoint through that character.

Let's illustrate with two poems, the first a lyric focusing on the
concept of music, and the second, a character sketch based on a person
who would be intensely interested in such a topic:

MUSIC

I cannot hold a note in my hand,
Though the singer does in her throat.
I cannot hold a grace note
On lined paper and hear it,
Though the singer waves
Her sheet music like a flag.

But I can hold the makers
Of music, the singer by the palm,
The silver of flute or piccolo,
Buff nickle keys of a clarinet.
If I breathe on them, I can
See my own image in the maker.

It's true. I can stroke
The pipework of sax and trombone,
Tip a chalice of trumpet, sort
The pots of horn, cornet to tuba.
I find myself stacking
Cymbals like Waterford

And grasping harems of mandolins,
Bellies aburst, necks ringed
With abalone, mother of pearl.
My violins and violas drip
With purfling so tiger-striped,
I keep them in velvet.

Unlike music, these can be mine.

Watch how this poem is transformed into a character study by focusing on the essence of a person who might feel this way about music

and by filtering voice and viewpoint through that person:

THE MUSIC MISER

The silver I shine comes in two denominations:
Flute and piccolo. Otherwise give me nickle,
The buff keys of a clarinet that fog so splendidly

And then glitter back the karats of my grin.
Give me brass, the pipework of sax and trombone,
Chalice of trumpet, and assorted pots of horn,

Cornet to tuba. Give me a china closetful
Of cymbals stacked like Waterford. Utensils?
Tuning forks. A connoisseur of woodwind and wood,

I'm the Picasso of varnish: violins that drip
With purfling, violas and cellos so tiger-striped
They're caged in velvet. I keep a harem

Of mandolins, their bellies aburst, elegant
Necks ringed with abalone, mother-of-pearl.
Then, the ebony and white — spinet to baby grand —

With ivory like contraband tusk. I can't play
A lick, tone-deaf. If you enter my villa,
Keep quiet. I have one rule: don't touch.

The lyric is clearly distinguishable from the character study, even though the latter employs many of the same devices: the topic, the intensity, the lack of time-passage, the first person, and shared images and metaphors. But the title of the second work — "The Music Miser" — grounds the piece in the dramatic mode by informing the reader about the voice on the page and by setting the stage for the topic to follow. Again, voice and viewpoint are aligned with the fictive entity of the miser.

Now that the character study has been distinguished from the lyric mode, here's how you can compose one:

1. Approach the character study as you would a lyric poem about a moment, object, living thing, concept or experience. Instead of writing about any of those basic topics, however, generate a dramatic work by contemplating a person who would be intensely interested in any of those topics. The person, of course, is not you but some invented, historical or composite entity. For example, William Blake (a historical entity) composed lyrics about a myriad of subjects. A little research also shows that he occasionally heard voices, foresaw the impact of the machine on people living during the Industrial Era, and could be

ornery. A character sketch about him would focus on personality traits that might have caused Blake to investigate the world so vigorously.

2. Once you have the character in mind, make a sketch (in prose) of that person, describing aspects of his or her personality. Later this will help you create an appropriate voice. For example:

Blake, of course, heard voices dictating his poems and had weird visions. He hated the machine. He'd walk the streets in an artist's cap and played devil's advocate with anyone who questioned him.

3. Now imagine such a person witnessing or re-creating a moment, an object, a living thing, a concept or an experience. To illustrate, let's take the person of William Blake and imagine him hearing a tiger roar (moment), seeing a tiger rug (object), contemplating the tiger (living thing), pondering the extinction of tigers (concept) and touring the zoo (experience). Decide which topic best suits your character and then research that topic as you would before composing a lyric work.

4. Create an appropriate title to introduce your character and to forebode what the character will be discussing in your poem. Consider these examples:

- William Blake Hears a Tiger Roar
- William Blake Steps on a Tiger Rug
- William Blake Sees His First Tiger
- William Blake Envisions the Extinction of Tigers
- William Blake Tours the Cat's Den at the Denver Zoo

5. Once you have sketched your character, researched your topic and composed your title, imagine how your character might treat the content of your poem. Keep in mind that, unlike a lyric in which the poet is charged with discovering the true essence of a topic, the character's viewpoint in a dramatic work should be limited so that a sense of irony ensues. Write a paragraph about how you might see the topic and how your character might. For example:

In my world, the extinction of the tiger is a concept that I can understand but not accept. Even in my lifetime I thought that the buffalo, eagle and whale might be extinct one day. But I cannot imagine William Blake thinking like this. His tiger, of course, is a symbol of the Creator's awesome power. His view of man destroying such a creature would be limited, at best, and might result in irony about our own destructive tendencies.

6. Now imagine the tones of voice that your character might employ when discussing, investigating or re-creating your chosen topic. Consult your character sketch and write a few adjectives to indicate the tone. Now write a few lines in the voice you would use to discuss

your topic and the voice your character would use, distinguishing both voices. (Later this will serve as a check to make sure you are filtering tones through your entity.) For example:

(My voice)

The tiger is dead. It began with the destruction of
habitat in Africa and ended, like most extinctions,
in zoos.

(Blake's voice)

Africa awake! arise! The tiger, caged?
The hand that made the tiger is caged.
Dead? The mind that made the tiger is dead.

7. Evaluate all your sketches and journal entries about personality, content, topic, research, tones of voice, etc. Note any irony, truth or common thread running through them. (For instance, you should be able to connect personality traits with viewpoint and voice quite easily.) Then, scan your material to see what information might appeal naturally to your entity. Write about this in your journal. For example:

My research shows that the Bali and Caspian tigers are extinct. The Java, Sumatran, Siberian and Indian subspecies are endangered. Tigers haunt the ruins of courts and temples. Given Blake's acumen about ancient places and use of symbols, I should be able to focus on lands of endangered tigers and to use the ruined temples as a symbol for the fate of mankind.

8. Envision the poem and compose.

To help you envision dramatic episodes and character studies, I've included some of my favorites in the mini anthology:

• In "The Homunculus," a character study that opens Fred Chappell's *Castle Tzingal* (Louisiana State University, 1984), you can see all the elements at work: an invented character speaking through an obviously fictive voice about a concept (espionage). The poem's best feature is a sense of irony and doom.

Chappell — a poet, writer and critic — has this advice about voice, especially as it applies to a longer dramatic work: "Sometimes I've found it useful, when two or more speakers talk in a dramatic poem, to identify their voices with musical instruments, flutes, cellos, trumpets and so forth. This technique reminds me of the necessity of variety in tonal values and offers a way to characterize."

• In "Sister Mary Appassionata Lectures the Eighth Grade Boys and Girls: *Every Day Another Snake*," David Citino blends elements of the episode (a lecture) with a character study of a nun. He forebodes all that in his clever dramatic title.

• In "Larry Corners the Psychiatrist," the dramatic piece that opens the sequence "The Psychiarist at the Cocktail Party" found in Frederick Feirstein's *City Life* (Story Line, 1991), Feirstein employs contemporary language in rhymed and metered stanzas, creating additional tension. Feirstein says that long dramatic works usually use meter because the poem "requires a repetitive base to play off and create variations in the speaking voice." He adds, "Because the long dramatic poem is meant for the stage or the stage inside the reader's head, its diction should be colloquial."

• In "Miss Intensity Thinks About Her Name," a perfect work to illustrate the difference between lyric, narrative and dramatic work, Katherine Murphy, whose verse we encountered in the chapter on extranatural poetry, bases her episode on an experience she had losing her wallet "and realizing I had no way, on my own, to identify or name myself." Murphy says that she employs a dramatic persona because "somehow this allows me to write even more autobiographically, using images that seem less poetic. In my poem here," she observes, "pregnancy tests, car repair, and the calluses on my heels aren't usual material for lyric/narrative poems."

Mini Anthology of Dramatic Poems

THE HOMUNCULUS

I'm hardly the first man to live in a bottle
And see the world through a different size.
I'm the King's most privy counselor,
And know the secrets lisped at midnight
By love-performing ministers
And cunning courtesans. I spy the spies
Who never seek beneath their beds
Or in the arras-folds hard by the banisters
Of the shadowed gallery. Wiser heads
Than yours are indiscreet when all intent
On easing the vexed blood-itch. I tell
No one but the King the things I hear,
Who poisoned whom, and where the florins went.

A dirty trade, you say. Well,
What's a bit of a fellow to do?
In high-heeled boots I'm eighteen inches tall,
A whole intelligence force in miniscule.

My father was a mage, my mother a pour

Of mystery chemicals. I was born
On a table bright with flame and glassware,
And had no childhood except an ignorance
Of politics and gossip. And what a boring year
My childhood was. No company
But the pottering alchemist, his cat
Who wanted to gobble me up, and three
Disgusting nodules of melting flesh
That were earlier attempts at being me.
I was happy to be set to work,
To know who knows, and how he knows, and why.
— Fred Chappell

SISTER MARY APPASSIONATA LECTURES
THE EIGHTH GRADE BOYS AND GIRLS:
EVERY DAY ANOTHER SNAKE

And God gave Adam hands, fingers
smooth enough to soothe, deft enough
to create, arms long enough to reach,
but Adam sinned by trying to please
himself alone, so God made Eve, and
to her too gave hands, fingers, arms,
but Eve sinned by wanting to please
herself before all else, so God was forced
to make the snake, but by this time
He'd learned a lesson, and made it
limbless, and its slither and hiss
made Adam work, and Eve, until
their hands grew rough as pumice,
fingers gnarled from scrabbling for roots
in rocky soil, sewing greasy skins
callous-tough with blunt bone needles,
arms bent from a winter's weight
of firewood, a spring field's
depth of stone and clay.

Still today women and men come
into the world with the means to soothe,
create and reach, but a burning lust
to please nobody else. Every day
God's forced to make another snake.
— David Citino

LARRY CORNERS THE PSYCHIATRIST
(an excerpt*)

Look who's standing in my bedroom door!
Give me your coat, Ben. Glad you could come
To one of my fund-raising bashes.
This one is for that man from Quistador.
Startling, these guys in khaki and mustaches.
Try an hors d'oeuvres. The catering is yum.

Where's Mary . . . , Jeez, does she have a fever?
I hope it's just the flu and nothing more.
Even you'd be a hypochondriac
With my mother—it was so hard to leave her.
I wish Mary wasn't flat on her back;
I wanted her to see my new decor.

It's Pop-Colonial, a parody:
Brighton bamboo, but painted Third World red.
The knicknacks are from 42nd Street,
Las Vegas, and Disneyland: *our* ivory
But crafted out of plastic—Go on, eat—
And not one single elephant shot dead.

Mary would have loved our rebel guest,
An illustration of her Ph.D.
On Latin intellectuals *cum* killer.
I think this baby far outstrips the rest.
He has a Harvard social work degree
And still reads shrink books. God, I think he'd thrill her. . . .
                                        —Frederick Feirstein

MISS INTENSITY THINKS ABOUT HER NAME

Centuries ago at EST, when I waved my hand,
praying the Trainer would choose me—as lost
as my friend Helen who got married and now her name
isn't in the phone book anymore—for the Birth Process
because he was teaching all 300 of us, simultaneously,

to get in touch with our bodies and the Self
(I'd heard it was like being reborn, alive again,
assertive, experiencing—wailing *Oh Moon of Alabama*
in the tub, charging that fringy sequin dress,

---

*This excerpt originally was from a larger poem that was part of a seventeen-part
dramatic sequence.*

feeling, instead of being a machine and just meshing gears

even though they don't let you go to the bathroom
and keep you in folding chairs until 4 AM), the Trainer
pointed, "You — Miss Intensity — in the red sweater,
Sweetheart, up here," and I sat in the director's chair,
high as a bar stool, with a microphone like his,

close enough to smell his aftershave lotion,
and I was Miss Intensity for two whole weekends
even though it wasn't on my name tag —
it wasn't like he just gave me my name,
it was finally somebody knew who I was, even though

I might have been suspicious of another name
from another man — usually some animal name first
like Bunny, or Pussy Cat, then you marry them
and take theirs (unless of course you hyphenate)
and then they begin to speak in the imperative voice —

it's a common problem, for instance, last winter
when I went for pregnancy tests every month,
the nurse read my name one day and said
"Aren't you related to Dr. So-and-so?"
and I said "What? That's not my real name,"

and she gave me the funniest look and just
set the bottle on the counter and we both laughed
and she wiped her eyes and said "Gee, none of us
have real names," and when I came back she said
"Dearheart, you're not pregnant, you're just old,"

so all spring I bought those home tests
at the drug store, but they wouldn't turn blue,
and then I forgot about my name, I guess, until
that day at the gas station I was trying to put air
in my right front tire and somebody stole my purse

(reached right in and picked it up off the car seat),
and my driver's license and all my credit cards,
my social security card — all with my married name —
and I thought how will I prove who I am and then
poems, nobody else could have written my poems

because once in a workshop this famous poet said I
had an individual voice and I thought Honey I haven't even
started talking, but now I wondered do words have different

kinds of whorls for everybody, like finger prints
and then I thought well, they'll believe my husband,

but instead of going home I drove to the mall—
a ½ price sale—and tried on a paisley maternity dress
(marked down for the third time, completely lined,
a famous maker although the label was cut off), scared
he'd be angry, and then I searched the lot for the car

and sat on the curb in front of Saks 5th Avenue
looking up at the clouds, wondering where's the car
and how in the world did I get too old to have a baby
and what will I say if he yells at me, when I suddenly saw
my face, my own face in the clouds, an alabaster statue

and then, slowly she turned, and she was still me
—down to my nose and the silver lame scarf tied
around my throat in a bow and my hair avant garde
like Ricardo did it at the Fall Make-Over
when he transformed me into the real me

and I wondered is seeing my face an omen
for getting pregnant or winning the lottery
or even finding the car, but the clouds disappeared
and I thought most people wouldn't believe
Miss Intensity is my real name, but they are wrong.

                                        —Katherine Murphy

Notebook

LEVEL ONE

1. Evaluate drafts of poems in your "Work in Progress" file that seem suited to the dramatic mode. Revise them according to precepts learned in this chapter.

2. From your "Work in Progress" file, take drafts of poems from each of the Notebook exercises in the narrative and lyric chapters. Revise the narrative drafts into dramatic episodes and the lyric drafts into character studies, using techniques explained in this chapter. Compare drafts. Afterward in your journal discuss the experience and evaluate which transformation—narrative to dramatic episode, lyric to character study—was the most and least effective.

3. Select ideas from your "Idea File" that seem suited to a dramatic episode and to the character study and compose one of each.

LEVEL TWO

1. Read your journal entries from the Level One, Exercise Two. If you found the narrative-to-dramatic-episode transformation the least effective, take your drafts again from the notebook exercise on narrative poems and transform them into episodes. (Do likewise with lyric drafts to character studies if you found that transformation the least effective.) Afterward determine whether you can personalize methods explained in this chapter so they are more in line with your muse.

2. Select two ideas from your "Idea File" and compose dramatic episodes or character studies — whichever mode you're having more trouble with — according to your new, personalized methods. (Note: If you are no longer experiencing any difficulty, select an idea for a dramatic episode and another for a character study and compose them.)

LEVEL THREE

Read any journal entries generated by Level One and Two exercises. Re-evaluate the composition process and personalize it, if appropriate. Then select three more ideas from your "Idea File" for dramatic episodes and/or character studies and compose them.

Chapter Seventeen

Free Verse

F ree verse features an irregular cadence instead of standard meter. Unfortunately, the words that make up the term *free verse* suggest a kind of poetry that lacks distinctive form or tradition. Although its history dates back to early English versions of the Bible, serious discussion of the form usually begins with Robert Frost who said he would rather play tennis without a net than compose free verse. Ever since, some people have seized on that analogy to argue that free verse really isn't poetry.

That's not the case, and that's not what Frost meant.

In an interview on *Meet the Press*, he elaborated on the remark. Asked why he took so many images and metaphors from the world of games, Frost replied, "I don't think anyone could think right in this world who didn't play games sometime in his life. I'd as soon write free verse as play tennis with the net down. That brought tennis in."

True, Frost didn't care much for free verse. But he was defining the type of verse that *he* wanted to write. He became a poet during an era that featured the innovative moderns — Pound, Eliot, H.D., Williams, Stevens and many others — who wrote many of their best poems in the first decades of the twentieth century and who argued against the formal verse in vogue in the Victorian era. They said the sound of poetry was stilted and blamed it, in part, on the forms of traditional verse; but they also accused Milton and the influence of his *Paradise Lost*, a brilliant epic in iambic pentameter (or blank verse), which, alas, lacks the tonality of the human voice:

> To whom, with healing words, Adam replied:
> "Daughter of God and Man, immortal Eve!
> For such thou art, from sin and blame entire
> Not diffident of thee do I dissuade
> Thy absence from my sight, but to avoid
> Th' attempt itself, intended by our foe. . . .

The paradox, as it concerns Frost, is that he had similar ideas about voice. Although Frost may have embraced the old forms, he rejected artificiality and recaptured a natural New England tone in his work. He was an innovator, too — of formal poetry. Meanwhile, moderns like Pound were rebelling against the traditions of the previous century, save one, as this Pound lyric suggests:

A PACT

I make a pact with you, Walt Whitman —
I have detested you long enough.
I come to you as a grown child
Who has had a pig-headed father;
I am old enough now to make friends.
It was you that broke the new wood,
Now is a time for carving.
We have one sap and one root —
Let there be commerce between us.

Pound was honoring the influence of Whitman, whose uneven lines caused a sensation in his day. Here's an excerpt from Whitman's free verse poem, "I Hear America Singing:"

I hear America singing, the varied carols I hear,
Those of mechanics, each one singing his as it should be blithe
                                        and strong
The carpenter singing his as he measures his plank or beam,
The mason singing his as he makes ready for work, or leaves
                                        off work,
The boatman singing what belongs to him in his boat, the
                    deckhand singing on the steamboat deck,
The shoemaker singing as he sits on his bench, . . .

In his usual celebratory fashion, Whitman ends his poem by depicting all manner of Americans singing "with open mouths their strong melodious songs."

Whitman is widely acknowledged as the founding father of free verse. After all, the Civil War era was perfect for it, an emotional time whose theme was freedom and whose subject matter — death and destruction — did not fit tidy patterns of formal poetry. But the paradox of Whitman is that his influence seems as great in the twentieth century as Milton's was in the last; moreover, while Milton will forever be known as a religious poet, it was Whitman who looked to the Bible, particularly Psalms, to hone his voice. Based on ancient Hebrew patterns, the Psalms were translated freestyle in 1611 in the King James version. Here is a typical passage (Psalm 137:1-2):

By the rivers of Babylon, there we sat down, yea,
    we wept,
    when we remembered Zion.
We hanged our harps upon the willows in the midst.

As you can see, Whitman laid the groundwork for the moderns. Two schools of free verse evolved. Pound, Eliot, H.D., Williams, Stevens and others experimented further with voice and form but focused primarily on image (at the expense of clarity, some claim). Other poets, such as Carl Sandburg and Edgar Lee Masters — refer to the latter's poem "Editor Whedon" on pages 253-254 — followed Whitman's lead and simply employed the tones and cadences of language without becoming obscure in the process. Thus, Sandburg and Masters were among the first poets to capture true American diction, using free verse as the vehicle and structure as the frame.

STRUCTURED FREE VERSE

If you have been composing free verse and following guidelines about idea, voice, title, line, stanza and other elements of craft as presented in the second section of this text, then your free verse really isn't free. It's structured. In other words, it has a preconceived form.

In traditional verse using rhyme and/or meter, the length of the line, and sometimes the shape of the stanza and the duration of the poem, are determined without your help. For instance, if you follow a rhyme scheme, rhymes also determine where lines end. If you employ a regular meter, the length of the line is automatically set for you. If you compose a sonnet or form poem (covered in upcoming chapters), the line, stanza and duration of the poem also are fixed. In free verse, however, you have to decide when and how to break a line, make a stanza and end a poem.

That's the so-called "freedom" of free verse.

If you are not making such decisions, you may or may not be writing poetry. You certainly are not writing structured verse. In general, more structure results in better poems; less structure approaches prose, which can be defined as "words spoken or written for an audience, using sentences and paragraphs." Let's illustrate:

(Prose)

Malta, 1943. My family suffers the ironies of war. German bombs explode day and night. Food is rationed. We are always hungry.

At dawn my father goes to the harbor, carrying a broom. He cannot stand his children starving. The British sailors unload sacks of flour, and dust settles on the docks. He

sweeps so my mother can bake bread full of grit and
splinters.

But we eat. Then the British arrest my father and
we don't know anymore who the enemy is.

(Unstructured free verse)

MALTA 1943

My family
suffers the ironies of
war. German bombs explode day and night. Food is
rationed. We are always hungry. At
dawn my father goes to the harbor, carrying a
broom. He cannot stand his
children starving. The
British sailors unload sacks of flour,
and dust
settles on the docks. He sweeps so
my mother can
bake bread full of grit and splinters. But we
eat. Then the British arrest my father and
we don't know anymore who the enemy is.

(Structured free verse)

DURATION
Malta 1943

My family suffers the ironies of war.
German bombs explode
day and night. Food is rationed.

We are always hungry. At dawn
my father goes to the harbor,
carrying a broom. He cannot

stand his children starving.
The British sailors unload
sacks of flour, and dust

settles on the docks. He sweeps
So my mother can bake bread
full of grit and splinters.

But we eat. Then the British
arrest my father and we don't
know anymore who the enemy is.

Analyze these samples for evidence of structure. In the prose piece, sentences and paragraphs provide the form. Because it is self-contained, the passage can be labeled a prose poem — a short, textured piece of writing without the added meaning derived from lines and stanzas. In the unstructured sample, irregular lines provide a pattern, but no discernable element of craft seems involved in these line breaks. Thus, the poem is weak. But in the structured sample, the title, line and stanza combine to make a stronger work than either the prose poem or unstructured version.

The above samples are meant only to show how structure alone can make a poem out of a prose passage. In actuality, each was based on this lyric whose line breaks help evoke a voice in Whitman's tradition, employing angry, repetitive and ironic tones and transforming the entire work:

A BLESSING
Malta 1943

I will eat your grey-speckled bread
because I am one of nine children
because our father has been arrested
for sweeping flour dust from the docks
because they cannot ration need
even now — their bombs popping
like small hungers — I want to go
belly full of this world.

Once again, form makes free verse.

"No poem exists without form," says Jim Barnes, whose structured poem "For Roland, Presumed Taken" appears in the chapter on extra-natural poetry. According to Barnes, "Anyone writing with no regard to structure is writing prose (not free verse!), and most likely bad prose at that." He says that writers who call themselves poets should be interested in the structure of language. "There are cadences, rhythms, echoes that poets have to control. They cannot be controlled *by* them, or prose will take over."

Similarly, poet Sharon E. Martin, whose structured free verse appears regularly in literary magazines, states: "A poem without structure of some kind is prose in masquerade. Theories on the line break, for instance, where word choices give lines multiple meanings, are about structure. Poems that lend themselves to oral readings and dramatics, written for delivery, have structure.

"I don't really believe in the 'prose poem.' I love short-short stories and vignettes (literary sketches), and most prose poems I see fall into one of these categories. I want structure, not margins.

"Poetry is high art, and poets who can shape their thoughts to fit an exacting form, whether that form is rhymed or unrhymed, are true artists."

Martin says she doesn't always achieve such artistry, but strives for it in poems like this one:

TO MY SON, GROWING UP

That I love you has never been enough,
child more me than I am,
son who claims my soul as his own.

Last night I held you as you cried
dry, shoulder-shaking tears
for the long-distance father

who won't come again this year.
It has always been the same—his excuses,
and you, so young, defending them.

Until now.
This time his excuses,
like my solo love, are not enough.

Consider the elements of craft involved in this seemingly simple, eloquent poem. First, the matter-of-fact voice (rather than a gushy or maudlin one) is appropriate for the occasion because it avoids sentimentality. Second, the poet shapes her lines into crisp units of speech and uses uniform stanzas (tercets) that forebode the ending. The final stanza begins with a short pivot line—"Until now"—to convey the epiphany.

To put all this into perspective, and to emphasize the effects of form on free verse, let's look at the creation of one more poem.

CASE STUDY: WRITING "BROWN SHOES"

I met Grace L. Rutledge at a writer's conference. She had an individual critique session with me, and instead of bringing a poem, she brought a vignette that contained a rhymed fragment. She had composed a few poems, she said, but thought her prose showed more promise:

Brown shoes. Looks like a little boy's shoes, they said. I didn't care—if it was from my daddy, it was above ridicule and I above humiliation. Me and my daddy didn't care together.

I loved my brown shoes, they were kind of a rich dark brown, round-toed, buster-brownish, but not quite. I would later concede, grudgingly, that they might look like little boys' shoes—so what? What was disturbing was not so much that people could laugh at something funny-looking, but how could they laugh at something you loved? And it was clear that I loved my brown shoes.

In time the house that inhabited seven people would be condemned as uninhabitable. Seven people. Torn to the ground, leveled. In the rubble where the foundation had been, crushed and broken, but still whole, I found one brown shoe, waiting to be carted away with the glass and memories. Where is the other one—alone somewhere; how sad to be without your partner in a crisis. A tearful goodbye, clutching stroking—alone with my shoe, me and my daddy's shoe. Yes, it was unmistakable now that it is a boy's shoe. So what?

House gone, in another year, daddy too
But me and my dad and my brown shoe
With laughter and tears we made it through
Me and my daddy and my brown shoe

How I wanted my shoes and the time back. They were mine.

I agreed with her—the vignette showed promise—*as a poem*. Her diction was too repetitive (and sentimental) for prose and her paragraphs concealed some fine lyrical moments. So we circled phrases in her vignette and recast them as lines and stanzas to convey greater levels of meaning. Finally, we tightened and added a few phrases and employed a better structure to imply the passage of time and forebode the epiphany.

In ten minutes, we assembled this poem:

BROWN SHOES

1.
Looks like little boy's shoes,
they said. I didn't care—
if they were from daddy,
I liked them: rich dark
brown round-toed, not quite
Buster-Brownish. If they looked
like little boy's shoes—
so what? I wore them.
2.
In time, the house that held
7 people was condemned:
uninhabitable. 7 people, torn
to the ground. Levelled.
In the rubble
where the foundation had been,

crushed and broken,
but still whole, I found

one brown shoe. I took it.

After we had revised her vignette, I asked Rutledge to comment on the experience: "I had used rhyme in writing poetry almost exclusively to lay an emotional foundation for my themes. So it was with wonder that I followed you into my prose piece, written totally without rhyme or poetic intention, as we transformed it into a poem.

"By, first of all, recognizing the more valid form for this piece as poetry — indeed, it is focused tightly on one metaphor — one can begin to 'hear' a musical strain, or emotional resonance. It carries a bittersweet memory that, with the strength of the metaphor and the key words to illustrate them, establish my theme and tone.

"What was left, then, was to give the words order and place them on the page to give them their emotional resonance, or music. The breakdown of stanzas, and the length and density of each line, suggest a natural rhythm and finally give the piece another layer of emotional resonance.

"You made a believer out of me."

That is my intention in this chapter — to make believers out of opposite camps — poets who think free verse really isn't poetry and ones who think it is but abandon form in the process.

In conclusion, let's introduce poems in the mini anthology that emphasize many of the points made in this chapter:

• "Inside the Light, the Figure That Holds Us" by Lucia Cordell Getsi, whose free verse has brought her a National Endowment for the Arts fellowship (among other honors). In this poem she employs structure as a frame and vehicle for her work. First, the idea — a painting in words whose beauty rivals Monet's — is, in itself, an epiphany about the power of poetry to capture the essence of art. Second, her lines are so well-crafted that they imply several levels of meaning or serve as precise units of speech. Third, her use of stanzas — a couplet pattern — eliminates the need for excessive punctuation; in fact, her poem consists of one sentence of more than one hundred eighty words! Finally, her first line is alluring and her last, even more so; the diction throughout the poem is brilliant — an intelligent, descriptive, sonorous voice.

• "Night Pleasures" by Dave Smith, a poet and writer who has authored more than twenty books. The poem featured here differs from his usual long narrated lyrics, combining elements of story with heightened lyrical moments. Says Smith, "I have begun to desire to write a new sort of poem" — one in which he attempts to "minimalize the story even more" and derive a "spare eloquence" in the process. But the focus on voice is not the only evidence of structure in his poem. Its irregular rhythm suits the topic: a little boat rocking against the "rhythmic landscape." Moreover, Smith uses stanza patterns to augment the effect, another brushstroke — wavelike on the page — that lets the reader see *and* hear that he is in full control of the poem.

  • "$" by Joyce Carol Oates, a versatile writer and author of some fifty books. Her lyric has a perfect title — so perfect, in fact, that when I discuss this poem I often call it "Money," although that word never appears. Instead she uses the symbol $ and the pronoun *it* so her lines meld into each other like thoughts in one, long, breathless sentence (which, incidentally, slows down when commas are inserted in the last two lines, signaling the ending). Oates also controls other elements of her lyric. Her first line plays off the title, standing alone as a statement worthy of our attention, establishing the theme — *it* — and then sallying forth. Every other line thereafter, it seems, has a horizontal meaning and combines with the line beneath it, enhancing meaning.

  This verse about money is, alas, hardly "free."

Mini Anthology of Free Verse Poems

INSIDE THE LIGHT, THE FIGURE THAT HOLDS US

  Monet's poplars slide through the bright surfaces of water
their slender wands; they rise through sky

    the color of the water, opaque, substantial
enough to hold the V-curve of leaf canopy

      that suggests perspective, flattened into painting
after painting, blurred to background or focussed,

        distinct, as though by telephoto eye so mesmerized
by sun the shape has burned into the lens and left a scar

          overlaid by a rhythmic imaging of light that hunts the soul
of the scar by reflection, the way the water reflects

            the sky, the way the eye hardly notices
the blue-green smudges of bank where the image

              reverses, sending the long stems like roots
into the viscous gelatin of retina; it requires

                an edge, the edge a frame, that we may see inside
the curving billow of leaves the classic form, like a chevron

                  of geese going south or north with the alterations

of light, that has flown into the very window

    of the eye, broken it a little in tiny cracks, so that the gaze
prefigures the repetitions, like a memory of home, a mirror.
— Lucia Cordell Getsi

NIGHT PLEASURES
(Poquoson, Virginia)

Where I come from land lies flat as paper.
    Pine, spruce, holly like dark words
left from a woods. Creeks coil, curve,
    enigmatic as women. To know the depths
you must dream. In the mountains
    for college I walked up and could see
barns, cows, housesmoke, but no boats.
    Hillsides of winesaps, still, perfect.

Here my little boat takes the night Bay.
    One far neon light tosses, a city
    people walk alone, its rhythmic
    landscape cut from marshes and cries.
On black water it is all mine, first
    beginnings, endings, love's beauties.
So when I move, it moves under me, and knows me.
— Dave Smith

$

If you have it you don't think about it
so acquiring it is the means of forgetting it
because if you don't have it you'll think about it
and you're embittered thinking about it because
to think about it is to acknowledge yourself
incomplete without it because you know you are
better than that, surely you are better
than the many who have it thus need not
think about it the way, after Death,
you won't think about Death either.
— Joyce Carol Oates

Notebook

LEVEL ONE

1. Evaluate drafts of poems in your "Work in Progress" file that
you cast in free verse. (If you have only metered poems, recast three of

those into free verse.) In any case, revise drafts according to precepts learned in this chapter.

2. Take three ideas from your "Idea File" and compose each one in prose, using sentences and paragraphs so you end up with three self-contained prose poems. In each work, circle phrases, images, individual words — whatever intrigues you in the piece — and reprint them on a separate sheet of paper. Using techniques illustrated in this chapter, cast those excerpts as lines and stanzas of a structured free verse poem, and title it. Then revise each work again, paying particular attention to voice (as you learned in chapter eight). Compare this method of composition to the one you have been using thus far when writing verse. Discuss the experience in your journal.

LEVEL TWO

Review the journal entry you made doing the Level One, Exercise Two. This time select three ideas from your "Idea File" and reverse the process, composing structured free verse poems first and then eliminating lines and stanzas in each draft to make prose poems. Compare drafts. Discuss the experience in your journal.

LEVEL THREE

1. Read your journal entries from the Level One and Two exercises. Select two similar ideas from your "Idea File." (Two lyric ideas involving a concept, say.) Do the Level One, Exercise Two again with one idea, composing a prose poem first and then revising it into structured free verse. Do the Level Two exercise again with the other idea, composing structured free verse first and then revising it into a prose poem. Discuss the methods of composition one more time and decide which one you prefer and why, using this as a guide for future work.

2. Select three ideas from your "Idea File" whose content somehow is related to movement. For instance, you might use ideas that involve the flight of birds at dawn (or bats at dusk!), waves of a river at full or low tide (or when a tug passes) or the arc of a falling tree (or a rising column of smoke). Try to mimic that movement with line break and stanza and be sure to employ a voice whose cadence also complements the topic of each idea.

Chapter Eighteen

The Sonnet

Villiam Shakespeare is as beloved for his sonnets as he is for his thirty-seven plays. Four centuries later, many of us know one or more of his sonnets by heart. In a word, the sonnet — or "little song" — strikes a universal chord within us. When we think of the immortality of poetry, we usually think of a sonnet like this one by the Bard:

Shall I compare thee to a summer's day?
Thou art more lovely and more temperate:
Rough winds do shake the darling buds of May,
And summer's lease hath all too short a date:
Sometimes too hot the eye of heaven shines,
And often is his gold complexion dimmed;
And every fair from fair sometimes declines,
By chance or nature's changing course untrimmed;
But thy eternal summer shall not fade,
Nor lose possession of that fair thou ow'st;
Nor shall death brag thou wander'st in his shade,
When in eternal lines to time thou grow'st:
So long as men can breathe, or eyes can see,
So long lives this, and this gives life to thee.

With lyrics like the one above, Shakespeare helped promote the sonnet in England. (The form has roots in continental Europe.) But others after him also did their part in passing along the grand tradition of composing sonnets to celebrate or bemoan an array of topics and occasions. For instance, Robert Browning composed some of the most accomplished poems in the English language, but his underrated lady Elizabeth Barrett Browning eclipsed the lot of Victorian laureates with this immortal song:

How do I love thee? Let me count the ways.
I love thee to the depth and breadth and height
My soul can reach, when feeling out of sight

For the ends of Being and ideal Grace.
I love thee to the level of everyday's
Most quiet need, by sun and candle-light.
I love thee freely, as men strive for Right;
I love thee purely, as they turn from Praise.
I love thee with the passion put to use
In my old griefs, and with my childhood's faith.
I love thee with a love I seemed to lose
With my lost saints — I love thee with the breath,
Smiles, tears, of all my life! — and, if God choose,
I shall but love thee better after death.

Finally, Edmund Spenser — known for his masterpiece *The Faerie Queene* — also helped popularize the sonnet by adapting its continental patterns to English, using an intricate but accessible rhyme scheme, illustrated in this sonnet from his famous sequence *Amoretti*:

My love is like to ice, and I to fire;
How comes it then that this her cold so great
Is not dissolved through my so hot desire,
But harder grows the more I her entreat?
Or how comes it that my exceeding heat
Is not delayed by her heart-frozen cold;
But that I burn much more in boiling sweat,
And feel my flames augmented manifold?
What more miraculous thing may be told,
That fire, which all things melts, should harden ice;
And ice, which is congealed with senseless cold,
Should kindle fire by wonderful device?
　　Such is the power of love in gentle mind,
　　That it can alter all the course of kind.

Using the above poems by Shakespeare, Elizabeth Barrett Browning and Spenser, let's define each of the sonnet's fundamental forms:

- *Shakespearean*, rhyming *abab cdcd efef gg*, each quatrain progressing toward a surprising turn of events in the ending couplet.
- *Italian* (or *Petrarchan*), rhyming *abbaabba* in the octave, or first eight lines, and *cdecde* in the sestet, or last six lines (or *cdcdcd* or other variation in the sestet, avoiding any couplets). The idea or question is presented in the octave and the resolution of the idea or question unravels in the sestet.
- *Spenserian*, rhyming *abab bcbc cdcd ee* with each quatrain developing a metaphor, conflict, idea or question, and the couplet resolving or concluding the matter.

The Italian form persists because the beauty of the octave and the vehicle of the sestet combine to express truth in a way no other poetic form can quite match. The Shakespearean remains popular because the form is simpler and the couplet, when executed well, packs the power of a punch line. The Spenserian has proved less popular than its cousins over time, but the form is easier than the Italian and more difficult than the Shakespearean, a kind of compromise between the two.

Finally, although we will focus on the above types, poets have been varying the forms of the sonnet for centuries — as you'll see reading sonnets in this chapter. Contemporary poets often vary the rhyme scheme or employ near rhymes, combine elements of the three basic forms, and even compose freestyle fourteen-line "sonnets" that eliminate rhyme altogether, along with the standard iambic pentameter beat. For such poets, varying the form eases restrictions and enhances content.

Furthermore, because of the sonnet's popularity and variations, we'll study it in depth and apart from fixed forms like the sestina, pantoum and villanelle (presented in the next chapter). The latter repeats lines or words in patterns that restrict certain types of topics. The thing to keep in mind about formal poetry in general, and sonnets in particular, is that content is crucial.

TYPES OF TOPICS

Each sonnet form was designed as a vehicle to convey certain topics or situations, using rhyme and scheme to enhance a message. Thus, you should know the tradition before attempting to compose such a poem. Simply, certain subjects do not fit the short form. While a skilled poet can break tradition and employ the sonnet to explain, say, why Communism failed in Eastern Europe, a novice probably should choose a freer form to convey such a notion.

A check of several major poetry anthologies puts the matter in perspective. In the past, the subject matter of the sonnet has clustered into these broad categories:

1. The love sonnet à la Shakespeare, Elizabeth Barrett Browning, Spenser (and just about everyone else).
2. The meditative sonnet à la Donne, Herbert, Milton (and just about everyone else).
3. The nature sonnet à la Surrey (who, by the way, introduced into English what we now call the Shakespearean sonnet).
4. The elegiac sonnet à la Gray and Longfellow (the first American master sonneteer).
5. The celebratory sonnet à la Arnold and Poe, praising a person

or thing (often the sonnet itself).

Here's a selection of sonnets representing each type. First, an untitled love sonnet by Lady Mary Wroth, using contemporary — instead of Elizabethan — spelling (to read Wroth's sonnets in the original, see *The Poems of Lady Mary Wroth*, edited by Josephene Roberts [Louisiana State University, 1983]).

> Good now be still, and do not me torment
>   With multitudes of questions, be at rest,
>   And only let me quarrel with my breast
>   Which still lets in new storms my soul to rent;
>
> Fie, will you still my mischiefs more augment?
>   You say I answer cross, I that confessed
>   Long since, yet must I ever be oppressed
>   With your tongue-torture which will ne'er be spent?
>
> Well, then, I see no way but this will fright
>   That devil-speech; alas, I am possessed,
>   And mad folks senseless are of wisdom's right,
>
> The hellish spirit-absence doth arest
>   All my poor senses to his cruel might,
>   Spare me then till I am my self, and blessed.

George Meredith's "Lucifer in Starlight" is a meditative sonnet:

> On a starred night Prince Lucifer uprose.
> Tired of his dark dominion swung the fiend
> Above the rolling ball in cloud part screened,
> Where sinners hugged their spectre of repose.
> Poor prey to his hot fit of pride were those.
> And now upon his western wing he leaned,
> Now his huge bulk o'er Afric's sands careened,
> Now the black planet shadowed Arctic snows.
> Soaring through wider zones that pricked his scars
> With memory of the old revolt from Awe,
> He reached a middle height, and at the stars,
> Which are the brain of heaven, he looked, and sank.
> Around the ancient track marched, rank on rank,
> The army of unalterable law.

"The Vantage Point," by Robert Frost, is a nature sonnet:

> If tired of trees I seek again mankind,
>   Well I know where to hie me — in the dawn,
>   To a slope where the cattle keep the lawn.

There amid lolling juniper reclined,
Myself unseen, I see in white defined
　　Far off the homes of men, and farther still,
　　The graves of men on an opposing hill,
Living or dead, whichever are to mind.

And if by noon I have too much of these,
　　I have but to turn on my arm, and lo,
　　The sun-burned hillside sets my face aglow,
My breathing shakes the bluet like a breeze,
　　I smell the earth, I smell the bruised plant,
　　I look into the crater of the ant.

"Mezzo Cammin," by Henry Wadsworth Longfellow, is an elegiac sonnet:

Half of my life is gone, and I have let
　　The years slip from me and have not fulfilled
　　The aspiration of my youth, to build
Some tower of song with lofty parapet.
Not indolence, nor pleasure, nor the fret
　　Of restless passions that would not be stilled,
　　But sorrow, and a care that almost killed,
Kept me from what I may accomplish yet;
Though, halfway up the hill, I see the Past
　　Lying beneath me with its sounds and sights,
　　A city in the twilight dim and vast,
With smoking roofs, soft bells, and gleaming lights,
　　And hear above me on the autumnal blast
The cataract of Death far thundering from the heights.

Finally, William Wordsworth's "Scorn Not The Sonnet" is a celebratory sonnet:

Scorn not the sonnet; critic, you have frowned,
Mindless of its just honors; with this key
Shakespeare unlocked his heart; the melody
Of this small lute gave ease to Petrarch's wound;
A thousand times this pipe did Tasso sound;
With it Camöens soothed an exile's grief;
The sonnet glittered a gay myrtle leaf
Amid the cypress with which Dante crowned
His visionary brow; a glow-worm lamp,
It cheered mild Spenser, called from Faeryland
To struggle through dark ways; and, when a damp
Fell round the path of Milton, in his hand

The thing became a trumpet; whence he blew
Soul-animating strains — alas, too few!

As you can see, the five major categories of sonnet are broad. Nonetheless, before you compose a sonnet, you should contemplate your
subject matter to see if it will suit the particular turn — an element of
craft that makes the sonnet more elusive, perhaps, than any other type
of poem.

TURNS OF THE SONNET

In any sonnet, the turn is that point in the poem where theme or
conflict is addressed and resolved. As such, the turn must be foreboded
by lines preceding it. Foreboding means that the ideas or images before
the turn prepare the reader for the ending . . . without exhausting
theme or revealing punch line — a tall order.

To execute this phase of the sonnet, you need to reflect again on
epiphany and peak experience (as explained in chapter one). Like all
poems, sonnets deal with these moments of truth. The octave or quatrains introduce an idea or emotion, signaling the reader that a turn
of events is forthcoming in the sestet or couplet. Then, the realization
of truth is expressed in the turn.

In a Petrarchan sonnet, the poet tries to develop content philosophically so the beauty of an idea in the octave is felt or envisioned in the
sestet. Epiphany dawns on the poet. The Shakespearean turn makes
a leap in logic. We progress slowly via each quatrain, laying the
groundwork leading to epiphany, and suddenly have one in the couplet. In the Spenserian form, the quatrains usually develop a concept,
situation or theme much like the octave of an Italian form; finally, the
couplet satisfies us with resolution (or statement of epiphany).

To show how epiphany operates in each type of sonnet, let's analyze
ones that began this chapter: "Shall I Compare Thee to a Summer's
Day?" by Shakespeare, "How Do I Love Thee?" by Elizabeth Barrett
Browning and "My Love Is Like to Ice" by Spenser.

In his sonnet, Shakespeare compares his love to a summer's day in
each quatrain. The first one claims that the lover is more consistent
than the weather; the second continues to find fault with nature, indicating all beauty must end; and the third makes a bold statement that
cannot possibly be true — his love will outlast summer, keep her beauty
and transcend death — leading to the epiphany: "So long as men can
breathe, or eyes can see,/So long lives this, and this gives life to thee."

In her Italian sonnet, Elizabeth Barrett Browning describes the
depth, breadth and height of her love in the octave. In the sestet, she
discusses how she can accomplish such love, remembering her passion, grief and lost saints, indicating that her spirit has been renewed

and leading slowly to the epiphany: "and, if God choose,/I shall but love thee better after death."

In each quatrain of his sonnet, Spenser simply expounds on the paradox of unrequited love — his fire cannot melt her ice — and, seemingly, scratches his head in mock confusion. Then he comes up with a logical conclusion: "Such is the power of love in gentle mind,/That it can alter all the course of kind."

All three sonnets feature turns that occur in the perfect place, at the beginning of the ninth line in the Italian and the thirteenth lines in the Shakespearean and Spenserian. This indicates that each sonnet was carefully thought out before the poet composed it. Likewise, you should resist the impulse to sit down and type when the muse strikes, and spend a few moments contemplating the turn of your sonnet. Ask yourself how you felt when you first realized a certain truth and how you plan to spring that truth on your readers: slowly as in the Italian model, swiftly as in the Shakespearean, or logically as in the Spenserian. To accomplish this, I find it helpful to sketch out what I intend to reveal in each section of a sonnet. This way, I can envision the piece before I compose it and prepare adequately for the turn.

Here's an example of such an outline from my notebook and the sonnet that ensued:

Three quatrains explaining how my father hated roses and how my mother loved them.

Quatrain One: develop image of mother's arch of roses above Virgin Mary statue in her garden

Quatrain Two: relate how my father clipped the roses

Quatrain Three: image of red petals on the lawn

Turn: father's coffin covered with roses, just reward

HIS LAST ROSES

The only roses my father liked were looped
Around a horse's head in the winner's circle.
My mother's garden bloomed with roses, roped
In an arch above a madonna won by raffle
At a parish bazaar. I watched him take shears
To the bushes one Sunday she lingered at mass;
Clipped every bud. He even used pliers
To get at ones tangled in thorns, till at last
The lawn bled with petals fallen from limbs
To madonna with Christ-child cradled at her bosom.
When mother strolled in the yard, still humming hymns,

And saw his handiwork, the pool of blossoms,
She sighed and turned away, just as she did
Today when we closed his rose-covered lid.

The final product above deviates somewhat from my notebook entry, as it should. No outline, however clever, ought to control the muse when it wants to take a better route. Nonetheless, the outline helped me compose a sonnet whose quatrains progress nicely via lyric and narrative moments to the forboded turn.

Let's summarize the process to compose a sonnet:

1. Know the rhyme scheme and structure of the basic forms (Shakespearean, Italian, Spenserian).
2. Become familiar with the broad categories of sonnets (love, nature, meditative, elegiac, celebratory).
3. Align your topic with the sonnet form that best conveys your epiphany via the turn (slowly as in the Italian, swiftly as in the Shakespearean or logically as in the Spenserian).
4. Think through the turn by outlining what you hope to accomplish in each segment of your sonnet (as I did in my journal entry for "His Last Roses").
5. Write.

Once you know the process, you can perfect, vary or experiment with the basic form. Toward this end, I have assembled a mini anthology of contemporary sonnets to illustrate these concepts:

• *Structure and Voice in an Italian Sonnet Variation.* Art Homer — poet, creative writing teacher and poetry editor — varies the sonnet form to capture the essence of an overheard conversation. In "At the Heartland Cafe," note how the structure of his variation (the octave uses four rhymes instead of two) augments diction: the perspectives of two women playing off each other in the octave and sestet.

• *Structure and Epiphany in an Italian/Spenserian Variation.* In T.R. Hummer's "A Crazy Girl Brings the Rural Carrier a Dime," note how the poet combines elements of the Italian (octave/sestet) and Spenserian (rhyme/turn) to convey his italicized epiphany.

• *Use of Line in an Italian/Shakespearean Variation.* In David Baker's "Driving Past the Nuclear Plant," note how the poet begins lyrically and shifts to the narrative mode, using midline stanzas to serve as transitions. Observe as well how he combines the Italian structure (octave/sestet) with the Shakespearean rhyme scheme to unravel his truth in the turn.

• *Voice, Rhyme, Meter and Structure.* In Diane Ackerman's "How Like a Virus Entering a Cell," note the scientific diction that creates a unique metaphor for love, the surprising rhymes and turn that echo elements of the Spenserian, and the lines that deviate from the the traditional pentameter, augmenting the final epiphany.

Mini Anthology of Sonnets

AT THE HEARTLAND CAFE

Carol says "His automatic's really cool,"
blows her coffee "but that .38
is one sweet weapon." She got state
twice, went to nationals. "Only a fool
like Gerry forgets to tighten his scope down—
sighting it in and it damn near tore
his nose off. God, what a mess. He wore
that gauze like Nicholson in *China Town*."

But Sandy's not so sure. "You know my Jeff
wakes up hard. I wouldn't want to scare
him awake. If I just snap my fingers,
he jumps up and throws the covers off.
He says if the kids come in there,
'Hell, I won't shoot any two-foot intruders.' "
— Art Homer

A CRAZY GIRL BRINGS
THE RURAL CARRIER A DIME

Every day she meets me at the mailbox, holding
Her hand out. It's not the mail she wants.
I've tried to give it to her, but she won't
Take it—just stretches her arm toward me, unfolding
Her fingers from the palm. And there's the dime.
She wants me to have it. I ask her *What do you need?*
She won't answer. She reaches toward me, shaking her head
Like there's something we both know. Time after time

I've shrugged my shoulders at her and driven on.
A ten-cent stamp, a cigarette—nothing satisfies her.
Every day, no matter what, she's there.
God, the way she looks, waiting for me in the rain!
Once I thought she followed me home. I started
To take her in my arms, hold her: *Is this what you wanted?*
— T.R. Hummer

DRIVING PAST THE NUCLEAR PLANT

How often have you heard it: tornado
rips through trailer court leaving dozens dead,

homes demolished. Shoot of straw burrows
into pine fence post. Or: family killed,
dog found barking on roof.
                        So last night
as the rain rattled off my hood like rocks,
I looked, and there, black in the few hundred feet
between storm clouds and ground, the twister dropped.

I pulled over, cut the engine, covered
my head to wait it out.
                        But no wind roared.
The rain let up. When I looked once more,
only the reactor's tower funneled
in the dark. I left. I drove so fast
I swear I rose, swirling in the window's blast.
                        — David Baker

HOW LIKE A VIRUS ENTERING A CELL

How like a virus entering a cell,
libertine, blasé, pollen-thighed,
you threw your coat aside
and pumped your salty cargo pell-mell
through my delicate biosphere.
In that tidal basin where life's begun,
your twin orchids blazed like suns:
white heat eclipsing but to reappear.
And how I sculled through your mind-lagoons
(vetchy, radiant, thick with fauna),
regaled by egret-flight and japonica,
deadsummer, when in arctic rooms
time rode the floe of our imaginings,
and my heart beat faster for its clipped wings.
                        — Diane Ackerman

Notebook

LEVEL ONE

Select three ideas from your "Idea File" (preferably one related to
love, nature, extranatural or occasion poetry). Adapt *each* idea to the
Italian, Shakespearean and Spenserian form by making an outline,
showing how you plan to execute key stanzas and turns. Compose
drafts of each idea in each sonnet form. Compare versions. In your
journal, discuss what you learned from the exercise, particularly any

observations about each style of sonnet and the respective turn affecting/augmenting content.

LEVEL TWO

Using one idea from each category of verse covered in part one of this book (love, nature and environmental, extranatural, war, political, occasion), follow the process to compose a sonnet as outlined at the end of this chapter. Afterward you should have six sonnets. In your journal, discuss each category above and focus on how the topic of your sonnet harmonized (or failed to harmonize) with the form.

LEVEL THREE

Devise sonnet variations by mixing the rhyme schemes, stanzas and turns of the basic forms described in this chapter. For instance, you might combine the octave and sestet of an Italian sonnet with the Spenserian rhyme scheme. Or alter the Italian sestet so you end with a couplet. Use your imagination, design at least six variations and analyze them. Above all, determine how the turn should unravel. Then select ideas from your "Idea File" and execute drafts of these variations.

Chapter Nineteen

Form Poems

A form poem has a fixed scheme. You have to follow it like a road map and hope it leads you to a destination. In sum, a form poem has a pattern that sets it apart from other types of rhymed poems like the ballad or ode whose lengths or styles vary.

The form poems we will discuss in this chapter had their origins in France, typically in the fourteenth century, or were introduced into Europe through France. That means they do not naturally suit the English language. Consequently, these forms — which tend to operate on only a few rhymes or which repeat entire lines — are considered the most difficult to compose.

Before you become discouraged, however, consider this: The act of *attempting* to write any form poem will help you craft powerful lines and stanzas. Even if your goal is to write only free verse, you will write a more structured, impressive free verse if, every now and then, you sharpen your skills by composing a few form poems.

To help you do that, I have devised step-by-step methods to demystify the various forms. You'll be able to compose them, too, or, if you already are familiar with them, compose them more easily than you have in the past. Let's see how.

THE VILLANELLE

Although it is known as a French form, the roots of the villanelle actually go back to medieval Italy. The bards there sang about pastoral settings. Soon the French were singing, too. By the time the villanelle arrived in England, though, it was used for light-verse topics. In this century, modern and contemporary poets began employing the form for more serious fare.

Next to the sonnet, the villanelle probably is the most common type of formal poem. Its scheme is said to be more difficult to master than that of a sonnet because the villanelle operates on only two rhymes and repeats lines. That's why some experts claim that a villanelle is better suited to French and Italian whose words rhyme more easily than English ones.

I'm not so sure about that. Look up entries in your rhyming dictionary and you'll find English words that have dozens (if not hundreds) of rhymes and slant rhymes. How many do you need?

A form poem needs a *formula*, plain and simple. Without one, it will be hit-and-miss. You cannot always create a villanelle by sitting at your desk or computer and composing from the top down (as you would a free verse poem). Neither can you rely much on discovery, letting the muse dictate a villanelle from on high. The scheme is too fixed to do that.

Instead you have to plot out your villanelle the way a short story writer or novelist plots a manuscript — *before* writing it. When you do, you will decrease the chances of wrenching rhyme or forcing lines and increase the chances of composing a masterful villanelle.

Follow this method:

Know the Pattern

The villanelle uses two rhymes (designated by a and b), five tercets and one ending quatrain (or five three-line stanzas and one four-line stanza), and two repeating lines (designated by A^1 and A^2 — the first and third lines of the first tercet, which repeat alternately as the third line of each following tercet and, finally, as the ending two lines).

Thus, the form: $\underline{A^1}b\underline{A^2}\,ab\underline{A^1}\,ab\underline{A^2}\,ab\underline{A^1}\,ab\underline{A^2}\,ab\underline{A^1}\,\underline{A^2}$.

If you are having difficulty visualizing the pattern, check this villanelle that I composed earlier according to methods outlined here:

BURIAL

A^1 The stalks of wheat appear to writhe and bow
b   As funnel clouds descend upon the plain.
A^2 The farmer ends his dreaming with a plow.

a   The sirens in the village always blow,
b   As if to synchronize his life of pain.
A^1 The stalks of wheat appear to writhe and bow

a   Then burst into a thunderclap of crow.
b   They flap against sky but do not gain.
A^2 The farmer ends his dreaming with a plow.

a   The funnel clouds increase, the shadows grow.
b   A gust of wind revolves the weathervane.
A^1 The stalks of wheat appear to writhe and bow.

a   His family beckons but he will not go
b   To shelter as the twister tills the grain.

A^2 The farmer ends his dreaming with a plow

a   To meet his fate in fields. He does not know
b   The apparitions bobbing in the rain.
A^1 The stalks of wheat appear to writhe and bow.
A^2 The farmer ends his dreaming with a plow.

Even though I am well acquainted with the form of a villanelle, I always type out the pattern on a worksheet so I have it handy without trying to memorize it. (You want to muster all your mental energy into composing the villanelle, not remembering the pattern.)

Combine Meter With Content

The villanelle works best using a four-foot or five-foot line. (Trimeter starts to call attention to the pattern instead of the poem's content because of shorter line lengths.)

Serious villanelles usually employ iambs or a combination of iambs and trochees. Lighter ones use more anapests for a tripping meter or dactyls for a haunting, childlike or marching meter.

Before you pick a meter for your poem, be sure to align it with content. The villanelle is an ideal form to express a nagging or recurring thought or idea. You might use anapestic pentameter, say, for a light verse villanelle about rejection slips or dactyllic tetrameter for a villanelle about marching to the mailbox awaiting a manuscript. Or iambic pentameter for a villanelle about the struggle to fulfill your dreams as an artist, questioning your sacrifices in the recurring lines.

If you need to brush up on the basics of prosody, review the "Meter Primer" in chapter six.

Know the Method

Because the first and third lines of the villanelle repeat according to a pattern and then must come together as ending lines in the final quatrain, compose the ending (as you would a couplet) *first*.

Many villanelles fail because the first and third lines of the first stanza are not strong enough to sustain the structure and then serve as a conclusion. By composing the last two lines first, you'll save yourself time and energy and virtually guarantee a first draft.

Compose your final lines carefully so that each reads as a unit of thought or speech. (This will make it easier to insert a line between them in the first stanza and to improvise in the middle stanzas.) Then pick end words that generate many rhymes.

Let me illustrate. Before I began to write this chapter, I outlined the idea for the villanelle "Burial." I wanted to write a villanelle about a farmer who cuts down his crop rather than risk losing it in a storm. I decided to use iambic pentameter because this was a serious poem.

Moreover, I had hoped that the repeating lines of my villanelle would serve as warnings about the storm throughout the piece.

Knowing this, I was able to fashion each line as a unit of speech encompassing or suggesting an idea.

So far so good.

But I wouldn't have gotten far with this couplet:

> The stalks of wheat appear to bow and writhe.
> The farmer ends his dreaming with the scythe.

In my rhyming dictionary, I found only four other rhymes for "writhe" and "scythe." Then I reversed the verbs to read "writhe and bow" and ended up with forty-two words that rhymed with "bow" and twice as many that near-rhymed: "blow, snow, etc."

The new lines still complemented my theme because a plow suggests "plowing under" or burying one's dreams:

> The stalks of wheat appear to writhe and bow.
> The farmer ends his dreaming with a plow.

Now I was able to return to the top of my worksheet and insert a line between them:

> The stalks of wheat appear to writhe and bow
> As funnel clouds descend upon the plain.
> The farmer ends his dreaming with a plow.

Voila! The beginning and end of my villanelle now were done. All I had left was the body of the poem. Because I chose my rhyme words carefully, I knew at this point that completing the entire poem wouldn't be a problem.

Let Rhyme Work for You

If you are composing a light-verse villanelle, consider multisyllabic words especially with falling (light stress) endings: "baloney/spumoni/matrimony." Villanelles about serious subjects usually employ monosyllabic (hard stress) end words: "bow/plow/how."

Villanelles using a combination of falling multisyllabic and rising monosyllabic rhymes also are excellent if you are composing satire. (See Ron Wallace's "State Poetry Day" in the mini anthology.)

Study all your rhyme and near-rhyme words. Then make a list of ones associated with the topic of your villanelle or common enough to use in a variety of ways. For instance, here's part of my list of farm-related and common words rhyming and near-rhyming with *bow: cow, bough, how, row, somehow, blow, crow, doe, flow, know, no, slow, grow, hoe, mow, tow, whoa, rainbow.*

I composed a similar list for *plain,* my second rhyme word. (Notice that I didn't use the word *field* at the end of the second line because, like the earlier *scythe*, it doesn't yield many rhymes.)

Finally, see what images or meanings your lists of rhyming words suggest and then go about using them to compose the body of your villanelle.

Visualize Your Villanelle

Analyze your repeating lines. In the case of the villanelle being discussed here, the first line — "The stalks of wheat appear to writhe and bow" — suggests images of agony, nightmare and wind. The other line — "The farmer ends his dreaming with a plow" — suggests a reaction by the farmer to such an image or situation.

After I realized this, I plugged those lines into the form on my worksheet. It looked like this:

A^1 The stalks of wheat appear to writhe and bow
b   As funnel clouds descend upon the plain.
A^2 The farmer ends his dreaming with a plow.

a   **(Compose lines related to agony, nightmare**
b   **or wind)**
A^1 The stalks of wheat appear to writhe and bow.

a   **(Compose lines that trigger a reaction**
b   **by the farmer)**
A^2 The farmer ends his dreaming with a plow.

a   **(Compose lines related to agony, nightmare**
b   **or wind)**
A^1 The stalks of wheat appear to writhe and bow.

a   **(Compose lines that trigger a reaction**
b   **by the farmer)**
A^2 The farmer ends his dreaming with a plow.

a   **(Compose lines that relate to agony, etc.,**
b   **and that trigger a reaction)**
A^1 The stalks of wheat appear to writhe and bow.
A^2 The farmer ends his dreaming with a plow.

Do that throughout the entire poem, and you'll get a sense of which rhyme words to use. For example, in what became the second stanza of my villanelle, I imagined a tornado warning (wind-related image) being sounded to heighten suspense. When I looked at my list, my eye fixed on the word *blow*. The second rhyme word was easy — *pain* — in keeping with the idea of agony.

Then I worked on lines using those words until they scanned, rhymed and made sense:

The sirens in the village always blow
As if to synchronize his life of pain.
The stalks of wheat appear to writhe and bow.

Finally, I followed the same process to complete the remaining three tercets and first two lines of the ending quatrain. The result was a villanelle whose very form helped me generate the poem "Burial" without wrenching rhyme or forcing lines.

In fact, the entire process took less than two hours. I credit that to the fact that I know the formula.

Now let's devise a formula for a poem that can stump the most accomplished formalist.

THE SESTINA

The sestina usually is regarded as the most difficult fixed form of the French lyric poets of the eleventh to thirteenth centuries. These poets were called *troubadours*.

The sestina's structure is ornate. It contains six six-line stanzas with an ending three-line envoy (extra stanza). Worse, you only get to use six words (or their homonymic counterparts) at the end of each line in a preconceived pattern. Even *worse*, that three-line envoy doesn't let you off the hook, either; you have to use three of your end words, one at the end of each line, *and* one of the three remaining end words somewhere within each line . . . according to a specific pattern.

Here's what the pattern looks like if we designate A, B, C, D, E, and F as the end words of the first stanza:

1. ABCDEF
2. FAEBDC
3. CFDABE
4. ECBFAD
5. DEACFB
6. BDFECA
7. ECA *or* ACE (with BDF within each line of the envoy).

Don't panic. At least not yet. It's obvious that the sestina doesn't translate well into English. (The sestina is difficult in French, too.) The intricate, interrelated form usually is too repetitive for the modern ear, especially as the sestina unravels toward the envoy and becomes increasingly forced.

These are shortcomings, perhaps, but they have solutions. Let's devise some, step by step:

Pick a Subject That Melds With the Form

Many sestinas fail because the poet uses this complex form to express any old idea. If you like formal poetry, you should know that each form was meant to convey different moods or subject matter. In the case of the sestina, the topic has to be inherently *repetitious*. For instance, the last two sestinas I have written and published depicted:

• A trip north along Interstate 29 in the Midwest, chronicling a family trip in which the same road signs, diners, smells, cities, animals, and other similarities and phenomena seemed to recur with every mile.

• My daughter getting lost in a maze at an Austrian castle, which actually happened when she was three. I could hear her voice echoing in the chambers as she ran from place to place, giggling as in a game of chase (which it, eerily, was).

So before you even consider composing a sestina, make sure your subject suits the repetition. If it doesn't, cut your losses right now.

Decide Whether Your Sestina Will Be Metered

Because the sestina contains such a strong pattern, you can compose one without meter. It won't be free verse because the end words of each line repeat and will have a rhymelike effect on the ear. Nonetheless, deciding to meter your sestina is a top priority.

If you meter your sestina, you should avoid trimeter and even tetrameter. The repeating end words will start to call attention to themselves in small lines, detracting from your poem's meaning. Pentameter is the meter of choice, but hexameter also works nicely in a sestina. The longer lines de-emphasize the repetition that so often results in an artificial-sounding sestina.

Again, if you don't meter your sestina, you should avoid short line lengths. Varying the line lengths not only can be visually appealing on the page, but also can appeal to the ear; it adds an element of surprise or anticipation because we never quite know when the repeating end words will resound. (This effect can be combined with content to produce a startling sestina about, say, negotiating a mine field in a war poem or describing thunder in a nature one.) Finally, long freestyle lines undercut the effect of repetition, making the sestina sound less forced. (See Diane Wakoski's freestyle "Elvis at the Dollar Slotbank Sestina" in the mini anthology.)

Pick Your End Words Carefully

Since these words are going to appear in your sestina so often, you want them to have special qualities. First, the end words should be common enough to serve different sentences. (For instance, you won't get too far with *consequently*, which is apt to grate on the ear or call attention to itself after the second use.) Second, the words should have different meanings or work in different ways (as a noun, verb and adjective, as in the word *fast*, for example).

Now the English language can help you. Its richness often results in homonyms (words that sound and are spelled the same but that have different origins or meanings) and other related sound effects (heteronyms, homophones, contronyms and charades).

With the help of wordsmith and author Richard Lederer, I have compiled abbreviated lists of such words from portions of his excellent books *Get Thee to a Punnery* (Wyrick, 1988) and *Crazy English* (Pocket Books, 1990):

• *Homonyms* (also known as homographs): ace, back, ball, bat, bill, blues, bluff, board, change, coat, county, court, dart, dash, draw, dull, fair, fall, fast, felt, file, fine, fire, free, fresh, go, hand, hard, ill, jam, lash, litter, lose, mad, match, minor, mint, odd, old, pants, partial, pit, pitch, pitcher, plot, poor, present, pupil, rare, record, rest, ring, right, rough, ruler, seal, set, short, single, soft, spirits, spring, stake, strike, take, tie, top, waffle

• *Heteronyms*: Words with the same spelling as other words but with different pronunciations and meanings: axes, bow, buffet, console, content, converse, deserts, does, entrance, incense, lead, minute, number, peaked, present, putting, ragged, recreate, resigned, resorting, row, secretive, sewer, slaver, slough, sow, tower, wind, wound

• *Homophones*: Words that sound alike but have different meanings and spellings: alter/altar; ant/aunt; ascent/assent; banned/band; barred/bard; base/bass; better/bettor; bizzare/bazaar; boar/bore; bored/board; boarder/border; bolder/boulder; booze/boos; capital/capitol; cellar/seller; cent/scent; cheap/cheep; choral/coral; cite/sight/site; coarse/course; coax/Cokes; colonel's/kernels; coward/cowered; crew's/cruise; dear/deer; does/doze; dual/duel; elicit/illicit; eight/ate; ewes/use; fare/fair; flees/fleas; flower/flour; foul/fowl; genes/jeans; gorilla/guerrilla; great/grate; grisly/grizzly; grosser/grocer; guest/guessed; hare/hair; heals/heels; hear/here; heard/herd; hoarse/horse; hoes/hose; idle/idol; isle/aisle; knave/nave; lead/led; lox/locks; lynx/links; lyre/liar; male/mail; maize/maze; manner/manor; meet/meat; mewl/mule; minor/miner; mite/might; moose/mousse; mourning/morning; mussel/muscle; mustered/mustard; naval/navel; nights/knights; one/won; our/hour; ooze/oohs; pain/pane; pair/pare/pear; pale/pail; patient's/patience; paws/pause; peak/peek; plain/plane; prince/prints; purchase/perches; rain/rein/reign; raise/rays/raze; right/rite/write; roe/row; roomer/rumor; sail/sale; sees/seas; slays/sleighs; sole/soul; stationary/stationery; Sunday/sundae; sun's/sons; sweet/suite; sword/soared; tacks/tax; tail/tale; tease/tees; thrown/throne; tied/tide; to/too/

two; towed/toad; whale/wail; whole/hole; whirled/world; who's/whose; wine/whine

- *Contronyms*: Words that have two distinctly opposite meanings: awful (awe-inspiring/terrible), bolt (secure/dart); buckle (fasten together/fall apart); certain (definite/difficult to specify); cleave (separate/adhere to); clip (fasten/separate); critical (opposed/essential to); dress (put on/take off); dust (remove/spread on); fast (firmly in one place/moving place to place); fix (restore/remove); give out (produce/ stop producing); hold up (support/hinder); left (departed from/remaining); moot (debatable/not worthy of debate); mortal (deadly/subject to death); oversight (careful supervision/neglect); put out (generate/ extinguish); qualified (competent/limited); scan (study/glance); screen (view/hide from view); sanction (give approval of/censure); strike (secure in place/remove); temper (soften/harden); trim (add to/ cut away); trip (to stumble/move gracefully); wear (endure/decay); weather (withstand/wear away)

- *Charades*: Words that contain two or more words or suggest ones by pronunciation: allowed (all owed), amaze (a maze), armour (arm our), appear (up here), diet (dye it), healthy (heal thy), hijack (hi jack), mustache (must ache), manslaughter (man's laughter), superbest (super best), withstand (with stand)

Keep in mind that these are *abbreviated* lists. You should add to them as you hear new words. Repeated homonymic and related words startle, humor or intrigue the listener. If you skillfully employ them in a sestina, you'll be able to execute the form in the grand tradition of the French troubadours . . . while you develop a keener love and appreciation for English.

Look Up Definitions of End Words and Chart Their Uses

After you have selected your end words, look up all possible definitions and uses in the dictionary and make a chart.

Before writing this chapter, I composed a new sestina according to the steps I have outlined here. I had just seen a fabulous documentary on Lourdes, the city in France where the Virgin Mary is said to appear and where miracles reportedly are performed. The mystic appearances and cures seemed ideal for the repetition of a sestina.

Using the list above, I chose a related set of end words — ones that appeared custom-made for the subject matter *and* that could yield multiple sounds or meanings (including, coincidentally, the city's own name). I allowed myself one slant rhyme — a word that was close but not exact in sound (tale/teal, for instance) — for each word, in case I wanted to vary the sound in a certain stanza. (Typically, the use of a slant rhyme or two in an entire sestina is permissible.)

Then I looked up my words in the dictionary, including compound words that, when hyphenated, could be used as an end word on one line and then as the beginning word of the next line (as in tail-/gate). Here's my chart:

1. *Tale/Tail*: tale (story/rumor/falsehood), tell-tale, tail-coat, tail-gate, tail-light, tail-pipe, tail-spin. *Slant rhyme*: teal.
2. *Lourdes/Lords*: Lourdes (place name), lords (noun: royalty/verb: rules), Lord's, House of Lords, the Lord's Day, the Lord's prayer, the Lord's supper. *Slant rhyme*: lured.
3. *Resort*: resort (noun: vacation spot, attempt/verb: to try), re-sort. *Slant rhyme*: rest or.
4. *Walks*: walks (noun: paths, distance, characteristic feature, status/verb: to go, to follow), woks, walk-in, walk-on, walk-out, walk-over, walk-up. *Slant rhyme*: wax.
5. *Heal/Heel*: heal (verb: make whole, settle, cure, mend), heal-thy, heel (noun: part of foot, shoe, a fool/verb: to follow as a dog, to lean as a ship). *Slant rhyme*: hell.
6. *Appear*: appear (verb: come into view, to be in court, to seem), up here. *Slant rhymes*: A pear, a pair.

After making my chart, I was ready to compose my sestina . . . but not in the usual manner, composing the opening lines first.

Do the Envoy First

The problem with most attempts at writing sestinas is that few people ever get to reach the envoy. Doing it first accomplishes three things:

1. You'll have an envoy.
2. You'll have a sense of direction (what you have to achieve in the poem and where you will have to end).
3. You'll have the scheme of the poem (where you will place each end word in each stanza of the sestina).

Using my end words, I came up with this envoy:

She walks on mist, not water, as she heals
Mortality. The tale at the resort,
When she appears, is: *Make your peace at Lourdes.*

Because I was writing a traditional sestina, the envoy (ECA) dictates that "walks," "tale" and "appears" (BDF) will fall within each line, respectively. According to the scheme, these words also will be the end words of my second, fourth and sixth lines of the first stanza, respectively. And the words "heals," "resort" and "Lourdes" will be the end words of my fifth, third and first lines of the first stanza, respectively.

But it wasn't time to compose yet.

Plug in the Scheme

Once you have your end words, take six pieces of paper (or make six pages in a file on your computer disk) — one for each stanza. Insert your end words on each page according to the prescribed scheme for that stanza. Using a page for each stanza helps you concentrate, as if it was a separate poem. This way, you'll emphasize every stanza as a complete unit of thought and avoid the tendency to lose interest in the sestina when it progresses and becomes more difficult to compose.

Here's how my six pages looked:

1. Lourdes, walks, resort, tales, heals, appears (Pattern: ABCDEF)
2. appears, Lourdes, heals, walks, tales, resort (Pattern: FAEBDC)
3. resort, appears, tales, Lourdes, walks, heals (Pattern: CFDABE)
4. heals, resort, walks, appears, Lourdes, tales (Pattern: ECBFAD)
5. tales, heals, Lourdes, resort, appears, walks (Pattern: DEACFB)
6. walks, tales, appears, heals, resort, Lourdes (Pattern: BDFECA)

Reading my end words, I had an inkling how each stanza would progress. This became my outline. For instance, the end words suggested that my first stanza would begin with the city and end with an appearance of the Virgin Mary. The second stanza would echo that appearance and end up, somehow, back at the resort. By the third stanza, I realized I would want to vary some of these end words using my chart of homonymic variations. This would reduce the artificial effects of repetition and enhance the subject matter of mystic appearances as the various end words melded into homonymns and homophones. In essence, I wanted each stanza to flow logically into the next, and concentrating on each stanza helped me achieve that.

Do the First Draft

Don't worry about composing a perfect sestina on the first go-around. It won't happen. The first draft is important because you'll have a sense of the ultimate success of your sestina; you can worry about meter and clarity of end words later. Your goal, simply, is to get a draft using your end words in the prescribed pattern. That is, by far, the most difficult aspect of composing a traditional sestina.

Here's my first draft:

They come on wheel or crutch to pray at Lourdes.
The millions set up camp along the walks.
They line the wells that lead to the resort,

Awaiting miracles or mercy. Tales
About Saint Bernadette abound, whose heels
Mark the spot on which Our Lady first appeared.

Today in town a rainbow arch appears
On the horizon, sudden light at Lourdes,
And then is gone. The holy water heals.
You catch it as it drips upon the walks
In magic puddles, mop it up in shirt tails,
Or buy it bottled, shopping at a resort.

Inside chalets, the Jesuits re-sort
Accounts of cures, deciding which appear
Miraculous, divine, or fairy tale.
The Vatican's verdict always lords.
It doesn't matter that a woman walks
Among the mass of worshippers and heals.

The pilgrims try to follow on the heels
Of another sighting, their last resort.
They dip their fingertips in marble woks
And somehow make the one-mile trek up here
To see how Mary manifests at Lourdes.
Her silken hood is white, her robe is teal;

The scent of roses, a truer tell-tail
Sign. And she is silent. She won't say *Heal
Thyself* to people healthy with the Lord's
Light already in them. She won't resort
To greater acts of awe. When she appears,
That is awe enough for those who see her walk

Through her own spectra. In the end, all walks
Of life depart with a parable or with a tale
Of how a saint appeared or did not appear.
Of how they healed or later could not heal.
Of how they traveled to France at a resort
And saw or did not see the Lady at Lourdes.

She walks on mist, not water, as she heals
Mortality. The tale at the resort,
When she appears, is: *Make your peace at Lourdes*.

The first draft had its problems. I wanted my iambic pentameter to
mimic the "walking" of pilgrims at Lourdes, but in some lines the
meter was rough. For instance, the sixth line had six hard stresses and

read like hexameter. The meter *and* the sense of lines sometimes sounded forced (particularly in the fifth stanza).

Despite the obvious problems, however, the prospects for a publishable sestina were good. Some lines intrigued me and the stanzas seemed to move easily or logically into each other. I let my first draft cool for a day or so, and then I revised it.

You should do the same. If you attempt to revise a sestina too soon, the original hard-fought lines of your first draft may still be echoing in your ear. It will be easier to conceive new lines to replace awkward ones if you wait a while.

Instead, think about a title.

Title and Polish the First Draft

While I was letting my sestina cool, I thought about using these titles: "Pilgrims," "Mortality" and "Sightings." The first title seemed too simple in that it did not contain a second level of meaning, as all good titles should. The second title, "Mortality," seemed undercut by that word being used so effectively in the envoy. The last title, "Sightings," suggested several levels of meaning: the *site* of Lourdes, *sighting* the Virgin Mary, and *citing* the poem as a chant (a homophone!). I chose "Sightings" because its shades of meaning suited the repetition of the sestina.

Then I went to work smoothing the meter and clarity of each line and came up with the following final draft:

SIGHTINGS

They come on wheel or crutch to pray at Lourdes.
The millions set up camp along the walks.
They line the wells that lead to the resort,
Awaiting wonderment or mercy. Tales
About Saint Bernadette abound. Her heels
Engrave the stone where Mary first appeared.

Today in town a rainbow arch appears
On the horizon, sudden light at Lourdes,
And then is gone. The holy water heals.
You catch it as it drips upon the walks
In magic pools or mop it up in tails
Of blouse or handkerchief. At the resort,

Inside chalets, the Jesuits re-sort
Accounts of cures, deciding which appear
Miraculous, divine, or fairy tale.
The verdict of the Vatican still lords.
It doesn't matter that a woman walks

Among the paralytic hordes and heals.

The pilgrims flock, then scatter on the heels
Of other sightings. As a last resort,
They dip their fingertips in bowls and woks
And cross their brows. They have to hike up here
To witness Mary manifest at Lourdes.
Her silken hood is white, her robe is teal;

The scent of roses, one more tell-tail
Sign. She is always silent when she heals.
And people always hail her with the Lord's
Prayer on their lips. She won't resort
To larger acts of awe. When she appears,
It is enough for those who see her walk

To revel in her spectra. Then all walks
Of life depart with parable or tale
Of how a vice or vision did appear.
Of how they healed or later could not heal.
Of how they ended up at a resort
And saw or did not see the Light at Lourdes.

She walks on mist, not water, as she heals
Mortality. The tale at the resort,
When she appears, is: *Make your peace at Lourdes.*

There you have it — a publishable sestina whose end words and pattern serve instead of detract from the form.

Now let's tackle one of the most elusive form poems.

THE PANTOUM

Although I think it's more difficult to compose a good sestina, some critics argue that the pantoum is more elusive. The reason, simply, is the complex form.

Written in quatrains (four-line stanzas), the pantoum repeats the second and fourth lines of each stanza as the first and third lines of the following stanza, respectively. The pattern is continued for as many stanzas as you like. But when you end a pantoum, you should repeat the first and third lines of the first stanza as the fourth and second lines, respectively, of the last stanza. So the pantoum begins and ends with the same line.

Because a pantoum doesn't have to have rhyming end words, numbers are used to indicate the pattern. Here is one for a sixteen-line pantoum: 1234 2546 5768 7381.

Some poets vary the repetition of a few lines or choose not to end the pantoum in the traditional way, using its pattern to generate a mood. Essentially, these writers improvise on tenets of traditional pantoums because they want their variations to enhance meaning in some way. As an example, see Joyce Carol Oates's "Welcome to Dallas!" in the mini anthology.

The pantoum is actually a Malayan verse form that is often lumped with traditional French forms such as the villanelle and the rondeau, triolet and ballade (more on them later). But because a pantoum can be any length, its form is not really fixed. Moreover, you can rhyme and meter the pantoum (which adds a pinch of salt to the wound of writing one). You can meter it without rhyme. Or rhyme it without meter. Or you can compose a freestyle version.

But as in the villanelle and sestina, all you need is a formula to help you focus on each element of the poem.

Here's a formula for the pantoum:

Pick a Subject That Suits the Form

This is paramount if you ever hope to write a pantoum. Consider how Joyce Carol Oates describes the pantoum's ability to convey certain subjects: "The pantoum is a poetic form marvelously suited for conveying extreme states of mind — mania, paranoia, delusion. Writing a pantoum is quite an experience: I've only written two in my entire life, and felt each time as if I were descending into madness, and holding on only by way of a rigorous discipline — in itself a bit mad."

Of course, pantoums don't have to be serious or insane. In fact, Oates observes, "If successful, the pantoum comes across as a comic form. Its gravity, even its tragedy, is transmuted into comedy."

When I write pantoums, sometimes I pick topics that imply a type of mania, paranoia or delusion. Sometimes I don't. But I do make sure my topic suggests something that *recurs* because my lines will recur throughout the poem.

For example, here are brief descriptions of the last two pantoums that I published:

• "Orphic Chant" concerns the circular layout of the Austrian city of Salzburg. My narrator is lost and thinks that he is walking out of town, miles from his original starting point. Suddenly, landmarks start reappearing and he realizes "I can't escape my life."

• "Mistaken Identity" concerns an American tourist being mistaken for a bank robber in Salzburg. During the arrest, a detective interrogates in German (a good scene for repetition):

He explains the civil code in German:
Sie sind verhaftet, verstehen Sie mich?
You are a suspect. You don't believe this.

Zeigen Sie mir schon Ihre Papiere!

Sie sind verhaftet, verstehen Sie mich?
A bad move. He wants to see your papers:
Zeigen Sie mir schon Ihre Papiere!
You could be staring at a stiff sentence. . . .

I have also written pantoums about recurring nightmares and sleep-walking, other topics in which repetition can be rich. The pantoum that I composed before writing this chapter focused on hurtful phrases that come back to haunt us all our lives.

But before I even composed the first stanza, I had to consider which type of pantoum would best convey my subject matter.

Decide Whether You Want Your Pantoum to Rhyme, Scan or Be Free

Because your lines will repeat, your pantoum will sound as if it is rhymed anyway. If you rhyme it, however, you will add another layer of sound so the effect is fuguelike. In music, a fugue is a composition that blends one, two, or more sounds or melody lines. In psychiatry, a fugue can be a symptom of amnesia in which a person has a forgotten and a remembered life — or two life lines. Both meanings of *fugue* are found in the *rhymed* pantoum, probably the eeriest-sounding poem in the English canon.

A metered pantoum sounds very deliberate and serves themes in which control is paramount: a person trying to solve a mystery, for example, or to overcome an addiction. This sound effect occurs because lines not only repeat, but repeat according to a distinct beat.

A freestyle pantoum surprises us and serves themes in which the unanticipated is paramount: jarring images of a nightmare, for example, or a punch line of a joke. This sound effect occurs because lines of varying length repeat in irregular intervals — some a long while for the setup and others, a short while for the jolt.

Once you have picked the mode, you're ready to write. For my particular pantoum, I decided to use rhyme and meter because I wanted my lines about hurtful phrases to reverberate in the heads of my listeners.

Make Sure Each Line of the First Stanza Serves the Structure of the Pantoum

Remember, the first and third lines will be repeated in the last stanza as the fourth and second lines, respectively. The second and fourth lines of your first stanza will be repeated as the first and third lines of your second stanza, respectively. That makes the first stanza key in completing the poem.

Let's diagram how:

1. The first line also is the ending.
2. The second line also makes a transition.
3. The third line also sets up the ending.
4. The fourth line also propels the poem.

To illustrate, here's the first stanza of my pantoum, "Boomerang":

Our lives are like pantoums. Those lines come back
To haunt us. Say your mantras, make your peace.
Every slur you heard is elegiac:
Something dies within. Something is released. . . .

It took me thirty-five minutes to come up with that stanza and to align it with the title. At first glance you can probably see how the first line foretells the ending: "Our lives are like pantoums. Those lines come back." The third line sets up that ending in the last stanza, foreboding another hurtful phrase. Meanwhile the second line — "To haunt us. Say your mantras, make your peace." — was conceived to hook up well with the fourth line and propel the poem to the second stanza.

When I had composed my first stanza, I was ready to proceed with the pantoum according to its scheme.

Don't Forget to Plug in Repeating Lines in the Following Stanza

This will keep you on track so you don't have to memorize the pattern of a pantoum. For instance, after creating my first stanza, I knew what the first and third lines of my second stanza would be. I also knew that the second and fourth lines would be new, again containing dual functions:

To haunt us. Say your mantras, make your peace.
(Compose second line that also makes transition)
Something dies within. Something is released.
(Compose fourth line that also propels the poem)

I concentrated on the new lines. The second one not only had to connect with the line above it but also had to serve as a transition for the stanza to follow. The fourth line not only had to connect with the line above it, completing the stanza, but also had to propel the poem to the next stanza.

Sensing that, I decided to pun the phrase "Say your mantras, make your peace" and continued the pantoum with this stanza:

To haunt us. Make your mantras, say your piece:

You were worthless then, dear. And worthless now.
Something dies within. Something is released.
In time you'll learn to let your goodness go. . . .

So far so good. I was on a roll. Because I had written pantoums
before, I knew that my lines should take on new meaning when repeated in following stanzas. To help that, I fashioned lines that could
be broken into phrases or that employed homonyms and homophones — words that sound the same but have different meanings — to
propel the poem.

I continued in this manner until I hit a snag, which always happens.
In my first draft, the snag occurred one stanza before the ending:

BOOMERANG

Our lives are like pantoums. Those lines come back
To haunt us. Say your mantras, make your peace.
Every slur you heard is elegiac:
Something dies within. Something is released

To haunt us. Make your mantras, say your piece:
You were worthless then, dear. And worthless now.
Something dies within. Something is released.
In time you'll learn to let your goodness go —

You were worthless then, dear, and worthless now —
And concentrate on arts of pain instead.
In time you'll learn, too. Let your goodness go
To waste on every partner in your bed,

And concentrate on arts of pain. Instead
Of needing love, remember you have lines
To waste on every partner in your bed:
You disappoint me. You show all the signs

Of needing love, remember? You have lines
To lock the heart and no one has the key.
You disappoint me. You show all the signs.
If you're nothing, you have nothing to lose. . . .

Oops. Try as I might, the transitional line "To lock the heart and
no one has the key" would not repeat as the first line of the next
stanza, no matter how I played with or varied it. Worse, the line seemed
too sentimental anyway. It had to go.

But revising a line in a pantoum is like removing a can from a
stacked pyramid in the grocery store. The pyramid may tumble down.

Let's see how you can revise and prevent that from happening.

Rewrite and Polish the Offending Line

When you are as deep as I was in a traditional pantoum, you don't want a clunky line to scrap the entire effort. I've known poets who have come within *one word* of completing a pantoum, only to abandon the effort because a line wouldn't serve two stanzas.

When that happens, throw out the entire line. Don't try to save it no matter how brilliant your images or extended your metaphors. Kill it, or it will kill your pantoum.

When you consider lines to replace it, focus again on ones that break well into phrases or employ homonymns or homophones. This will give you several options for new lines and transitions. Above all, resist the impulse to go with a line that simply salvages the pantoum. You want a slick line that propels the poem.

For instance, here's the first possible replacement line I conceived to make my pantoum work: "To keep a person from getting close." The meter was wrong, so I changed it to "To prevent a person from getting close." It didn't connect well with the repeating line—"If you're nothing, you have nothing to lose/To prevent. A person from getting close"—but, with a little polish, it suggested a real winner.

Look at the phrase *"A person from getting close"* and consider how that can stand independently: *A person's getting close.* Now consider the possibilities of my new line: "To prevent a person's getting close." The meter was wrong again, but easy to fix: "To undermine a person's getting close."

At last, I could complete the pantoum:

Of needing love, remember? You have lines
To undermine a person's getting close:
You disappoint me. You show all the signs.
If you're nothing, you have nothing to lose,

To undermine. A person's getting close.
Every slur you heard is elegiac.
If you're nothing, you have nothing to lose.
Our lives are like pantoums. Those lines come back.

Presto! A pantoum! After I had composed it, I rewrote "Boomerang" into metered and freestyle versions. Compare the sound effects. Here's the metered version:

THOSE LINES COME BACK

Our lives are like pantoums.
You'd better make your peace.
Any slur can slay you:
Something dies within.

You'd better make your peace:
You are worthless, dear.
Something dies within.
Let your goodness go —

You are worthless, dear —
And concentrate on pain.
Let your goodness go
To waste on one-night stands

And concentrate on pain.
You remember words
To waste on one-night stands:
What a disappointment.

You remember words,
So sabotage the heart:
What a disappointment.
You have nothing to lose

So sabotage the heart.
Any slur can slay you.
You have nothing to lose.
Our lives are like pantoums.

Here's the free-verse version:

OUR LIVES ARE LIKE PANTOUMS

Those lines come back.
Say your mantras, make your peace.
Any slur can slay you:
Something dies within and is released.

Make your mantras, say your piece:
You are worthless, dear.
Something dies within and is released.
Let your goodness go —

You are worthless, dear —
And learn to deepen pain of lovers.
Let your goodness go
To waste on all those one-night stands

And learn to deepen pain of lovers.
You remember lines
To waste on all those one-night stands:
You're a real letdown.

You remember lines . . .
So sabotage the heart:
You're a real letdown.
If you're nothing, you have nothing to lose

So sabotage the heart.
Any slur can slay you.
If you're nothing, you have nothing to lose.
Those lines come back.

The metered pantoum still conveys a sense of control, each line repeating according to a beat. But it has lost that extra layer of sound without rhyme. The free-verse version emphasizes certain lines, giving them more clout; but the loss of meter undermines the theme. I wanted a sense of control *and* sound to enhance my pantoum, and so I still prefer the original version.

Let's end the chapter by considering lesser-known form poems.

OTHER FORM POEMS

The villanelle, sestina and pantoum are more popular than the ballade, triolet and rondeau. Nonetheless, you should know about these, too, and may want to try your hand at them. Here is a brief summary of how to compose them and other related forms:

The Ballade

Form: Three eight-line stanzas rhyming *ababbcbC* with a four-line envoy (extra stanza) rhyming *bcbC*. The capital letter *C* indicates a repeating line whose end word rhymes or slant rhymes with the end word in line *c*. For example:

BRAINCHILD

I.

Hind

Let us celebrate the cerebellum
In a ballade melodious as a lullaby
And interlock our limbs until we come
To accept fate or infertility.
Let the medulla make this child the way
It makes the lungs inflate to help us breathe
In unison: involuntarily.
Maybe then we will conceive.

II.

Mid

Let us key the lobes of equilibrium
And sing about umbilicals, accompany
The chamber music of the cranium.
Or let the pons compose a symphony
Sans a conductor, so we may occupy
The seats of all-being and make-believe,
Left and right. If we exalt the nuclei,
Maybe then we will conceive.

III.

Fore

Let us sculpt the thalamus and cerebrum
With palms and mold the primordial clay
In our own image, a mixed medium.
We can put our creations on display
And marvel at our motor and sensory
Powers. Even specialists will perceive
The marriage of art and anatomy
And maybe then we will conceive.

IV.

Stem

Inside the hemispheres of ecstasy
A brainchild is easier to achieve.
Let us link up the parts and prophesy:
Maybe then? Will we conceive?

Approach:

1. For best results, pick a topic that can be analyzed in three parts (one per stanza) and then summed up or concluded in the envoy.

2. Consider end words that yield lots of rhymes because the ballade only operates on three through twenty eight lines.

3. Pick rhyme words that enhance the topic or suggest lines in keeping with the topic. Don't be afraid to slant rhyme, if necessary. Use a thesaurus and rhyming dictionary to help isolate rhymes.

4. Write your repeating line *C* first. You want to fashion a line that can be used to evoke different moods (as in the villanelle) or that can be broken into phrases (as in the pantoum).

5. Once you have your repeating line, figure out four uses or mean-

ings that it evokes. Contemplate those uses or meanings and put them in a logical order. For instance, in the above ballade, the repeating line "maybe then we will conceive" suggests these uses and meanings:

- *First stanza*
  If we give up control, maybe then . . .
- *Second stanza*
  If we celebrate the brain, maybe then . . .
- *Third stanza*
  If we marry art and science, maybe then . . .
- *Envoy*
  If we do all of the above, maybe then? Will we conceive?

The above serves like an outline for each stanza, indicating what I need to accomplish.

- Plug in your repeating line and rhyme scheme for each stanza on a separate page or file in your computer (as suggested for the sestina).
- Compose the ballade.

Other related form: Chant Royal. Form: Five eleven-line stanzas rhyming *ababccddedE* with *E* as the repeating line, followed by a five-line envoy rhyming *ddedE*. Use the same approach as in the ballade with even greater care choosing your five rhyme words since they have to span sixty lines.

Triolet

Form: An eight-line, four-stanza poem with repeating lines (indicated by capital letters) and rhyming *AB aA ab AB* (with stanzas optional). For example:

HABITAT

"The woodpecker's back there on the feeder,
The endangered one," she says. "I told you

About his red cone head like a hatter.
The woodpecker's back there. On the feeder,

Bigger than I remember and brighter,
Too. Come quick to the window. What a view!

The woodpecker's back. There, on the feeder.
The endangered one." She says, "I *told* you."

Approach:

1. For best results, pick a fleeting topic that is repetitious.

2. Compose your first stanza that contains your repeating lines. Craft the lines so that they can be broken into phrases that connect with other lines or so they can shift in meaning when used elsewhere.

3. Plug those lines into the scheme. Now you have only three new lines to create.

4. Compose the triolet so the repeating lines play off the nonrepeating lines.

Other related form: Rondel. Form: A thirteen-line, three-stanza poem with repeating lines indicated by capital letters and rhyming *ABba abAB abbaA*. Follow the same approach as the triolet with more emphasis on the two rhyme words that have to span thirteen lines.

Rondeau

Form: A thirteen-line, three-stanza poem operating on two rhymes and a word or phrase — indicated by *(R)* — that begins the first line and (ideally) rhymes or slant-rhymes with the end word of the first line. The word or phrase is repeated at the end of the second and third stanzas, indicated now by *R*, and exists apart from any set meter. Commonly, each line should have eight syllables (or each may have ten). The rondeau, in German, is known as *ringelrime* (wrap-around rhyme). Here's the rhyme scheme: *(R)aabba aabR aabbaR*.

For example:

RINGELREIM

Baker's Dozen. Bless the women
Kneading flour at the oven
Every night, working overtime:
They know the alley-people come
Empty-handed at break of dawn

Waiting for the inn to open,
To smell the scent of cinnamon
Remembering home. Ringelreim: baker's dozen.

The racks of rolls, croissant and scone
In the window display again
Raise their hunger and hope. This time
Someone leaves a batch in their name.
Our lives are interwoven: baker's dozen.

Approach:

1. For best results, pick a topic that defines, deconstructs or puns a word or phrase. (In my poem I use *baker's dozen* to allude to the

homeless alley-people, along with its standard meaning—extra or thirteenth piece.)

2. Use the word or phrase to begin your first line. Make sure the first line ends with a rich rhyme word. Or slant rhyme the word for more possibilities.

3. Pick another rich or unusual sound for the second rhyme word.

4. Plug in the word or phrase *(R)* at the end of the second and third stanzas.

5. Contemplate the word or phrase and envision the poem. The word or phrase enhances and shapes content. When repeated at the end of the eighth line, it should take on new meaning. When repeated at the end of the last line, it should suggest an epiphany or express a punch line.

6. Compose the poem.

Other related form: Rondeau Redouble. Not only does this poem contain a partial repetition of the opening word or phrase from the first line, indicated by *(R)* — which should rhyme with the end word of the first line—but it also has repeating rhyming lines as in a villanelle, indicated by A^1 and A^2 and by B^1 and B^2.

All the repeating lines are in the opening four-line stanza and recur, one after the other, as the last lines in the following four stanzas. The entire poem operates on two rhymes, so you have to pick exceptionally rich ones. You also have to shape the lines of the first stanza as you would lines of a pantoum.

Once the first stanza is written, plug in the lines according to this rhyme scheme: $(R)A^1B^1A^2B^2$ babaA^1 abaB^1 babaA^2 abaB^2 babaR.

As you can see, the very structure of the poem shapes its content: a proposition put forth in the first stanza, with each condition (line) of that stanza developed in the following four stanzas, with the final stanza coming to a firm conclusion.

Finally, in the mini anthology, you'll be reading a traditional villanelle by Ronald Wallace, a freestyle sestina by Diane Wakoski and a freestyle pantoum by Joyce Carol Oates.

Mini Anthology of Form Poems

STATE POETRY DAY

The mayor couldn't be here, but he sends his grand whereases,
and his best regards take their places in the rear.
Another year closes with a villanelle's razzmatazzes.

Outside, in sunlight, with their stunted squash and radishes,
farmers wonder what the going rate is for crop failure and despair.
The mayor couldn't be here but he sends his grand whereases.

In the legislative chambers with their dactyls and caesuras
the local poet laureates sing in praise of cheese and beer.
Another year closes with a villanelle's razzmatazzes.

On the South Side, poverty makes another of its passes.
A bag lady lifts her breakfast from a trash can on the square.
The mayor couldn't be here but he sends his grand whereases.

Now the poetry club presidents show their poems off like badges
to the hard-of-hearing, blue-haired citizens gathered here.
Another year closes with a villanelle's razzmatazzes.

No one mentions Nicaragua, acid rain, cocaine, or Star Wars,
as the couplets and quatrains maintain a pleasant atmosphere.
The mayor couldn't be here, but he sends his grand whereases.
Another year closes with a villanelle's razzmatazzes.
                                        — Ronald Wallace

ELVIS AT THE DOLLAR SLOTBANK SESTINA

It wasn't only Beethoven whom I found in Las Vegas,
though the sound of silver dollar money —
thunk, thunk, thunk, thunk — clanking
into the metal pans is a sound
similar to his Fifth symphony. We hear it
coming from the bank of dollar slots next to the Keno Bar

Where Steelman likes to sit, drinking soda. It's a bar
where he can see the Keno board, watch Las Vegas
characters — clowns, Elvis impersonators, old ladies in gold lame. It
is part of his story, this rattle of money,
American poetry or truth. The sound
of the Rolling Stones must also be part of what he hears, clanking

Fire, satisfaction, millions of dollars in records. What he feels clanking
out of the slots when he lines up triple bars
on any machine. Steelman likes the sounds
of winning. While Twenty-one is my Las Vegas
game, he scorns a pursuit where you can only double your money.
A thousand to one is the way he prefers it.

That must be how he discovered old fashioned Elvis. It
wasn't as if Steelman even thought of Elvis as important. Clanking
heavy metal or sentimental crooner ballads: both irrelevant. His money
was on the limey mavericks until he saw Elvis behind prison bars,
jailhouse rock denim, not eagle or studded white and leather Las Vegas
suits. Then he began to hear in Elvis the same sounds

The Beatles heard in 1963 when they first came to the US. Sounds
that made them request a meeting with The King. It
didn't impress Elvis, these Liverpool boys. Tom Jones in Las Vegas
was his model. And all the money, clanking
into the Colonel's pockets to pay gambling debts, the old man barred
from traveling abroad. Poor Elvis earning money

For everyone. But there was never enough money
and he—oh, why am I telling this story of sounds?
We left Steelman sitting at the Keno Bar
perhaps thinking of gamblers, musicians. He too knows it
is money and music, the thunk, the ring, the clank
of the dollar slot machines that sums up all of Las Vegas.

Difficult in Las Vegas to find Beethoven's music or to win money.
But I can imagine both in the slot machine's clanking sound;
that it's not just dollars, but Elvis humming The Moonlight Sonata, there
                                                      by the Keno Bar.
                    — Diane Wakoski

WELCOME TO DALLAS!

Welcome to Dallas!—this place is wild!
Nothing's more than five years old!
24 HAPPY HOURS 'ROUND THE CLOCK!
He died, his lungs was Dutch Boy Glitter-Gold!

Nothing's more than five years old—
our city bird's the CONSTRUCTION CRANE!
He died, his lungs was Dutch Boy Glitter-Gold!
Nothing's been built that can't be sold!

Our city bird's the CONSTRUCTION CRANE!
InterFirst Plaza & ThanksGiving Square!
Nothing's been built that can't be sold!
Dallas/Ft. Worth Airport is bigger than Zaire!

InterFirst Plaza & ThanksGiving Square!
World Trade Center & John Neely Bryan Restored Log Cabin!
Dallas/Ft. Worth Airport is bigger than Zaire!
"When we got there, we forgot where we were going!"

World Trade Center & John Neely Bryan Restored Log Cabin!
OOOOOOOhhhhhh man—it's how you *fly!*
"When we got there, we forgot where we were going!"
The custom-built helicopter's here a *habit!*

OOOOOOOhhhhhh man—it's how you *fly!*

One good huff of Black Flag you want to *die!*
The custom-built helicopter's here a *habit!*
"When we got there, we forgot where we were going!"

One good huff of Black Flag you want to *die!*
When the going gets tough the tough go shopping!
Drinks in Deep Ellum, you forget where you've *been!*
See my new Nieman-Marcus boots made for STOMPING!

When the going gets tough the tough go SHOPPING!
The MOON so dam' big you step on his dam' FACE!
See my new Nieman-Marcus boots made for STOMPING!
The Ferrari headlights flashed and there shone—NO DUMPING!

The MOON so dam' big you step on his dam' FACE!
We'll rendezvous in bankruptcy court—just in case!
The Ferrari headlights flashed and there shone—NO DUMPING!
Is there a life, she pondered, after shopping?

We'll rendezvous in bankruptcy court—just in case!
Pittsburgh Black & Dutch Boy Glitter-Red!
Is there a life, she pondered, after shopping?
"Hector looked so peaceful, how'd we know he was dead?"

We didn't smell no thing, man, the Rodriquez family said!
All them smells, man, already in the air!
"Hector looked so peaceful, how'd we know he was dead?"
Airplane glue & turpentine & Day-Glo Glitter-Red!

Welcome to Dallas!—this place is wild!
(She talked so cool, man, how'd we know she was a *child!*)
                                        —Joyce Carol Oates

Notebook

LEVEL ONE

1. Using ideas from your "Idea File," select ones that can be adapted to the villanelle, sestina and pantoum. (Or conceive new ideas.) Then go through the step-by-step method as outlined for each type of poem. For the sestina and pantoum, use meter, if you like, or cast them in a freestyle a la Diane Wakoski's sestina or Joyce Carol Oates's pantoum.

2. In your journal, note difficulty with any step involved during the composition of a villanelle, sestina and pantoum.

LEVEL TWO

1. Read your journal entry from the Level One, Exercise Two to prepare you for any difficulty involving a villanelle, sestina or pantoum. Then select ideas from your "Idea File," or conceive new ideas, and compose these form poems again. (Note: If you did a freestyle sestina and/or pantoum, do a traditional one now — or vice versa.)

2. In your journal, note any continuing difficulty with any step involved during the composition of the above form poems.

3. Using ideas from your "Idea File," or conceiving new ideas, attempt a ballade, triolet and rondeau.

LEVEL THREE

1. Read your journal entries from the first two levels to prepare yourself for any lingering difficulty in composing a villanelle, sestina or pantoum. Then, using ideas from your "Idea File," or conceiving new ideas, compose these form poems one more time.

2. Using ideas from your "Idea File," or conceiving new ideas, try your hand at a chant royal, rondel and rondeau redouble.

Chapter Twenty

The Sequence

A sequence is a poem in parts — as few as two or as many as the muse can muster. Other names include *suite, series, cycle,* and *numbered* or *sectioned* poem. More importantly, a sequence is made up of individual poems that can stand alone but, when grouped together under one title, become a greater work.

There are dozens of ways to explain how a sequence should function, but I like this one best by poet-teacher Sharon Klander, whose verse we read in the chapter on nature poetry: "When a student asks me why and when a poem should be divided into sections, I begin by comparing the decision to that of whether to use a semicolon or a period between two sentences. In this analogy, two sentences divided by a period represent two independent poems that perhaps share a subject; even though content is related" — e.g., two poems about divorce — "they are each self-contained and benefit from white space on the page holding them in on all sides. A sentence divided by a semicolon, however, can be split grammatically into two separate sentences, and yet still benefits by being connected. This, of course, corresponds to the poem divided into sections" — e.g., two opposing viewpoints about divorce — "wherein each section can stand alone if it weren't for the depth, richness or the tension gained by the proximity of part to part."

Typically, novice poets divide a long work into parts because they admire how it appears on the page. So designed, a sequence becomes an ornament rather than an element of craft: Either its parts cannot stand alone or, when grouped, they fail to constitute a better poem.

To illustrate these pitfalls, let's analyze different versions of one of my sequence poems, a lyric in two parts:

FLUENTLY

1.
My pen-pal cousin used to send me
Photographs, heavy in those blue envelopes

Stamped "par avion." She posed in the sea,
Small whitecaps splashing up her sundress.
I think I loved her, even when she wrote
In that strange tongue — so many Ks, Js and Zs
My father had to translate.
2.
I expected another blue envelope
Announcing the birth of her child;
Instead I get this card, my cousin's picture
Printed alongside a cross, heavy with Jesus.
I don't call for my father,
Scan the inscription full of Ks, Js and Zs —
At once making terrible sense.

An early work, the poem is self-explanatory. The narrator has had
a foreign pen-pal cousin since childhood and can't understand her
language, asking his father to translate; years later, anticipating another letter, the narrator receives a funeral announcement, and this
time he doesn't have to ask his father to interpret his grief (which he
feels "fluently").

The sequence succeeds because its two parts suggest a passage of
time, can stand alone, and, when grouped, make a better poem.

Let's divide it into several parts that *cannot* stand alone:

FLUENTLY

1.
My pen-pal cousin used to send me
Photographs, heavy in those blue envelopes
Stamped "par avion." She posed in the sea,
Small whitecaps splashing up her sundress.
2.
I think I loved her, even when she wrote
In that strange tongue — so many Ks, Js and Zs
My father had to translate.
3.
I expected another blue envelope
Announcing the birth of her child;
Instead I get this card, my cousin's picture
Printed alongside a cross, heavy with Jesus.
4.
I don't call for my father,
Scan the inscription full of Ks, Js and Zs —
At once making terrible sense.

Now the numbers call attention to themselves. The second section cannot stand alone because the poetic phrase needs more elaboration and the fourth seems to share the same time element with the third (and thus cannot stand alone, either). Mostly the four parts obfuscate the passage of time that deepens the narrator's love and grief; in fact, when divided this way, the poem overemphasizes the funeral card which doesn't need a translation.

Now let's read the original sequence as a single work:

FLUENTLY

My pen-pal cousin used to send me
Photographs, heavy in those blue envelopes
Stamped "par avion." She posed in the sea,
Small whitecaps splashing up her sundress.
I think I loved her, even when she wrote
In that strange tongue — so many Ks, Js and Zs
My father had to translate.

I expected another blue envelope
Announcing the birth of her child;
Instead I get this card, my cousin's picture
Printed alongside a cross, heavy with Jesus.
I don't call for my father,
Scan the inscription full of Ks, Js and Zs —
At once making terrible sense.

The stanza break above does not emphasize the passage of time the way numbers do in the original. Instead the two stanzas suggest that the narrator may be a boy (or at best, a teenager) with a "pen pal," confusing the issue of the cousin's pregnancy. The original is superior because the passage of time implies a deeper bond between the cousins and a deeper sense of grief at her passing.

In sum, the best way to make a sequence is not to *divide* a poem but to preconceive and *build* one, choosing topics that suit the form. Before you compose a sequence, determine whether your topic has:

- *Significant time elements.* For instance, another of my sequence poems titled "The Extinction of Species" is based on the creation story and thus has seven parts, representing the seven days it took to make the world as recorded in the Bible.
- *Definitive parts.* Another one of my sequence poems, titled "Articles of Insurrection," is a series of lyrics based on the Bill of Rights, the first ten amendments to the Constitution.
- *Logical concepts.* Another sequence poem titled "Platonic Love" analyzes four definitions of that term and so has four parts.

Those broad categories encompass most sequences. Another way to envision them is to consider ten basic groupings of such poems. I'll define each grouping and cite examples by famous poets whose sequences are too long to reprint here (though you should read them in books or anthologies).

1. *The Stanza Grouping.* Usually found in an ode, this type of sequence calls attention to the stanza as a self-contained unit. In "Intimations of Immortality," Wordsworth puts his life experience into perspective in eleven irregular stanzas. He begins by recalling the world "Apparelled in celestial light" and, ultimately, re-embraces the innocence of childhood.

2. *The Narrative Grouping.* Usually found in ballads, this sequence uses numbers to designate scenes or episodes that make up a story. In his "The Rime of the Ancient Mariner," Coleridge announces in a subtitle that his ballad will be told "In Seven Parts" or seven numbered episodes of a tale that the hero relates at a wedding feast, beginning with his killing of the albatross — "the pious bird of good omen" — and culminating in penance.

3. *The Lyric Grouping.* This type of sequence combines lyric poems that imply a story, probe a moment or reflect the mind. In his "Thirteen Ways of Looking at a Blackbird," Wallace Stevens (as the title suggests) presents thirteen perspectives on the bird, probing what it evoked in his mind (or imagination).

4. *The Dramatic Grouping.* One character (or several) speaks or interacts with others, as in a play. In Robert Browning's "Dramatis Personae," carrying the subtitle "James Lee's Wife," we overhear the character addressing her husband in nine settings ("James Lee's Wife Speaks at the Window," "By the Fireside," "In the Doorway," etc.).

5. *The Song Grouping.* An assembly of song lyrics that, when read in sequence, weaves melodies that resonate like a fugue. In "Three Songs of Shattering," Edna St. Vincent Millay presents three such lyrics about a singer who no longer is enchanted by spring, because of a severed relationship.

6. *The Fragment Grouping.* A poem divided by one or more asterisks (or other mark) and signifying disjointed thoughts, scenes or episodes. In "From the Sea," a type of love journal, Sara Teasdale jumps from thought to thought — through stanzas separated by rows of six asterisks — reminiscing on six aspects of a love affair.

7. *The Argument Grouping.* Each part of the sequence represents an argument whose sum equals an epiphany or reaches a conclusion. In Ralph Waldo Emerson's two-part poem, "The Informing Spirit," he asserts that the soul cannot be defined in physical terms, and he

proposes that if we accept such an argument, a person can own everything, from Christ's heart to the cosmos.

8. *The Mosaic Grouping.* A mosaic sequence describes each part of a person, place or thing so we have to piece it together again to acquire new understanding of the whole. In "Transformations," D.H. Lawrence describes "The Town," "The Earth" and "Men," revealing a decaying universe.

9. *The Seasonal Grouping.* A person, place or thing is viewed in different seasons so that its true essence is revealed. In "Bronzes" by Carl Sandburg, the poet views statues in Lincoln Park in summer and in winter, setting them against the urban landscape and revealing their absurdity.

10. *The Symbolic Grouping.* An image is presented in each part and their sum is symbolic, depicting or implying a greater truth. In her two-part "Garden," H.D. ponders a rose "cut in rock" and the wind cutting "apart the heat" so "fruit" may drop. The rose/rock, wind/heat and tree/fruit images also symbolize truths about life, imagination and hope.

After you become familiar with these basic types of sequences, you should be able to conceive a topic, align it with a grouping and build such a poem. But don't compose yet. You still need to envision what each section of your sequence has to accomplish and what, exactly, it will contribute to the whole.

PREPARING TO WRITE THE SEQUENCE

Outline each section of your sequence in your journal. If you rough out the poem first, you'll save time by identifying weak spots and eliminating or adding parts as needed. Finally, with overview of the sequence, you can move or rearrange parts to enhance theme or add clout to message.

For example, in a six-part villanelle sequence (a combination of symbolic and dramatic groupings), I researched passages in the Bible relating to trees in general and the fig tree in particular. I found several citations, choosing ones with a theme of betrayal. This indicated how many parts my sequence would contain. I decided to tell the poems in voices: my own, Peter's and Judas's. Although I knew the citations, the theme, the voices and number of parts to make the sequence, I still needed to ascertain the particular order of poems and how each one would contribute to the whole.

Now the outline came in handy. Here's an abbreviated version from my journal:

1. **Hunger and the Fig Tree**
   Citation: "Seeing in the distance a fig tree in leaf,

Jesus went to find out if it had any fruit."
Action: He curses the tree and it withers.
Voice: Peter as witness.
Theme/Epiphany: Innocence and betrayal.

2. **Fate and the Fig Tree**
Citation: "He remembered and said to Jesus, 'Rabbi,
look! The fig tree you cursed has withered!' "
Action: Show of power.
Voice: Peter as witness.
Theme/Epiphany: Warning: "Don't Betray Me."

3. **Fate and the Tree**
Citation: "And Judas cast down the pieces of silver in the
temple, and departed, and went and hanged himself."
Action: Judas hangs himself on a redbud tree.
Voice: Spirit of Judas.
Theme/Epiphany: Betrayal and remorse.

4. **Judas at the Table**
Citation: "Jesus dipped the piece of bread and gave it
to Judas. At that instant, Satan entered him."
Action: An argument at the table.
Voice: Judas as witness.
Theme/Epiphany: Betrayal as challenge.

5. **Fate or Fulfillment**
Citation: "For it is by your words you will be justified
and by your words condemned."
Action: Contemplation of family tree.
Voice: Narrator.
Theme/Epiphany: Betrayal since Eden.

6. **Faith and the Fig Tree**
Citation: "Look at the fig tree and all trees. . . .
Heaven and earth will pass away, but
my words will never pass away."
Action: Apocalypse.
Voice: Narrator.
Theme/Epiphany: Words are eternal, a kind of *ars poetica*.

Each description above filled a page in my journal. Now that I could
visualize the poems clearly, I could shuffle and rearrange those pages
and assemble the poems in the best order. As it happened, I switched
outlines (3) and (4) so Judas betrays before he hangs himself, changed
the citation in (3) to a more compassionate psalm, made outline (5)
the first poem in the sequence, and left (6) as the last because of its
apocalyptic overtones.

In sum, the process of preparing the sequence involved:

1. Choosing a topic (Biblical trees) that suited the form.
2. Choosing citations similar in theme, unifying the poem and indicating how many parts or sections would be involved.
3. Outlining each poem to envision its place in the sequence.
4. Arranging outlines for added unity and momentum.

The hard part done, I could compose my sequence.

WRITING THE SEQUENCE

Once you have broken the sequence into its respective parts, compose each as you would a regular poem. The problem now, however, is that the typical poet normally writes good, bad and mediocre poems, and each part of a sequence has to be good . . . or the chain will have a weak link. It is one thing to eliminate a weak link during the outlining phase and another to do so after a part has been composed. After you invest so much time composing a sequence, you might be tempted to leave in a weak poem or section that (a) cannot stand alone, (b) doesn't play off other parts or (c) fails to serve the entire work.

Consequences can be immense. One defective part of a sequence can ruin the entire effort, confusing readers so they lose interest and stop reading after a certain point. When this happens, all those weeks of preparation and composition are wasted. Think of each part in a sequence as gears of a car engine. One defective gear can bring the entire vehicle to a grinding halt.

Thus, after you compose your sequence, determine whether any part can be eliminated without affecting unity or theme. If it can, you may not need the part. (The more concise you make the sequence, the more efficiently it will convey its message or truth.) Then determine whether all the parts are equally strong. If not, improve the weak link(s) until each contributes substantially to the poem. After you rewrite any part of a sequence, evaluate that part again; if it still seems weaker than other parts, keep improving it until you are satisfied with the new part and the entire sequence.

Let's preview successful sequences in the mini anthology:

• "Here and Back," by Sharon Klander. The title, she says, "does not suggest 'Here' in the first section and 'Back' in the second; rather, they represent two enlarged moments from the 'Here,' or the present, which recall the 'Back,' or the past."

• "Three Ways to Tell a Story," by Laurel Speer, whose verse we read in chapter one. Speer says her sequence evolved after a friend told her a childhood experience. "In the different versions she gave me over the years, I was struck by how selection of particular details could skew the story in one direction or another. For me, the most important detail was her father's devastating observation that ends the poem. Everything in the sequence of stories leads up to that moment and those words."

Finally, this is the last anthology in the text. We've covered a lot of art and craft in our journey. In the final brief chapter, I'll discuss the revision process and try to put your poetic experience into perspective.

Mini Anthology of Sequence Poems

HERE AND BACK

i.
Not the moth-worn clouds moving left,
back-lit by some moon, but lightning
the more companionable light
giving edge to the deckled hills,
to a narrow road just wet,
with luminous yellow borders less boundary
than tease. Go ahead for the hell of it
off the side, windows down, nose down
to the unlucky cushion of oak and pine.
I'm tired. I imagine I'm going home.
ii.
The morning surrenders, finally, its storm.
Across the road a man hammers the door
back in place and calls for his wife.
They've lived here long enough to know
what a house can take. Now there's everything
to learn from frantic birds
caught like debris in the top branches,
from a porchlight left on. How the rain
slaps pavement like children's feet
running here, running back.

—Sharon Klander

THREE WAYS TO TELL A STORY

1.
I'm standing at the sink balanced on crutches
doing the dishes with a cast on my leg
after coming home from polio. This is my
regular chore and we all work. I'm washing
and my sister's drying and I slip because I'm
awkward still and can't get up. I'm pole-axed
on the floor and my sister starts crying.
She's always crying then, but my parents make

allowances. It's a difficult time.

2.

The hard part about losing the use of your
right side as a kid is the incapacity.
I'm washing dishes. My folks think everything
will be fine and they need the help because
they both work. I fall down on the linoleum,
crutches clattering and can't get up. My sister
has the t-towel balled in her fist and she's crying.
"Get Dad," I hiss, but it takes her the longest
time and I know nothing will ever be the same.

3.

One day after having polio, I fall down
on the kitchen floor and can't get up.
My sister's too small to lift me and she's
crying. After trying and falling back,
I tell her to get Dad. My father is perfect
physically. He works hard and hasn't an
ounce of fat. When he sees me helpless
on the floor, he shakes his head, "I guess
you'll always be a cripple now," and picks
me up like a piece of meat.

—Laurel Speer

Notebook

LEVEL ONE

1. Visit the library and read the poems mentioned under each of
the ten groupings in this chapter. After each poem, make notations in
your journal about the poem's success as a sequence. For instance,
evaluate the strength of each part and determine whether any part
could have been eliminated without affecting meaning or theme.

2. Select five ideas from your "Idea File" (or conceive new ideas)
that suit five of the ten groupings. Follow precepts explained in this
chapter about preparing to write a sequence. Compose yours. (After
you have composed your sequences, note any problems — or how you
overcame them! — in your journal.)

LEVEL TWO

Read journal entries about the sequence generated from Level One
exercises to remind you of touchstones, problems and/or solutions.
Then select five more ideas from your "Idea File" (or conceive new

ideas) for the remaining groupings of the ten described in this chapter. Compose them.

LEVEL THREE

Select five ideas from your "Idea File" (or conceive new ideas) for sequences that combine elements of the ten groupings explained in this chapter. For example, you might combine elements of the symbolic grouping with elements of the dramatic grouping. Then compose your sequences.

Chapter Twenty-One

The Total Poem

The total poem is one to which you have given your *all*. That means that you have considered the elements of craft when composing each draft—idea, voice, line, stanza, title, meter and rhyme. It means that you have analyzed the modes of expression—narrative, lyric, dramatic—and employed the appropriate methods and forms to convey your epiphanies and peak experiences. It means, ultimately, that you have respect for your readers, sharing your best ideas with the best words in the best order of presentation.

Of all the definitions of "total" or "pure" poetry, the one that impresses me the most was coined by Canadian poet George Whipple, whose lyric "A Hymn to God the Father" appears in the chapter on voice. Whipple, who composes as many as thirty drafts of each poem, advises: "When you revise, remember it is not what *you* feel that is important, but what you can make *others* feel."

An implied respect for audience has been the theme of each chapter in *The Art and Craft of Poetry*.

Unlike other texts, however, my discussion of revision in this chapter will be the shortest. You have been learning the discipline of revision by keeping a file labeled "Work in Progress" and by keeping all drafts of each poem. My goal has been to transfer to you the process of composing effective poetry via these methods:

1. *Conceiving effective ideas.* In notebook assignments in the first section, you learned that poets are expected to envision the inner and outer realms of life with universality. Truth emanates from powerful ideas. Without such ideas, your poems may seem static, trite, rambling, vague or obscure.

2. *Studying tools of craft.* In notebook assignments in the second section, you learned that the more tools a poet has at his or her disposal, the easier it is to convey those universal and visionary ideas. Moreover, you learned how to assemble the foundation of a total poem, aligning such elements as voice, line, stanza and title.

3. *Employing formats and forms.* Finally, in notebook assignments in the third section, you became familiar with methods of composition. If it was your first go-around, the Level One exercises also showed you how to adapt your drafts and ideas to narrative, lyric, dramatic, free and formal verse. If it was your second go-around, the Level Two exercises showed you how to identify your individual strengths and weaknesses when adapting your drafts and ideas. If it was your third go-around, the Level Three exercises should have pushed you to the edge of your ability, attempting to turn those weaknesses into strengths.

Now it's time to apply what you have learned to drafts of poems in your "Work in Progress" file.

REVISING YOUR POEMS

Take out drafts of poems and follow this step-by-step method to revise your work:

1. Lay drafts of each poem on a flat surface. Read them sequentially, from first draft to last, and choose the best draft. Usually (but not always) the *last* draft will be the most effective because you knew your poem intimately when you composed this version. In any case, put aside your most effective draft.

2. Review every word and line of your *lesser* drafts. Occasionally you'll find better passages in these attempts that somehow failed to make it into your most effective one. Or perhaps a stanza or title of a lesser draft seems, in retrospect, more powerful. Circle these passages or elements of craft on each lesser draft and put them aside.

3. Return to your most effective draft and compare it to lesser ones with circled passages and/or elements of craft. Consider whether you can insert or apply the circled elements to your most effective draft. Often it will be easy to insert a dropped word or line or to replace a title or revise a stanza. Sometimes it will be impossible because your most effective draft may be a sonnet or form poem or may contain a distinct meter or rhyme. Or perhaps your free-verse version took a different direction that no longer requires that word, line, passage or element of craft. If that is the case, take out your journal and save that word, line, passage or element for another day and another poem.

4. Insert your remaining word(s), line(s), passage(s) or craft element(s) into your most effective draft and then read the entire poem again. Smooth voice, sharpen line, evaluate your stanza preference and/or title — and whatever else you need to improve the draft — and set it aside for a few days. Make a new file titled "Old Drafts" and clip and store your earlier drafts of each poem here, so you can return to them later in your career to note your progress. As time goes on,

your "Old Drafts" file will contain a wealth of information about your strengths, weaknesses and work ethic as a poet.

5. Return to the draft of your most effective poem (which now contains improvements from other versions). Waiting a few days — or even weeks — to return to revised work will allow you to evaluate your poem more objectively. For instance, you may no longer remember your inserts or revisions, so you can read the poem as a single work. Make improvements, if needed, and repeat this step until you're satisfied with the poem.

FINAL WORDS

Let's wrap up. At this point you should have an "Idea File" with remaining ideas for poems. (Every poet should have more ideas for poems than he or she has time to compose.) You should have a lighter "Work in Progress" file and a heavy "Old Drafts" one.

Now it's time to reward yourself. If this is your first time through the text, the good news is that you need a new file: "Final Drafts." If this is your second or third time, you have such a file already and now will be able to add more poems to it. In any case, congratulations.

In a minute, it will be time to close this book and reflect on what you have learned thus far. Get out your journal and describe your poetic experience. If you have read this book more than once, describe your experience again and review your previous journal entries to determine how you have evolved as a poet and how you hope to continue to evolve.

Remember, the objective is to create art that will endure — and that takes time. If you have patience, you not only will be able to compose a total poem . . . but you will become a total *poet*.

INDEX

More Great Books for Poets!

1997 Poet's Market—Discover 1,700 listings for publishers, arts councils, contests and awards, publications, organizations and other markets for your work! You'll find advice on submission formats, cover letters and record keeping. Plus, interviews with editors and published poets illustrate the ins and outs of this field. *#10461/$22.99/576 pages*

The Writer's Survival Guide—Drawing on her own experiences, as well as those of her students and colleagues, Rachel Simon explores the whole writerly journey—offering ways to stay productive on a day-to-day basis, advice for navigating the publishing world and prescriptions for overall creative happiness. *#48025/$18.99/224 pages*

Discovering the Writer Within: 40 Days to More Imaginative Writing—Uncover the creative individual inside who will, with encouragement, turn secret thoughts and special moments into enduring words. You'll learn how to find something exciting in unremarkable places, write punchy first sentences for imaginary stories, give a voice to inanimate objects and much more! *#10472/$14.99/192 pages/paperback*

The Poetry Dictionary—This comprehensive book unravels the rich and complex language of poetry with clear, working definitions. Drury's discussions of poetic forms, elements, tools and traditions result in a volume that is the definitive source for today's poet. In many cases, several different poems are used to illustrate the many ways poets have put theories to work, making *The Poetry Dictionary* a unique anthology. *#48007/$18.99/336 pages*

Creating Poetry—Designed to encourage budding poets to explore and practice poetry writing skills, Drury's nuts-and-bolts instruction addresses all elements of creating poetry. Each chapter offers an overview of each element discussed, a definition of terms, poetry examples, plus hands-on exercises. *#10209/$18.99/224 pages*

The Poet's Handbook—Here's expert instruction on how to use figurative language, symbols and concrete images; how to tune the ear to sound relationships; the requirements for lyric, narrative, dramatic, didactic and satirical poetry and more. *#01836/$14.99/224 pages/paperback*